I0824725

"I am the way, and the truth, and the life."

Christ in the Gospel

The Life of Christ by the Four Evangelists

WITH
170
ORIGINAL
ILLUSTRATIONS

1949

Arranged by
Rev. Joseph B. Frey

CONFRATERNITY of the PRECIOUS BLOOD

Nihil Obstat:

Georgius A. Denzer, S.T.D.
Censor Duputatus

Imprimatur:

+ Thomas Edmundus Molloy, S.T.D.
Episcopus Brooklyniensis.

Brooklyni, XVIII Aprilis 1949.

First published in 1949 by Confraternity of the Precious Blood.

Cataloging-in-Publication data on file with the Library of Congress.

ISBN 978-1-61890-839-1

Confraternity of the Precious Blood is an imprint of TAN Books
PO Box 269
Gastonia, NC 28053
www.TANBooks.com

Printed and bound in India.

Contents

+ + + + + + + + + + + + + + + + + +

Foreword

IN THIS little volume we are presenting a different kind of book, one that contains the Life of Christ in word and picture. The words are the inspired words of the Four Evangelists woven into one complete story. This greatest of all stories falls into four convenient parts: the Birth and Infancy of Christ, the Public Life, the Passion and Death, the Resurrection and Ascension.

This book is so divided that it furnishes suitable reading for each day of the year. This division is based on "Readings from the Four Gospels" arranged by the late Monsignor Stedman, who lives on in the work of the Confraternity which he fostered with such marked success. Each open page of this book presents a picture and text for one day's reading and meditation. This, in turn, is supplemented by a corresponding section in the Appendix under the title "Study Guide and Daily Practice" which should prove very useful and fruitful for schools, study clubs, and Confraternities of Christian Doctrine.

IMPORTANCE OF THIS BOOK

THE LIFE, example and teaching of Jesus Christ recorded in the Four Gospels constitute a code of perfection for every Catholic. In the Gospels will be found the healing prescriptions of the Divine Physician of souls, the guideposts to eternal life, set up by the Divine Exemplar. Our Lord's precepts form the Jacob's Ladder of the Christian, reaching from earth to Heaven by which all may scale the heights of sanctity.

St. Ambrose writes: "In Christ are all things. Christ is everything to us. Hast thou wounds? Christ is the Physician. Dost thou need help? He is thy strength. Dost thou fear death? He is Life. Dost thou long for Heaven? He is the Way. Dost thou flee darkness? He is the Light. Dost thou hunger? Christ is thy Food." St. Jerome, who translated the Hebrew and Greek Scriptures into Latin, said: "Ignorance of the Bible means ignorance of Christ." So true is this that the Popes repeatedly have urged upon the laity the duty of serious biblical study, especially study of the Holy Gospel.

VISUAL INSTRUCTION

THIS pocket edition of *Christ in the Gospel* is a companion volume to other publications issued by the Confraternity of the Precious Blood in similar format. This convenient harmony of the Four Gospels presents "the greatest story ever told" in concise form. Its clear type can be read with equal ease at home, in Church, or while traveling. Illustrations by the same able artist whose drawings enrich "My Daily Psalm Book" contribute to a clearer understanding of the text. The noted Armenian artist, Ariel Agemian, has created these outstanding examples of Christian art expressly and exclusively for this book. There are 170 pictures which illustrate the various teachings and events of the life of the Divine Master. In paging through this volume you become an eyewitness of the life of Jesus.

LOOK AND LEARN

LEARN from this book the gospel story of the Master's Life; meditate upon this record of the Master's words. You will note that He speaks to you. He proclaims: "Blessed are the poor in spirit, the meek, those who mourn, those who hunger and thirst for justice, the merciful, the pure of heart, the peacemakers, and those who suffer persecution." Follow the path of Christ's teaching that you may experience the fulfillment of His promises. Obedience to Him will bring you to the "kingdom of Heaven" wherein you will "be comforted" and satisfied, obtain mercy, see God and be called the children of God.

HOW TO USE THIS BOOK

THIS volume is suited to many purposes. It may be employed as private, spiritual reading, as a school text, and as material for the work of study groups. When used in conjunction with the "Study Guide" found in the Appendix it provides a complete system and schedule of meditation. The illustrations will aid in forming the "composition of place" recommended by St. Ignatius; the text of the Gospel and the "Study Guide" will furnish material for reflection, application and resolution. Our hope is that the faithful will find it helpful in perfecting their Catholic lives by assisting them in their "imitation of Christ." In presenting this first edition of *Christ in the Gospel* we respectfully adopt, as our own, the words of Pope Benedict XV: "Our one desire for all the

Church's children is that being saturated with the Bible, they may arrive at the all surpassing knowledge of Jesus Christ."

GRATEFUL ACKNOWLEDGMENTS

To his Excellency, Most Reverend Thomas E. Molloy, S.T.D., we are deeply indebted for the gracious encouragement he has afforded us.

To the Reverend John A. O'Brien, Ph.D., of Notre Dame University we express our sincere appreciation of his painstaking labor in preparing the "Study Guide."

To the Sisters Adorers of the Precious Blood we offer our heartfelt thanks for their fine spirit of co-operation and ever ready assistance in proofreading the manuscripts—another example of their devotion to the "Word of God" written in letters of red—the Most Precious Blood of Jesus Christ.

Feast of St. Joseph (Rev.) Joseph B. Frey
March 19, 1949

PART I

+ + + The Birth and

Jesus Christ Is God

Introduction to Gospels

John's Mission Foretold

Redeemer's Coming Announced

Joy of Mary and Elizabeth

Infancy of Christ + +

birth of john the baptist

the virgin birth

angel announces good news

the child is called jesus

wise men seek heavenly king

the return from exile

JESUS CHRIST IS GOD

DEC. 1 or June 1

John 1 1-18 IN THE BEGINNING was the [1]Word, and the
Word was with God; and the Word was
2 God. He was in the beginning with God. All
3 things were made through him, and without

1. St. John employs the term "Word," in referring to the eternal co-existence of Jesus with the Father. This term "Word" designates the Son as a kind of intellectual emanation from the Father. He enjoys the divine nature and yet is distinct from the Father. It was this eternal divine Person who became man in order to reveal God to us, and to accomplish our redemption.

him was made nothing that has been made.
In him was life, and the life was the [1]light of 4
men. And the light shines in the darkness; and 5
the darkness grasped it not.

John Came to Witness This Truth

There was a man, one sent from God, whose 6
name was John. This man came as a witness, 7
to bear witness concerning the light, that all
might believe through him. He was not himself 8
the light, but was to bear witness to the light.
It was the true light that enlightens every 9
man who comes into the world. He was in 10
the world, and the world was made through
him, and the world knew him not. He came 11
unto his own, and his own received him not.

How Jesus Becomes Our Brother

But to as many as received him he gave the 12
power of becoming sons of God; to those
who believe in his name: who were born not 13
of blood, nor of the will of the flesh, nor of
the will of man, but of God.

---

1. *Light* is God's revelation and grace; *Darkness* is man's sinful nature. *Shines:* i.e., is always in the world, in both the past and the present. *Grasped:* this may refer to man's failure to appreciate the light

14 And the Word was made flesh, and dwelt
among us. And we saw his glory—glory as of
the only-begotten of the Father—full of grace
15 and of truth. John bore witness concerning
him, and cried, "This was he of whom I said,
'He who is to come after me has been set
above me, because he was before me.'"

We Are Called to Share His Life

16 And of his fullness we have all received, grace
17 for grace. For the Law was given through
Moses; grace and truth came through Jesus
18 Christ. No one has at any time seen God. The
only-begotten Son, who is in the bosom of
the Father, he has revealed him.

Zachary Prays

INTRODUCTION to GOSPELS

DEC. 2 or June 2

INASMUCH AS MANY have undertaken to draw Luke 1
up a narrative concerning the things that 1-13

2 have been fulfilled among us, even as they
who from the beginning were eyewitnesses
and ministers of the word have handed them
3 down to us, I also have determined, after following up all things carefully from the very
first, to write for thee, most excellent The-
4 ophilus, an orderly account, that thou mayest understand the certainty of the words in
which thou hast been instructed.

John's Birth Foretold

5 In the days of Herod, king of Judea, there was
a certain priest named Zachary, of the course
of Abia; and his wife was of the daughters of
6 Aaron, and her name was Elizabeth. Both
were just before God, walking blamelessly in
all the commandments and ordinances of the
7 Lord. But they had no son, for Elizabeth was
barren; and they were both advanced in years.

As Zachary Prays for Redeemer

8 Now it came to pass, while he was officiating
in the order of his course as priest before God,
9 according to the custom of the priest's office,
that he was chosen by lot to enter the temple
10 of the Lord to burn incense. And the whole

multitude of the people were praying outside
at the hour of incense.
And there appeared to him an angel of 11
the Lord, standing at the right of the altar of
incense. And Zachary, seeing him, was trou- 12
bled, and fear fell upon him. But the angel 13
said to him, "Do not be afraid, Zachary, for
thy petition has been heard, and thy wife Elizabeth shall bear thee a son and thou shalt call
his name John."

JOHN'S MISSION FORETOLD

DEC. 3 or June 3

Luke 1 14-25 "AND THOU shalt have joy and gladness, and many will rejoice at his birth. For

he shall be great before the Lord; he shall drink 15
no wine or strong drink, and shall be filled
with the Holy Spirit even from his mother's
womb. And he shall bring back to the Lord 16
their God many of the children of Israel, and
he shall himself go before him in the spirit and 17
power of Elias, to turn the hearts of fathers
to their children and the incredulous to the
wisdom of the just; to prepare for the Lord a
perfect people."

And Zachary said to the angel, "How shall 18
I know this? For I am an old man and my wife
is advanced in years."

And the angel answered and said to him, 19
"I am Gabriel, who stand in the presence of
God; and I have been sent to speak to thee and
to bring thee this good news.

Zachary Punished for Doubting

"And behold, thou shalt be dumb and unable to 20
speak until the day when these things come to
pass, because thou hast not believed my words,
which will be fulfilled in their proper time."

And the people were waiting for Zachary, 21
and they wondered at his tarrying so long in
the temple. But when he did come out he 22

could not speak to them, and they realized
that he had seen a vision in the temple. And he
kept making signs to them, but he remained
dumb.

23 And it came to pass, when the days of his
service were completed, that he departed to
24 his own house. Now after these days Elizabeth
his wife conceived, and she secluded herself
25 for five months, saying, "Thus has the Lord
dealt with me in the days when he deigned to
take away my reproach among men."

REDEEMER'S COMING ANNOUNCED

DEC. 4 or June 4

Luke 1
26-38
NOW IN the sixth month the angel Gabriel
was sent from God to a town of Galilee 27

called Nazareth, to a virgin betrothed to a
man named Joseph, of the house of David,
and the virgin's name was Mary.
28 And when the angel had come to her, he
said, "Hail, full of grace, the Lord is with thee.
29 Blessed art thou among women." When she
had heard him she was troubled at his word,
and kept pondering what manner of greeting
this might be.
30 And the angel said to her, "Do not be afraid,
Mary, for thou hast found grace with God.
31 Behold, thou shalt conceive in thy womb and
shalt bring forth a son; and thou shalt call
32 his name Jesus. He shall be great, and shall
be called the Son of the Most High; and the
Lord God will give him the throne of David
his father, and he shall be king over the house
33 of Jacob forever; and of his kingdom there
shall be no end."

Mary Gives Consent

34 But Mary said to the angel, "How shall this
happen, since I do not know man?"
35 And the angel answered and said to her,
"The Holy Spirit shall come upon thee and
the power of the Most High shall overshadow

thee; and therefore the Holy One to be born
shall be called the Son of God And behold, 36
Elizabeth thy kinswoman also has conceived
a son in her old age, and she who was called
barren is now in her sixth month; for nothing 37
shall be impossible with God."

But Mary said, "Behold the handmaid of 38
the Lord; be it done to me according to thy
word." And the angel departed from her.

JOY of MARY and ELIZABETH

DEC. 5 or June 5

Luke 1 39-55 NOW IN those days Mary arose and went
with haste into the hill country, to a
40 town of Juda. And she entered the house of
41 Zachary and saluted Elizabeth. And it came
to pass, when Elizabeth heard the greeting of
Mary, that the babe in her womb leapt.

And Elizabeth was filled with the Holy
Spirit, and cried out with a loud voice, saying, 42
"Blessed art thou among women and blessed
is the fruit of thy womb!
"And how have I deserved that the mother 43
of my Lord should come to me? For behold, 44
the moment that the sound of thy greeting
came to my ears, the babe in my womb leapt 45
for joy. And blessed is she who has believed,
because the things promised her by the Lord
shall be accomplished."

Mary's "Magnificat" of Thanksgiving

And Mary said, 46
"My soul magnifies the Lord,
and my spirit rejoices in God my Savior; 47
Because he has regarded the lowliness of 48
his handmaid;
for, behold, henceforth all generations
shall call me blessed;
Because he who is mighty has done great 49
things for me,
and holy is his name;
And his mercy is from generation to gen- 50
eration
on those who fear him.

51 He has shown might with his arm,
he has scattered the proud in the conceit of their heart.
52 He has put down the mighty from their thrones,
and has exalted the lowly.
53 He has filled the hungry with good things,
and the rich he has sent away empty.
54 He has given help to Israel, his servant,
mindful of his mercy—
55 Even as he spoke to our fathers—
to Abraham and to his posterity forever."

BIRTH of JOHN the BAPTIST

DEC. 6 or June 6

AND Mary remained with *Elizabeth* about Luke 1
three months and returned to her own 56-80
house.

Now Elizabeth's time was fulfilled that 57
she should be delivered, and she brought
forth a son. And her neighbors and kinsfolk 58
heard that the Lord had magnified his mercy
towards her, and they rejoiced with her.

And it came to pass on the eighth day, that 59
they came to circumcise the child, and they
were going to call him by his father's name,
Zachary. And his mother answered and said, 60
"Not so, but he shall be called John." And they 61
said to her, "There is none of thy kindred that
is called by this name."

Zachary Recovers His Speech

And they kept inquiring by signs of his father 62
what he would have him called. And asking 63
for a writing-tablet he wrote the words,
"John is his name." And they all marvelled.
And immediately his mouth was opened and 64
his tongue loosed, and he began to speak,
blessing God.

65 And fear came on all their neighbors; and
all these things were spoken abroad in all the
66 hill country of Judea. And all who heard them
laid them up in their heart, saying, "What then
will this child be?" For the hand of the Lord
67 was with him. And Zachary his father was filled
with the Holy Spirit, and prophesied, saying,

Zachary's Hymn of Thanksgiving

68 "Blessed be the Lord, the God of Israel,
because he has visited and wrought
redemption for his people,
69 And has raised up a horn of salvation for us,
in the house of David his servant,
70 As he promised through the mouth of his
holy ones,
the prophets from of old;
71 Salvation from our enemies,
and from the hand of all who hate us,
72 To show mercy to our forefathers
and to be mindful of his holy covenant,
73 Of the oath that he swore to Abraham our
father,
that he would grant us,
74 That, delivered from the hand of our enemies,
we should serve him without fear,

In holiness and justice before him all our days. 75
And thou, child, shalt be called the prophet of the Most High, 76
for thou shalt go before the face of the Lord to prepare his ways,
To give to his people knowledge of salvation 77
through forgiveness of their sins,
Because of the loving-kindness of our God, 78
wherewith the Orient from on high has visited us,
To shine on those who sit in darkness and 79
in the shadow of death,
to guide our feet into the way of peace."

And the child grew and became strong in 80
spirit; and was in the deserts until the day of
his manifestation to Israel.

The VIRGIN BIRTH

DEC. ▯ or June ▯

Matt. 1 18-25 NOW THE origin of Christ was in this
wise. When Mary his mother had
been betrothed to Joseph, before they came
together, she was found to be with child by
19 the Holy Spirit. But Joseph her husband, being
a just man, and not wishing to expose her to
reproach, was minded to put her away privately.
20 But while he thought on these things,
behold, an angel of the Lord appeared to him
in a dream, saying, "Do not be afraid, Joseph,
son of David, to take to thee Mary thy wife,
for that which is begotten in her is of the Holy
21 Spirit. And she shall bring forth a son, and

thou shalt call his name Jesus; for he shall save
his people from their sins."
Now all this came to pass that what was 22
spoken by the Lord through the prophet
might be fulfilled, "Behold, the virgin shall 23
be with child, and shall bring forth a son; and
they shall call his name Emmanuel"; which is,
interpreted, "God with us."
So Joseph, arising from sleep, did as the 24
angel of the Lord had commanded him, and
took unto him his wife. And he did not know 25
her till she brought forth her [1]firstborn son.
And he called his name Jesus.

At Bethlehem

Now it came to pass in those days, that a Luke 2 1-7
decree went forth from Cæsar Augustus that
a census of the whole world should be taken.
This first census took place while Cyrinus 2
was governor of Syria. And all were going, 3
each to his own town, to register.
And Joseph also went from Galilee out of 4
the town of Nazareth into Judea to the town

1. *Firstborn:* does not imply that Mary ever bore another child. Among the Jews this title belonged to an only child (if a son) to mark his rights and duties under the Law. Thus the apostolic doctrine of Mary's perpetual virginity is in no way denied by these words.

of David, which is called Bethlehem—because
he was of the house and family of David—to
5 register, together with Mary his espoused
wife, who was with child.
6 And it came to pass while they were there,
that the days for her to be delivered were
7 fulfilled. And she brought forth her firstborn
son, and wrapped him in swaddling clothes,
and laid him in a manger, because there was
no room for them in the inn.

ANGEL ANNOUNCES GOOD NEWS

DEC. 8 or June 8

AND THERE were shepherds in the same district living in the fields and keeping Luke 2 8-20

9 watch over their flock by night. And behold,
an angel of the Lord stood by them and the
glory of God shone round about them, and
they feared exceedingly.
10 And the angel said to them, "Do not be
afraid, for behold, I bring you good news of
11 great joy which shall be to all the people; for
today in the town of David a Savior has been
12 born to you, who is Christ the Lord. And this
shall be a sign to you: you will find an infant
wrapped in swaddling clothes and lying in a
13 manger." And suddenly there was with the
angel a multitude of the heavenly host praising God and saying,

Glory to God, Peace among Men

14 "Glory to God in the highest, and on earth
peace among men of good will."
15 And it came to pass, when the angels had
departed from them into heaven, that the
shepherds were saying to one another, "Let us
go over to Bethlehem and see this thing that
has come to pass, which the Lord has made
known to us."
16 So they went with haste, and they found
Mary and Joseph, and the babe lying in the

manger. And when they had seen, they under- 17
stood what had been told them concerning
this child. And all who heard marvelled at the 18
things told them by the shepherds. But Mary 19
kept in mind all these things, pondering them
in her heart. And the shepherds returned, glo- 20
rifying and praising God for all that they had
heard and seen, even as it was spoken to them.

The CHILD IS CALLED JESUS
DEC. 9 or June 9

Luke 2 21-38 AND WHEN eight days were fulfilled for his
circumcision, his name was called Jesus,
the name given him by the angel before he
was conceived in the womb.
22 And when the days of her purification
were fulfilled according to the Law of Moses,
they took him up to Jerusalem to present him
23 to the Lord—as it is written in the Law of the
Lord, "Every male that opens the womb shall
24 be called holy to the Lord"—and to offer a
sacrifice according to what is said in the Law
of the Lord, "a pair of turtledoves or two
young pigeons."

Simeon Rejoices to See Savior

And behold, there was in Jerusalem a man 25
named Simeon, and this man was just and
devout, looking for the consolation of Israel,
and the Holy Spirit was upon him. And it had 26
been revealed to him by the Holy Spirit that
he should not see death before he had seen
the Christ of the Lord. And he came by inspi- 27
ration of the Spirit into the temple. And when
his parents brought in the child Jesus, to do
for him according to the custom of the Law,
he also received him into his arms and blessed 28
God, saying,

"Now thou dost dismiss thy servant, O Lord, 29
according to thy word, in peace;
Because my eyes have seen thy salvation, 30
which thou hast prepared before the 31
face of all peoples:
A light of revelation to the Gentiles, 32
and a glory for thy people Israel."

Simeon Predicts Sorrows for Mary

And his father and mother were marvelling 33
at the things spoken concerning him. And 34
Simeon blessed them, and said to Mary his
mother, "Behold, this child is destined for the

fall and for the rise of many in Israel, and for
35 a sign that shall be contradicted. And thy own
soul a sword shall pierce, that the thoughts of
many hearts may be revealed."

Prophetess Anna Greets Redeemer

36 There was also Anna, a prophetess, daughter
of Phanuel, of the tribe of Aser. She was of a
great age, having lived with her husband seven
37 years from her maidenhood, and by herself
as a widow to eighty-four years. She never
left the temple, with fastings and prayers
38 worshipping night and day. And coming up
at that very hour, she began to give praise to
the Lord, and spoke of him to all who were
awaiting the redemption of Jerusalem.

WISE MEN SEEK HEAVENLY KING

DEC. 10 or June 10

NOW WHEN Jesus was born in Bethlehem of Matt. 2
Judea, in the days of King Herod, behold, 1-18
Magi came from the East to Jerusalem, saying,
"Where is he that is born king of the Jews? For 2
we have seen his star in the East and have come
to worship him." But when King Herod heard 3
this, he was troubled, and so was all Jerusalem
with him. And gathering together all the chief 4
priests and Scribes of the people, he inquired of
them where the Christ was to be born.

And they said to him, "In Bethlehem of 5
Judea; for thus it is written by the prophet,
'And thou, Bethlehem, of the land of Juda, art 6
by no means least among the princes of Juda;
for from thee shall come forth a leader who
shall rule my people Israel.'"

King Herod Pretends to Adore

Then Herod summoned the Magi secretly, 7
and carefully ascertained from them the time

8 when the star had appeared to them. And
sending them to Bethlehem, he said, "Go and
make careful inquiry concerning the child,
and when you have found him, bring me
word, that I too may go and worship him."
9 Now they, having heard the king, went
their way. And behold, the star that they had
seen in the East went before them, until it
came and stood over the place where the
10 child was. And when they saw the star they
11 rejoiced exceedingly. And entering the house,
they found the child with Mary his mother,
and falling down they worshipped him. And
opening their treasures they offered him gifts
12 of gold, frankincense and myrrh. And being
warned in a dream not to return to Herod,
they went back to their own country by
another way.

Holy Family Flees into Egypt

13 But when they had departed, behold, an angel
of the Lord appeared in a dream to Joseph,
saying, "Arise, and take the child and his
mother, and flee into Egypt, and remain there
until I tell thee. For Herod will seek the child
14 to destroy him." So he arose, and took the

child and his mother by night, and withdrew
into Egypt, and remained there until the death 15
of Herod; that what was spoken by the Lord
through the prophet might be fulfilled, "Out
of Egypt I called my son."

Slaughter of the Innocents

Then Herod, seeing that he had been tricked 16
by the Magi, was exceedingly angry; and he
sent and slew all the boys in Bethlehem and
all its neighborhood who were two years old
or under, according to the time that he had
carefully ascertained from the Magi.

Then was fulfilled what was spoken through 17
Jeremias the prophet, "A voice was heard in 18
Rama, weeping and loud lamentation; Rachel
weeping for her children, and she would not
be comforted, because they are no more."

The RETURN from EXILE

DEC. 11 or June 11

Matt. 2 19-23 BUT WHEN Herod was dead, behold, an
angel of the Lord appeared in a dream
20 to Joseph in Egypt, saying, "Arise, and take
the child and his mother, and go into the land
of Israel, for those who sought the child's life
are dead."
21 So he arose and took the child and his
22 mother, and went into the land of Israel. But
hearing that Archelaus was reigning in Judea
in place of his father Herod, he was afraid to
go there; and being warned in a dream, he
23 withdrew into the region of Galilee. And he
went and settled in a town called Nazareth;
that there might be fulfilled what was spoken
through the prophets, "He shall be called a
Luke 2 40-52 Nazarene." And the child grew and became

strong. He was full of wisdom and the grace
of God was upon him.

The Boy Jesus Lost and Found

And his parents were wont to go every year 41
to Jerusalem at the Feast of the Passover. And 42
when he was twelve years old, they went up to
Jerusalem according to the custom of the feast.
And after they had fulfilled the days, when 43
they were returning, the boy Jesus remained
in Jerusalem, and his parents did not know it.
But thinking that he was in the caravan, they 44
had come a day's journey before it occurred
to them to look for him among their relatives
and acquaintances. And not finding him, they 45
returned to Jerusalem in search of him.

And it came to pass after three days, that 46
they found him in the temple, sitting in the
midst of the teachers, listening to them and
asking them questions. And all who were lis- 47
tening to him were amazed at his understanding and his answers. And when they saw him, 48
they were astonished. And his mother said
to him, "Son, why hast thou done so to us?
Behold, in sorrow thy father and I have been
seeking thee."

49 And he said to them, "How is it that you
sought me? Did you not know that I must be
50 about my Father's business?" And they did not
understand the word that he spoke to them.

His Humility and Obedience

51 And he went down with them and came to
Nazareth, and was subject to them; and his
mother kept all these things carefully in her
52 heart. And Jesus [1]advanced in wisdom and age
and grace before God and men.

1. As God, our Lord has infinite knowledge; as man, He had from the beginning the greatest possible infused knowledge and also the beatific vision. His human mind, however, could advance in experimental knowledge, which is only acquired through the medium of mental faculties and bodily senses.

PART II

+ + + + The Public

Preparation

repentance for sin
jesus is the christ
jesus challenged by satan
jesus is god
jesus salutes peter
jesus at a marriage feast

First Year

money-changers cast out
jesus explains baptism
final testimony of john
necessity of spiritual worship
teaches from peter's ship
jesus prays, preaches
jesus forgives sin
jesus calls matthew (levi)

Life of Christ + + +

Second Year

jesus cures helpless invalid
jesus declares he is god
jesus justifies his claims
sermon on the mount
how to pray
necessity of a right motive
raises widow's son to life
the penitent woman

Third Year

peter's profession
transfiguration
the good samaritan
mary and martha
feast of the dedication
raising of lazarus
zacchaeus
anointing at bethany

REPENTANCE for SIN

DEC. 12 or June 12

Luke 3 THE WORD OF God came to John, the son of
2-3 Zachary, in the desert. And he went into
3 all the region about the Jordan, preaching a
Matt. 3 baptism of repentance for the forgiveness of
2-3 sins, and saying, "Repent, for the kingdom
3 of heaven is at hand." For this is he who was
spoken of through Isaias the prophet, when
he said,

“The voice of one crying in the desert, Luke 3
‘Make ready the way of the Lord, make 4-6
straight his paths. Every valley shall be filled, 5
and every mountain and hill shall be brought
low, and the crooked ways shall be made
straight, and the rough ways smooth; and all 6
mankind shall see the salvation of God.’”

And all the country of Judea went out to Mark 1
him, and all the inhabitants of Jerusalem; and 5-6
they were baptized by him in the river Jordan,
confessing their sins. And John was clothed in 6
camel’s hair, with a leathern girdle about his
loins, and he ate locusts and wild honey.

John Denounces Injustice

But when he saw many of the Pharisees and Matt. 3
Sadducees coming to his baptism, he said to 7-10
them, “Brood of vipers! who has shown you
how to flee from the wrath to come? Bring 8
forth therefore fruit befitting repentance, 9
and do not think to say within yourselves,
‘We have Abraham for our father’; for I say
to you that God is able out of these stones to
raise up children to Abraham. For even now 10
the axe is laid at the root of the trees; every
tree therefore that is not bringing forth

good fruit is to be cut down and thrown into
the fire."

He Urges Charity and Justice

Luke 3 10-14 And the crowds asked him, saying, "What
then are we to do?" And he answered and said
11 to them, "Let him who has two tunics share
with him who has none; and let him who has
food do likewise."

12 And publicans also came to be baptized,
and they said to him, "Master, what are we to
13 do?" But he said to them, "Exact no more than
what has been appointed you."

14 And soldiers also asked him, saying, "And
we—what are we to do?" And he said to
them, "Plunder no one, accuse no one falsely,
and be content with your pay."

JESUS IS the CHRIST

DEC. 13 or June 13

NOW AS the people were in expectation, Luke 3
and all were wondering in their hearts 15
about John, whether perhaps he might be John 1
the Christ, the Jews sent to him from Jeru- 19-26
salem priests and Levites to ask him, "Who 20
art thou?" And he acknowledged and did not
deny; and he acknowledged, "I am not the 21
Christ." And they asked him, "What then? Art
thou Elias?" And he said, "I am not." "Art thou
the Prophet?" And he answered, "No."

They therefore said to him, "Who art thou? 22
that we may give an answer to those who sent
us. What hast thou to say of thyself?" He said, 23
"I am the voice of one crying in the desert,

'Make straight the way of the Lord,' as said
Isaias the prophet."

24 And they who had been sent were from
25 among the Pharisees. And they asked him,
and said to him, "Why, then, dost thou baptize, if thou art not the Christ, nor Elias, nor
26 the Prophet?" John said to them in answer, "I
baptize with water; but in the midst of you
there has stood one whom you do not know.

Luke 3 16-18 [1]"But one mightier than I is coming, the
strap of whose sandals I am not worthy to
loose. He will baptize you with the Holy
17 Spirit and with fire. [2]His winnowing fan is in
his hand, and he will clean out his threshing
floor, and will gather the wheat into his barn;
but the chaff he will burn up with unquench-
18 able fire." So with many different exhortations
he kept on preaching the gospel to the people.

Heavens Testify Jesus Is God

Matt. 3 13-17 Then Jesus came from Galilee to John, at the
14 Jordan, to be baptized by him. And John was

1. The Messias will baptize with the Holy Spirit and *with fire;* cf. Mal. 3, 2. His action, symbolized by purifying fire, will be more penetrating and powerful than that of John.

2. Here Jesus is described in His capacity as judge. In this verse fire does not symbolize an agent of purification, as in v. 16, but rather a destructive agency.

for hindering him, and said, "It is I who ought
to be baptized by thee, and dost thou come
to me?" But Jesus answered and said to him, 15
"Let it be so now, for so it becomes us to fulfill all justice." Then he permitted him. And 16
when Jesus had been baptized, he immediately came up from the water.

And behold, the heavens were opened to
him, and he saw the Spirit of God descending
as a dove and coming upon him. And behold, 17
a voice from the heavens said, "This is my
beloved Son, in whom I am well pleased."

JESUS CHALLENGED by SATAN

DEC. 14 or June 14

Matt. 4 THEN Jesus was led into the desert by the
1-11 Spirit, to be tempted by the devil. And

after fasting forty days and forty nights, he 2
was hungry. And the tempter came and said 3
to him, "If thou art the Son of God, command
that these stones become loaves of bread."

First Temptation: Lust of the Flesh

But he answered and said, "It is written, 'Not 4
by bread alone does man live, but by every
word that comes forth from the mouth of
God.'"

Second Temptation: Pride of Life

Then the devil took him into the holy city 5
and set him on the pinnacle of the temple, and 6
said to him, "If thou art the Son of God,
throw thyself down; for it is written, 'He will
give his angels charge concerning thee; and
upon their hands they shall bear thee up, lest
thou dash thy foot against a stone.'"

Jesus said to him, "It is written further, 7
'Thou shalt not tempt the Lord thy God.'"

Third Temptation: Lust of the Eyes

Again, the devil took him to a very high 8
mountain, and showed him all the kingdoms
of the world and the glory of them. And he 9

said to him, "All these things will I give thee,
10 if thou wilt fair down and worship me." Then
Jesus said to him, "Begone, Satan! for it is
written, 'The Lord thy God shalt thou worship and him only shalt thou serve.'"
11 Then the devil left him; and behold, angels
came and ministered to him.

TESTIFIES JESUS IS GOD

DEC. 15 or June 15

THE NEXT day John saw Jesus coming to him, and he said, "Behold, the lamb of John 1 29-40

30 God, who takes away the sin of the world! This
is he of whom I said, 'After me there comes
one who has been set above me, because he
31 was before me.' And I did not know him. But
that he may be known to Israel, for this reason
have I come baptizing with water."
32 And John bore witness, saying, "I beheld
the Spirit descending as a dove from heaven,
33 and it abode upon him. And I did not know
him. But he who sent me to baptize with
water said to me, 'He upon whom thou wilt
see the Spirit descending, and abiding upon
him, he it is who baptizes with the Holy
34 Spirit.' And I have seen and have borne witness that this is the Son of God."

John's Disciples Now Follow Jesus

35 Again the next day John was standing there,
36 and two of his disciples. And looking upon
Jesus as he walked by, he said, "Behold the
37 lamb of God!" And the two disciples heard
him speak, and they followed Jesus.
38 But Jesus turned round, and seeing them
following him, said to them, "What is it you
seek?" They said to him, "Rabbi (which interpreted means Master), where dwellest thou?"

He said to them, "Come and see." They came 39
and saw where he was staying; and they stayed
with him that day. It was about the tenth hour.
Now Andrew, the brother of Simon Peter, 40
was one of the two who had heard John and
had followed him.

JESUS SALUTES PETER

DEC. 16 or June 16

John 1 41-51 HE FOUND first his brother Simon and said
to him, "We have found the Messias
42 (which interpreted is Christ)." And he led

him to Jesus. But Jesus, looking upon him,
said, "Thou art Simon, the son of John; thou
shalt be called [1]Cephas (which interpreted
is Peter)."

Jesus Calls Philip

The next day he was about to leave for Gal- 43
ilee, and he found Philip. And Jesus said to
him, "Follow me." Now Philip was from Beth- 44
saida, the town of Andrew and Peter.

Philip found Nathanael, and said to him, 45
"We have found him of whom Moses in the
Law and the Prophets wrote, Jesus the son of
Joseph of Nazareth." And Nathanael said to 46
him, "Can anything good come out of Naz-
areth?" Philip said to him, "Come and see."

Jesus saw Nathanael coming to him, and 47
said of him, "Behold a true Israelite in whom
there is no guile!"

Recognizing Jesus as Son of God

Nathanael said to him, "Whence knowest thou 48
me?" Jesus answered and said to him, "Before
Philip called thee, when thou wast under the

1. *Cephas:* in Aramaic this name means "rock."

49 fig tree, I saw thee." Nathanael answered him
and said, "Rabbi, thou art the Son of God,
thou art King of Israel."

50 Answering, Jesus said to him, "Because I
said to thee that I saw thee under the fig tree,
thou dost believe. Greater things than these
51 shalt thou see." And he said to him, "Amen,
amen, I say to you, you shall see heaven
opened, and the angels of God ascending and
descending upon the Son of Man."

JESUS at a MARRIAGE FEAST
DEC. 17 or June 17

AND ON the third day a marriage took John 2 1-12
place at Cana of Galilee, and the mother
of Jesus was there. Now Jesus too was invited 2
to the marriage, and also his disciples. And 3
the wine having run short, the mother of
Jesus said to him, "They have no wine." And 4
Jesus said to her, [1]"What wouldst thou have
me do, woman? My hour has not yet come."

1. *What wouldst thou have me do:* literally, "What to me and to thee." is an expression which can vary in meaning with its context, and with the speaker's

Performs First Miracle for Mary

5 His mother said to the attendants, "Do whatever he tells you."
6 Now six stone water-jars were placed
there, after the Jewish manner of purification,
7 each holding two or three measures. Jesus
said to them, "Fill the jars with water." And
8 they filled them to the brim. And Jesus said
to them, "Draw out now, and take to the chief
steward." And they took it to him.
9 Now when the chief steward had tasted the
water after it had become wine, not knowing
whence it was (though the attendants who had
drawn the water knew), the chief steward called
10 the bridegroom, and said to him, "Every man
at first sets forth the good wine, and when they
have drunk freely, then that which is poorer.
But thou hast kept the good wine until now."

Faith in Jesus through Mary

11 This first of his [1]signs Jesus worked at Cana of
Galilee; and he manifested his glory, and his

---

tone of voice. The circumstances show that it was not a rebuke. Woman: an honorable address in the language spoken by our Lord. *My hour:* is used of the opening of Christ's public ministry, or of that ministry as a whole.

1. *Signs:* St. John speaks always of Christ's miracles as "signs" or "works." We retain the term "sign," but it is to be understood in the same sense as "miracle" in the Synoptic Gospels.

disciples believed in him. After this he went 12
down to Capharnaum, he and his mother,
and his brethren, and his disciples. And they
stayed there but a few days.

MONEY-CHANGERS CAST OUT

DEC. 18 or June 18

John 2 13-25 NOW THE Passover of the Jews was at hand, and Jesus went up to Jerusalem.

And he found in the temple men selling oxen, 14
sheep and doves, and money-changers at their
tables. And making a kind of whip of cords, 15
he drove them all out of the temple, also the
sheep and oxen, and he poured out the money
of the changers and overturned the tables.
And to them who were selling the doves he 16
said, "Take these things away, and do not make
the house of my Father a house of business."

And his disciples remembered that it is 17
written, "The zeal for thy house has eaten me
up."

The Jews therefore answered and said to 18
him, "What sign dost thou show us, seeing
that thou dost these things?"

Jesus Gives Sign of His Authority

In answer Jesus said to them, "Destroy this 19
temple, and in three days I will raise it up." The
Jews therefore said, "Forty-six years has this 20
temple been in building, and wilt thou raise it
up in three days?" But he was speaking of the 21
temple of his body. When, accordingly, he had 22
risen from the dead, his disciples remembered
that he had said this, and they believed the
Scripture and the word that Jesus had spoken.

He Distrusts Their Weak Faith

23 [1]Now when he was at Jerusalem for the
feast of the Passover, many believed in his
name, seeing the signs that he was working.
24 But Jesus did not trust himself to them, in that
25 he knew all men, and because he had no need
that anyone should bear witness concerning
man, for he himself knew what was in man.

1. The faith of those attracted to Christ was imperfect, and He knew it. Hence He did not reveal Himself to them (Chrysostom), or admit them to a more intimate understanding of His teaching and Person.

JESUS EXPLAINS BAPTISM

DEC. 19 or June 19

NOW THERE was a certain man among the John 3
Pharisees, Nicodemus by name, a ruler 1-21
of the Jews. This man came to Jesus at night, 2
and said to him, "Rabbi, we know that thou
hast come a teacher from God, for no one
can work these signs that thou workest unless
God be with him." Jesus answered and said 3
to him, "Amen, amen, I say to thee, unless a
man be born again, he cannot see the kingdom of God."

Man Reborn through Baptism

Nicodemus said to him, "How can a man be 4
born when he is old? Can he enter a second
time into his mother's womb and be born
again?"

Jesus answered, "Amen, amen, I say to 5
thee, unless a man be born again of water
and the Spirit, he cannot enter into the kingdom of God. That which is born of the flesh 6

is flesh; and that which is born of the Spirit
is spirit.
7 "Do not wonder that I said to thee, 'You
8 must be born again.' The wind blows where
it will, and thou hearest its sound but dost not
know where it comes from or where it goes.
So is everyone who is born of the Spirit."
9 Nicodemus answered and said to him,
"How can these things be?"
10 Answering him, Jesus said, "Thou art a
teacher in Israel and dost not know these
11 things? Amen, amen, I say to thee, we speak
of what we know, and we bear witness to
what we have seen; and our witness you do
12 not receive. If I have spoken of earthly things
to you, and you do not believe, how will you
believe if I speak to you of heavenly things?
13 And no one has ascended into heaven except
him who has descended from heaven: the Son
of Man who is in heaven.

Necessity for Belief in Christ

14 "And as Moses lifted up the serpent in the
desert, even so must the Son of Man be lifted
15 up, that those who believe in him may not
perish, but may have life everlasting."

For God so loved the world that he gave his 16
only-begotten Son, that those who believe in
him may not perish, but may have life everlasting. For God did not send his Son into the 17
world in order [1]to judge the world, but that
the world might be saved through him. He 18
who believes in him is not judged; but he who
does not believe is already judged, because
he does not believe in the name of the only-
begotten Son of God.

Now this is the judgment: The light has 19
come into the world, yet men have loved the
darkness rather than the light, for their works
were evil. For everyone who does evil hates 20
the light, and does not come to the light, that
his deeds may not be exposed. But he who 21
does the truth comes to the light that his
deeds may be made manifest, for they have
been performed in God.

1. *To judge:* here in the sense of "to punish."

FINAL TESTIMONY of JOHN

DEC. 20 or June 20

John 3 22-36 AFTER THESE things Jesus and his disciples came into the land of Judea, and
he stayed there with them and baptized.
23 Now John was also baptizing in Aennon, near
Salim, for there was much water there. And

the people came and were baptized. For John 24
had not yet been put into prison.

Now there arose a discussion about puri- 25
fication between some of John's disciples and
the Jews. And they came to John and said to 26
him, "Rabbi, he who was with thee beyond
the Jordan, to whom thou hast borne witness,
behold he baptizes and all are coming to him."

John answered and said, "No one can 27
receive anything unless it is given to him
from heaven. You yourselves bear me witness 28
that I said, 'I am not the Christ but have been
sent before him.' He who has the bride is 29
the bridegroom; but the friend of the bridegroom, who stands and hears him, rejoices
exceedingly at the voice of the bridegroom.
This my joy, therefore, is made full. He must 30
increase, but I must decrease."

Testimony of Jesus to Us

He who comes from above is over all. He who 31
is from the earth belongs to earth, and of the
earth he speaks. He who comes from heaven
is over all. And he bears witness to that which 32
he has seen and heard, and his witness no one
receives. He who receives his witness has set 33

34 his seal on this, that God is true. For he whom
God has sent speaks the words of God, for not
by measure does God give the Spirit.
35 The Father loves the Son, and has given all
36 things into his hand. He who believes in the
Son has everlasting life; he who is unbelieving towards the Son shall not see life, but the
wrath of God rests upon him.

John 4 1-3 When, therefore, Jesus knew that the Pharisees had heard that Jesus made and baptized
2 more disciples than John—although Jesus
3 himself did not baptize, but his disciples—he
left Judea and went again into Galilee.

The SAMARITAN WOMAN
DEC. 21 or June 21

NOW HE had to pass through Samaria. He John 4 4-19
came, accordingly, to a town of Samaria 5
called Sichar, near the field that Jacob gave to
his son Joseph. Now Jacob's well was there. 6
Jesus, therefore, wearied as he was from
the journey, was sitting at the well. It was 7
about the sixth hour. There came a Samaritan
woman to draw water.

8 Jesus said to her, "Give me to drink"; for
his disciples had gone away into the town to
9 buy food. The Samaritan woman therefore
said to him, "How is it that thou, although
thou art a Jew, dost ask drink of me, who am a
Samaritan woman?" For Jews do not associate
with Samaritans.

Jesus Promises Living Water

10 Jesus answered and said to her, "If thou didst
know the gift of God, and who it is who says
to thee, 'Give me to drink,' thou, perhaps,
wouldst have asked of him, and he would have
11 given thee living water." The woman said to
him, "Sir, thou hast nothing to draw with, and
the well is deep. Whence then hast thou living
12 water? Art thou greater than our father Jacob
who gave us the well, and drank from it, himself, and his sons, and his flocks?"
13 In answer Jesus said to her, "Everyone
who drinks of this water will thirst again.
He, however, who drinks of the water that
14 I will give him shall never thirst; but the
water that I will give him shall become in
him a fountain of water, springing up unto
15 life everlasting." The woman said to him, "Sir,

give me this water that I may not thirst, or
come here to draw."

Jesus as a Searcher of Hearts

Jesus said to her, "Go, call thy husband and 16
come here." The woman answered and said, 17
"I have no husband." Jesus said to her, "Thou
hast said well, 'I have no husband,' for thou 18
hast had five husbands, and he whom thou
now hast is not thy husband. In this thou hast
spoken truly." The woman said to him, "Sir, I 19
see that thou art a prophet."

NECESSITY of SPIRITUAL WORSHIP

DEC. 22 or June 22

John 4 20-42 "OUR FATHERS worshipped on this mountain, but you say that at Jerusalem is
21 the place where one ought to worship." Jesus
said to her, "Woman, believe me, the hour is
coming when neither on this mountain nor
22 in Jerusalem will you worship the Father. You
worship what you do not know; we worship
what we know, for salvation is from the Jews.
23 But the hour is coming, and is now here,
when the true worshippers will worship the
Father [1]in spirit and in truth. For the Father
24 also seeks such to worship him. God is spirit,
and they who worship him must worship in
spirit and in truth."

I Am the Christ

25 The woman said to him, "I know that Messias
is coming (who is called Christ), and when he
comes he will tell us all things."
26 Jesus said to her, "I who speak with thee
am he."

---

1. *In spirit and in truth*: not merely with the external observances of Jews and Samaritans, but internally and according to God's will. *Such to worship him*: God desires as His worshippers those who have this internal disposition.

And at this point his disciples came; and they 27
wondered that he was speaking with a woman.
Yet no one said, "What dost thou seek?" or, 28
"Why dost thou speak with her?" The woman
therefore left her water-jar and went away into
the town, and said to the people, "Come and 29
see a man who has told me all that I have ever
done. Can he be the Christ?" They went forth 30
from the town and came to meet him.

Jesus Hungers to Do the Father's Will

Meanwhile, his disciples besought him, say- 31
ing, "Rabbi, eat." But he said to them, "I have 32
food to eat of which you do not know." The 33
disciples therefore said to one another, "Has
someone brought him something to eat?"

Jesus said to them, "My food is to do the will 34
of him who sent me, to accomplish his work.

And to Reap a Harvest of Souls

"Do you not say, 'There are yet four months, 35
and then comes the harvest'? Well, I say to
you, lift up your eyes and behold that the fields
are already white for the harvest. [1]And he 36

1. Under this agricultural figure Christ illustrates the whole plan of His mission. The sowers were God's earlier messengers, as Moses and the

who reaps receives a wage, and gathers fruit
unto life everlasting, so that the sower and
37 the reaper may rejoice together. For herein is
38 the proverb true, 'One sows, another reaps.' I
have sent you to reap that on which you have
not labored. Others have labored, and you
have entered into their labors."

39 Now many of the Samaritans of that town
believed in him because of the word of the
woman who bore witness, "He told me all
40 that I have ever done." When therefore the
Samaritans had come to him, they besought
41 him to stay there; and he stayed two days. And
far more believed because of his word.

42 And they said to the woman, "We no longer believe because of what thou hast said, for
we have heard for ourselves and we know that
this is in truth the Savior of the world."

---

prophets. The one who sows for this harvest is Christ. The reapers are the Apostles. In this spiritual harvest both sowers and reapers will rejoice together.

HIS OWN COUNTRYMEN BLIND

DEC. 23 or June 23

"NOW AFTER two days he departed from that John 4
place and went into Galilee, for Jesus himself 43-53
bore witness that a prophet receives no honor 44
in his own country. When, therefore, he had 45
come into Galilee, the Galileans received
him, having seen all that he had done in Jerusalem during the feast, for they also had gone
to the feast.

He came again therefore to Cana of Galilee, 46
where he had made the water wine. And there

was a certain royal official whose son was lying
47 sick at Capharnaum. When he heard that Jesus
had come from Judea into Galilee, he went to
him and besought him to come down and heal
his son, for he was at the point of death.
48 Jesus therefore said to him, "Unless you
see signs and Wonders, you do not believe."
49 The royal official said to him, "Sir, come down
before my child dies."

He Heals the Son of an Official

50 Jesus said to him, "Go thy way, thy son lives."
The man believed the word that Jesus spoke
51 to him, and departed. But even as he was now
going down, his servants met him and brought
52 word saying that his son lived. He asked of them
therefore the hour in which he had got better.
53 And they told him, "Yesterday, at the seventh
hour, the fever left him." The father knew then
that it was at that very hour in which Jesus had
said to him, "Thy son lives." And he himself
believed, and his whole household.

He Preaches Penance

Matt. 4 And leaving the town of Nazareth, he came and
13-17 dwelt in Capharnaum, which is by the sea, in

the territory of Zabulon and Nephthalim; that 14
what was spoken through Isaias the prophet
might be fulfilled: "Land of Zabulon and land 15
of Nephthalim, by the way to the sea, beyond
the Jordan, Galilee of the Gentiles: the people 16
who sat in darkness have seen a great light; and
upon those who sat in the region and shadow
of death, a light has arisen."

From that time Jesus began to preach, and 17
to say, "Repent, for the kingdom of heaven
is at hand." And the fame of him went out Luke 4
through the whole country. And he taught in 14-15 15
their synagogues, and was honored by all.

TEACHES from PETER'S SHIP

DEC. 24 or June 24

Matt. 4 18 As *Jesus* was walking by the sea of Galilee, he saw two brothers, Simon, who is

called Peter, and his brother Andrew, casting
a net into the sea (for they were fishermen).
Now it came to pass, while the crowds were Luke 5
pressing upon him to hear the word of God, 1-11
that he was standing by Lake Genesareth. 2
And he saw two boats moored by the lake,
but the fishermen had left them and were
washing their nets. And getting into one of 3
the boats, the one that was Simon's, he asked
him to put out a little from the land. And
sitting down, he began to teach the crowds
from the boat.

But when he had ceased speaking, he said 4
to Simon, "Put out into the deep, and lower
your nets for a catch." And Simon answered 5
and said to him, "Master, the whole night
through we have toiled and have taken nothing; but at thy word I will lower the net."

"Thou Shalt Catch Men"

And when they had done so, they enclosed 6
a great number of fishes, but their net was
breaking. And they beckoned to their com- 7
rades in the other boat to come and help
them. And they came and filled both the boats,
so that they began to sink.

8 But when Simon Peter saw this, he fell
down at Jesus' knees, saying, "Depart from
9 me, for I am a sinful man, O Lord." For he
and all who were with him were amazed at
10 the catch of fish they had made; and so were
also James and John, the sons of Zebedee,
who were partners with Simon. And Jesus
said to Simon, "Do not be afraid; henceforth
11 thou shall catch men." And when they had
brought their boats to land, they left all and
followed him.

ASTONISHED at HIS TEACHING

DEC. 25 or June 25

AND THEY entered Capharnaum. And Mark 1
immediately on the Sabbath he went 21-31
into the synagogue and began to teach them.
And they were astonished at his teaching; for 22
he was teaching them as one having authority,
and not as the Scribes.

Jesus Casts Out Unclean Spirit

Now in their synagogue there was a man with 23
an unclean spirit, and he cried out, saying, 24

"What have we to do with thee, Jesus of Nazareth? Hast thou come to destroy us? I know
25 who thou art, the Holy One of God." And Jesus
rebuked him, saying, "Hold thy peace, and go
26 out of the man." And the unclean spirit, con-
vulsing him and crying out with a loud voice,
went out of him.

27 And they were all amazed, so that they
inquired among themselves, saying, "What
is this? What new doctrine is this? For with
authority he commands even the unclean spir-
28 its, and they obey him." And rumor concerning
him went forth immediately into all the region
round about Galilee.

Jesus Cures Peter's Mother-in-law

29 And as soon as they came out of the synagogue, they, with James and John, came
30 to the house of Simon and Andrew. Now
Simon's mother-in-law was keeping her bed,
sick with a fever, and they immediately told
31 him about her. And drawing near, he took
her by the hand and raised her up; and the
fever left her at once, and she began to wait
on them.

He Restores Others to Health

Now when the sun was setting, all who had Luke 4 40
persons sick with various diseases brought
them to him. †And the whole town had gathered together at the door. ‡And he laid his
hands upon each of them and cured them;
*that what was spoken through Isaias the
prophet might be fulfilled, who said, "He
himself took up our infirmities, and bore the
burden of our ills." Matt. 8 16

They brought to him many who were Luke 4 41
possessed, and he cast out the spirits with a
word. And devils also came forth from many,
crying out and saying, "Thou art the Son of
God." And he rebuked them, and did not permit them to speak, because they knew that he
was the Christ.

† Mark 1, 33
‡ Luke 4, 40
* Matt. 8,17

OTHER MIRACLES

DEC. 26 or June 26

Mark 1 35-38 AND RISING UP long before daybreak, he
went out and departed into a desert

place, and there he prayed. And Simon, and 36
those who were with him, followed him. And 37
they found him and said to him, "They are all 38
seeking thee." And he said to them, "Let us
go into the neighboring villages and towns,
that there also I may preach. For this is why
I have come."

And the crowds were seeking after him, Luke 4
and they came to him, and tried to detain 42
him, that he might not depart from them.
And Jesus went about all Galilee, teaching in Matt. 4
their synagogues, and preaching the gospel of 23
the kingdom, and healing every disease and
every sickness among the people.

Jesus Heals a Leper

And it came to pass, while he was in one of Luke 5
the towns, that, behold, there was a man full 12
of leprosy. And when he saw Jesus he fell on
his face and besought him, saying, "Lord, if
thou wilt, thou canst make me clean."

And Jesus, having compassion on him, Mark 1
stretched forth his hand and touched him, 41-45
and said to him, "I will; be thou made clean."
And when he had spoken, immediately the 42
leprosy left him, and he was made clean.

43 Then he strictly charged him, and immedi-
44 ately drove him away. And he said to him,
"See thou tell no one; but go, show thyself to
the high priest, and offer for thy purification
the things that Moses commanded, for a wit-
45 ness to them." But he went out, and began to
publish and to spread abroad the fact, so that
Jesus could no longer openly enter a town,
but remained outside in desert places.

Luke 5 15-16 But so much the more the tidings spread
concerning him, and great crowds gathered
together to hear him and to be cured of their
16 sicknesses. But he himself was in retirement
in the desert, and in prayer.

JESUS FORGIVES SIN

DEC. 27 or June 27

AND AFTER some days, he again entered Mark 2
Capharnaum and it was reported that 1-3

2 he was at home. And many gathered together,
so that there was no longer room, not even
3 around the door. And he spoke the word to
Luke 5 17-19 them. There were Pharisees and teachers of
the Law sitting by, who had come out of every
village of Galilee and Judea and out of Jerusalem. And the power of the Lord was present
to heal them.

18 And behold, some men were carrying
upon a pallet a man who was paralyzed, and
they were trying to bring him in and to lay
19 him before him. And as they found no way
of bringing him in, because of the crowd,
they went up onto the roof and lowered him
through the tiles, with his pallet, into the
Matt. 9 midst before Jesus. And Jesus, seeing their
2 faith, said to the paralytic, "Take courage, son;
thy sins are forgiven thee."

Proves His Pardon by a Miracle

Luke 5 And the Scribes and Pharisees began to argue,
21 saying, "Who is this man who speaks blasphe-
mies? Who can forgive sins, but God only?"
Matt. 9 And Jesus, knowing their thoughts, said,
4-6 "Why do you harbor evil thoughts in your
5 hearts? For which is easier, to say, 'Thy sins

are forgiven thee,' or to say, 'Arise, and walk'?
But that you may know that the Son of Man 6
has power on earth to forgive sins"—then
he said to the paralytic—"Arise, take up thy
pallet and go to thy house." And immediately Luke 5
he arose before them, took up what he had 25-26
been lying on, and went away to his house,
glorifying God.

And astonishment seized upon them all, 26
and they glorified God and were filled with
fear, saying, "We have seen wonderful things Mark 2
today. Never did we see the like." 12

JESUS CALLS MATTHEW (LEVI)

DEC. 28 or June 28

Matt. 9 9 Mark 2 13-14 NOW AS Jesus passed on from there, he
went forth again by the water's edge,
and all the crowd kept coming to him, and
14 he taught them. And as he was passing along,
Luke 5 27-29 †he saw a publican, ‡named Matthew sitting in
the tax-collector's place, and he said to him,
28 "Follow me." And leaving all things, he arose
29 and followed him. And Levi gave a great feast
for him at his house.

He Eats with Publicans and Sinners

Mark 2 15 And it came to pass as he was at table in Levi's
house, that many publicans and sinners were

† Luke 5, 27
‡ Matt. 9, 9

at table with Jesus and his disciples, for there
were many and they also followed him. And Luke 5
the Pharisees and their Scribes were grum- 30
bling, saying to his disciples, "Why does your Mark 2
master eat and drink with publicans and sin- 16-17
ners?" And Jesus heard this, and said to them, 17
"I have not come to call the just, but sinners, Luke 5
to repentance." 32

The Question of Fasting

And the disciples of John and the Pharisees Mark 2
were fasting. And they came, and said to him, 18
"Why do the disciples of John fast often and Luke 5
make supplications, and likewise those of 33
the Pharisees, whereas thy disciples eat and
drink?"

[1]And Jesus said to them, "Can the wedding Mark 2
guests fast as long as the bridegroom is with 19-20
them? As long as they have the bridegroom 20
with them they cannot fast. But the days will
come when the bridegroom shall be taken
away from them, and then they will fast on
that day."

---

1. Jesus is the bridegroom, and His wedding guests (literally, children of the bridegroom) are His disciples. It is repugnant to Jewish custom to think of fasting and mourning during the period of the wedding festivities. But when He is taken away from them, then His disciples will fittingly fast and mourn.

Luke 5 36-39 [1]And he spoke a parable also to them, "No
one puts a patch from a new garment on an
old garment; else not only does he tear the
new one, but the patch from the new garment
37 does not match the old. And no one pours new
wine into old wine-skins; else the new wine
will burst the skins, and will be spilt itself,
38 and the skins ruined. But new wine must be
39 put into fresh skins, and both are saved. And
no man after drinking old wine immediately
desires new; for he says, 'The old is better.'"

1. In these two similes Jesus refers to the differences between the old dispensation, which was coming to an end, and the new order, which was foretold by the prophets and which He began to establish. These two orders are incompatible and cannot be made to match.

CURES HELPLESS INVALID

DEC. 29 or June 29

AFTER THIS there was a feast of the Jews, John 5
and Jesus went up to Jerusalem. Now 1-15
there is at Jerusalem, by the Sheepgate, a pool 2

called in Hebrew Bethsaida, having five porti-
3 coes. In these were lying a great multitude of
the sick, blind, lame, and those with shrivelled
limbs, waiting for the moving of the water.
4 For an angel of the Lord used to come down
at certain times into the pool, and the water
was troubled. And the first to go down into
the pool after the troubling of the water was
cured of whatever infirmity he had.

5 Now a certain man was there who had been
6 thirty-eight years under his infirmity. When
Jesus saw him lying there, and knew that he
had been in this state a long time, he said to
7 him, "Dost thou want to get well?" The sick
man answered him, "Sir, I have no one to put
me into the pool when the water is stirred;
for while I am coming, another steps down
before me."

8 Jesus said to him. "Rise, take up thy pallet
9 and walk." And at once the man was cured.
And he took up his pallet and began to walk.
Now that day was a Sabbath.

Accused of Violating the Sabbath

10 The Jews therefore said to him who had been
healed, "It is the Sabbath; thou art not allowed

to take up thy pallet." He answered them, 11
"He who made me well said to me, 'Take up
thy pallet and walk.'" They asked him then, 12
"Whois the man who said to thee, 'Take up
thy pallet and walk'?" But the man who had 13
been healed did not know who it was, for
Jesus had quietly gone away, since there was
a crowd in the place.

Afterwards Jesus found him in the temple, 14
and said to him, "Behold, thou art cured. Sin
no more, lest something worse befall thee."
The man went away and told the Jews that it 15
was Jesus who had healed him.

HE SHALL COME to JUDGE the WORLD

DEC. 30 or June 30

John 5 16-30 AND THIS is why the Jews kept persecuting Jesus, because he did such things on
17 the Sabbath. Jesus, however, answered them,
"My Father works even until now, and I work."
18 This, then, is why the Jews were the more anxious to put him to death; because he not only
broke the Sabbath, but also called God his own
Father, making himself equal to God.

He Discusses His Own Divine Character

In answer therefore Jesus said to them, 19
"Amen, amen, I say to you, the Son can do
nothing of himself, but only what he sees the
Father doing. For whatever he does, this the
Son also does in like manner. For the Father 20
loves the Son, and shows him all that he himself does. And greater works than these he
will show him, that you may wonder.

"For as the Father raises the dead and gives 21
them life, even so the Son also gives life to
whom he will. For neither does the Father 22
judge any man, but all judgment he has given
to the Son, that all men may honor the Son 23
even as they honor the Father. He who does
not honor the Son, does not honor the Father
who sent him.

"Amen, amen, I say to you, he who hears 24
my word, and believes him who sent me, has
life everlasting, and does not come to judgment, but has passed from death to life.

"Amen, amen, I say to you, the hour is 25
coming, and now is here, when the dead shall
hear the voice of the Son of God, and those
who hear shall live. For as the Father has life 26
in himself, even so he has given to the Son also

27 to have life in himself; and he has granted him
power to render judgment, because he is Son
28 of Man. Do not wonder at this, for the hour is
coming in which all who are in the tombs shall
hear the voice of the Son of God.

29 "And they who have done good shall come
forth unto resurrection of life; but they who
have done evil unto resurrection of judgment.
30 Of myself I can do nothing. As I hear, I judge,
and my judgment is just because I seek not my
own will, but the will of him who sent me."

JESUS JUSTIFIES HIS CLAIMS

DEC. 31 or July 1

IF I BEAR witness concerning myself, my John 5 31-47
witness is not true. There is another who 32
bears witness concerning me, and I know

that the witness that he bears concerning me
is true.
33 "You have sent to John, and he has borne
34 witness to the truth. I however do not receive
the witness of man, but I say these things that
35 you may be saved. He was the lamp, burning
and shining; and you desired to rejoice for a
while in his light.
36 "The witness, however, that I have is greater
than that of John. For the works which the
Father has given me to accomplish, these very
works that I do, bear witness to me, that the
37 Father has sent me. And the Father himself,
who has sent me, has borne witness to me. But
you have never heard his voice, or seen his face.
38 "And you have not his word abiding in you,
since you do not believe him whom he has
39 sent. You search the Scriptures, because in
them you think that you have life everlasting.
40 And it is they that bear witness to me, yet you
are not willing to come to me that you may
have life.

He Rebukes Them for Their Unbelief

41-42 "I do not receive glory from men. But I know
that you have not the love of God in you. I

have come in the name of my Father, and you 43
do not receive me. If another come in his own
name, him you will receive. How can you 44
believe who receive glory from one another,
and do not seek the glory which is from the
only God?

"Do not think that I shall accuse you to the 45
Father. There is one who accuses you, Moses,
in whom you hope. For if you believed Moses 46
you would believe me also, for he wrote of
me. But if you do not believe his writings, 47
how will you believe my words?"

Jesus heals a withered hand

JESUS EXCUSES HIS DISCIPLES

JAN. 1 or July 2

Mark 2 AND IT CAME to pass again as he was going
23 through the standing grain on the Sab-
Luke 6 bath, that his disciples were plucking and eat-
1 ing the ears of grain, rubbing them with their
Matt. 12 hands. But the Pharisees, when they saw it,
2 said to him, "Thy disciples are doing what it
is not lawful for them to do on the Sabbath."

By Example of Holy Men

Mark 2 And he said to them, "Have you never read
25-26 what David did when he and those who were
26 with him were in need, and hungry? how he
entered the house of God, when Abiathar was
high priest, and ate the loaves of proposition,
which he could not lawfully eat, but only the

priests? and how he gave them to those who
were with him?

By the Mind of God Himself

"Or have you not read in the Law, that on the Matt. 12
Sabbath days the priests in the temple break 5-7
the Sabbath and are guiltless? But I tell you 6
that one greater than the temple is here. But 7
if you knew what this means, 'I desire mercy,
and not sacrifice,' you would never have condemned the innocent."

And he said to them, "The Sabbath was Mark 2
made for man, and not man for the Sabbath. 27-28
Therefore the Son of Man is Lord even of the 28
Sabbath."

Jesus Heals a Withered Hand

And it came to pass on another Sabbath, that Luke 6
he entered the synagogue and taught. And a 6-7
man was there and his right hand was withered. And the Scribes and the Pharisees were 7
watching whether he cured on the Sabbath,
that they might find how to accuse him.

And they asked him, saying, "Is it lawful Matt. 12
to cure on the Sabbath?" But he knew their 10 Luke 6
thoughts, and he said to the man with the 8-9

withered hand, "Arise and stand forth in the
9 midst." And he arose and stood forth. But
Jesus said to them "I ask you, is it lawful on
the Sabbath to do good, or to do evil? to save
a life, or to destroy it?" †But they kept silence.

Matt. 12 11-12 But he said to them, "What man is there
among you who, if he has a single sheep and
it falls into a pit on the Sabbath, will not take
12 hold of it and lift it out? How much better is
a man than a sheep! Therefore, it is lawful to
Mark 3 9 do good on the Sabbath." And looking round
upon them with anger, and being grieved
at the blindness of their hearts, he said to
the man, "Stretch forth thy hand." ‡And he
stretched it forth, and it was restored, as
sound as the other.

† Mark 3, 4
‡ Matt. 12, 13

The choice of the Twelve

PHARISEES FILLED with FURY

JAN. 2 or July 3

†BUT THE Pharisees were filled with fury, Luke 6 11
and began to discuss among them-
selves what they should do to Jesus. The Phar- Mark 3 6
isees went out and immediately took counsel
with the Herodians against him, how they
might do away with him.

Jesus Withdraws

‡Then, knowing this, Jesus with his disci- Mark 3 7-10
ples withdrew to the sea; and there followed
him a large crowd from Galilee and Judea, 8
and from Jerusalem, and from Idumea, and
from beyond the Jordan. And of those about
Tyre and Sidon, a large crowd, hearing what
he was doing, came to him. And he told his 9

† Matt. 12, 14
‡ Matt. 12, 15

disciples to have a small boat in readiness for
him, because of the crowd, lest they should
10 throng him. For he healed many, so that as
many as had ailments were pressing upon him
to touch him.

Again He Cures Body and Soul

Matt. 4 24 And his fame spread into all Syria; and they
brought to him all the sick suffering from
various diseases and torments, those possessed, and lunatics, and paralytics; and he
Mark 3 11-12 cured them. And the unclean spirits, whenever they beheld him, fell down before him
12 and cried out, saying, "Thou art the Son
of God."

And he charged them strictly not to make
Matt. 12 17-21 him known; that what was spoken through
Isaias the prophet might be fulfilled, who
18 said, "Behold, my servant, whom I have chosen, my is beloved in whom my soul is well
pleased: I will put my Spirit upon him, and
19 he will declare judgment to the Gentiles. He
will not wrangle, nor cry aloud, neither will
anyone hear his voice in the streets.
20 "A bruised reed he will not break, and a
smoking wick he will not quench, till he send

forth judgment unto victory; and in his name 21
will the Gentiles hope."

After Prayer He Chooses Twelve Apostles

Now it came to pass in those days, that [*]see- Luke 6 12
ing the crowds, he went out to the mountain Luke 6 12-13
to pray, and continued all night in prayer to
God. And when day broke, he called to him Mark 3 13-14
men of his own choosing, and they came to
him. And he appointed twelve that they might 14
be with him and that he might send them
forth to preach.

Now these are the names of the twelve Matt. 10 2-4
apostles: [1]first Simon, who is called Peter,
and his brother Andrew; James the son of 3
Zebedee, and his brother John; Philip and
Bartholomew; Thomas and Matthew the
publican; James the son of Alpheus, and Thad-
deus; Simon the Cananean, and Judas Iscar- 4
iot, he who betrayed him.

---

* Matt. 5, 1

1. *First Simon, who is called Peter:* primacy in the Church belongs to Peter.

The SERMON on the MOUNT

JAN. 3 or July 4

Luke 6 17-20 AND COMING DOWN with them, he took his
stand on a level stretch, with a crowd
of his disciples, and a great multitude of people from all Judea and Jerusalem, and the sea
18 coast of Tyre and Sidon, who came to listen
19 to him and to be healed of their diseases. And
those who were troubled with unclean spirits

were cured. And all the crowd were trying to 20
touch him, for power went forth from him Matt. 5 2-12
and healed all. And he lifted up his eyes to his
disciples. And opening his mouth he taught
them, saying,

The Eight Beatitudes

"Blessed are the poor in spirit, for theirs is the 3
kingdom of heaven.
"Blessed are the meek, for they shall pos- 4
sess the earth.
"Blessed are they who mourn, for they 5
shall be comforted.
"Blessed are they who hunger and thirst for 6
justice, for they shall be satisfied.
"Blessed are the merciful, for they shall 7
obtain mercy.
"Blessed are the clean of heart, for they 8
shall see God.
"Blessed are the peacemakers, for they 9
shall be called children of God.
"Blessed are they who suffer persecution 10
for justice' sake, for theirs is the kingdom of
heaven.
"Blessed are you when men reproach you, 11
and persecute you, and, speaking falsely, say

all manner of evil against you, for my sake.
12 Rejoice and exult, because your reward is
great in heaven; for so did they persecute the
prophets who were before you.

Followed by Threats

Luke 6 24-26 "But woe to you rich! for you are now hav-
25 ing your comfort. Woe to you who are filled!
for you shall hunger. Woe to you who laugh
26 now! for you shall mourn and weep. Woe to
you when all men speak well of you! In the
selfsame manner their fathers used to treat
the prophets."

Hatred versus Charity

DISCIPLES COMPARED to SALT and LIGHT

JAN. 4 or July 5

YOU ARE the salt of the earth; but if the Matt. 5
salt loses its strength, what shall it be 13-26
salted with? It is no longer of any use but to
be thrown out and trodden underfoot by men.
"You are the light of the world. A city set 14
on a mountain cannot be hidden. Neither 15
do men light a lamp and put it under the

measure, but upon the lamp-stand, so as to
16 give light to all in the house. Even so let your
light shine before men, in order that they may
see your good works and give glory to your
Father in heaven.

17 "Do not think that I have come to destroy
the Law or the Prophets. I have not come to
18 destroy, but to fulfill. For amen I say to you,
till heaven and earth pass away, not one jot
or one tittle shall be lost from the Law till all
things have been accomplished.

19 "Therefore whoever does away with one
of these least commandments, and so teaches
men, shall be called least in the kingdom of
heaven; but whoever carries them out and
teaches them, he shall be called great in the
20 kingdom of heaven. For I say to you that
unless your justice exceeds that of the Scribes
and Pharisees, you shall not enter the kingdom of heaven.

Hatred versus Charity

21 "You have heard that it was said to the
ancients, 'Thou shalt not kill'; and that who-
22 ever shall kill shall be liable to judgment. But I
say to you that everyone who is angry with his

brother shall be liable to judgment; and whoever says to his brother, 'Raca,' shall be liable
to the Sanhedrin; and whoever says, 'Thou
fool!', shall be liable to the fire of Gehenna.
"Therefore, if thou art offering thy gift 23
at the altar, and there rememberest that thy
brother has anything against thee, leave thy 24
gift before the altar and go first to be recon-
ciled to thy brother, and then come and offer
thy gift. Come to terms with thy opponent 25
quickly while thou art with him on the way;
lest thy opponent deliver thee to the judge,
and the judge to the officer, and thou be cast
into prison. Amen I say to thee, thou wilt 26
not come out from it until thou hast paid the
last penny."

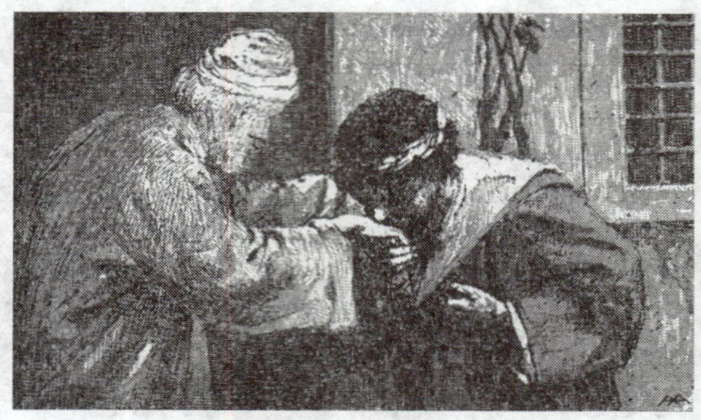

Pardon, not revenge

CHASTITY of MIND and BODY

JAN. 5 or July 6

Matt. 5 27-42 "YOU HAVE heard that it was said to the
ancients, 'Thou shalt not commit adul-
28 tery.' But I say to you that anyone who so much
as looks with lust at a woman has already committed adultery with her in his heart.

Occasions of Sin

29 "So if thy right eye is an occasion of sin to
thee, pluck it out and cast it from thee; for
it is better for thee that one of thy members
should perish than that thy whole body should
30 be thrown into hell. And if thy right hand is

an occasion of sin to thee, cut it off and cast
it from thee; for it is better for thee that one
of thy members should be lost than that thy
whole body should go into hell

Divorce

"It was said, moreover, 'Whoever puts away 31
his wife, let him give her a written notice of
dismissal.' [1]But I say to you that everyone who 32
puts away his wife, save on account of immorality, causes her to commit adultery; and he
who marries a woman who has been put away
commits adultery.

Perjury and Swearing

"Again, you have heard that it was said to the 33
ancients, 'Thou shalt not swear falsely, but
fulfill thy oaths to the Lord.' But I say to you 34
not to swear at all: neither by heaven, for it
is the throne of God; nor by the earth, for it 35
ishis footstool; nor by Jerusalem, for it is the
city of the great King. Neither do thou swear 36
by thy head, for thou canst not make one hair

1. Unfaithfulness justifies separation from bed and board, but the bond of marriage remains unbroken. This truth is clear enough from the conclusion of this verse, and still clearer in Mark 10, 11; Luke 16, 18; Rom. 7, 2; 1 Cor. 7, 10f. 39.

37 white or black. But let your speech be, 'Yes,
yes'; 'No, no'; and whatever is beyond these
comes from the evil one.

Pardon, Not Revenge

38 "You have heard that it was said, 'An eye for
39 an eye,' and, 'A tooth for a tooth.' But I say to
you not to resist the evildoer; on the contrary,
if someone strike thee on the right cheek, turn
40 to him the other also; and if anyone would go
to law with thee and take thy tunic, let him
41 take thy cloak as well; and whoever forces
42 thee to go for one mile, go with him two. To
him who asks of thee, give; and from him who
would borrow of thee, do not turn away."

Alms .. given in secret

LOVE YOUR ENEMIES

JAN. 6 or July 7

"YOU HAVE HEARD that it was said, 'Thou Matt. 5
shalt love thy neighbor, and shalt hate 43

Luke 6 thy enemy.' But I say to you who are listening:
27-28 Love your enemies, do good to those who
28 hate you. Bless those who curse you, pray for
Matt. 5 those who calumniate you, so that you may be
45 children of your Father in heaven, who makes
his sun to rise on the good and the evil, and
sends rain on the just and the unjust.

The Golden Rule

Luke 6 "And even as you wish men to do to you,
31 Matt. 5 soalso do you to them. For if you love those
46 that love you, what reward shall you have? Do
not even the publicans do that?

Luke 6 "And if you do good to those who do
33-36 good to you, what merit have you? For even
34 sinners do that. And if you lend to those
from whom you hope to receive in return,
what merit have you? For even sinners lend
to sinners that they may get back as much
in return.

35 "But love your enemies; and do good, and
lend, not hoping for any return, and your
reward shall be great, and you shall be children of the Most High, for he is kind towards
36 the ungrateful and evil. Be merciful, therefore, even as your Father is merciful.

Correct Motive for Your Charities

"Take heed not to do your good before men, Matt. 6 1-4
in order to be seen by them; otherwise you
shall have no reward with your Father in
heaven.

"Therefore when thou givest alms, do not 2
sound a trumpet before thee, as the hypocrites
do in the synagogues and streets, in order
that they may be honored by men. Amen I
say to you, they have received their reward.
But when thou givest alms, do not let thy left 3
hand know what thy right hand is doing, so 4
that thy alms may be given in secret; and thy
Father, who sees in secret, will reward thee."

"Give us . . . our daily bread"

HOW to PRAY

JAN. 7 or July 8

Matt. 6 5-21 "AGAIN when you pray, you shall not be
like the hypocrites, who love to pray
standing in the synagogues and at the street
corners, in order that they may be seen by
men. Amen I say to you, they have received
6 their reward. But when thou prayest, go into

thy room, and closing thy door, pray to thy
Father in secret; and thy Father, who sees in
secret, will reward thee.
"But in praying, do not multiply words, as 7
the Gentiles do; for they think that by saying
a great deal, they will be heard. So do not 8
be like them; for your Father knows what
you need before you ask him. In this manner 9
therefore shall you pray:

Lord's Prayer Is a Method of Prayer

"'Our Father who art in heaven, hallowed
be thy name. Thy kingdom come, thy will be 10
done on earth, as it is in heaven. Give us this 11
day our daily bread. And forgive us our debts, 12
as we also forgive our debtors. And lead us 13
not into temptation, but deliver us from evil.'
"For if you forgive men their offenses, 14
your heavenly Father will also forgive you
your offenses. But if you do not forgive men, 15
neither will your Father forgive you your
offenses.

How to Fast

"And when you fast, do not look gloomy like 16
the hypocrites, who disfigure their faces in

order to appear to men as fasting. Amen I say
17 to you, they have received their reward. But
thou, when thou dost fast, anoint thy head
18 and wash thy face, so that thou mayest not be
seen fasting by men, but by thy Father, who is
in secret; and thy Father, who sees in secret,
will reward thee.

Work for Eternal Treasures

19 "Do not lay up for yourselves treasures on
earth, where rust and moth consume, and
20 where thieves break in and steal; but lay up
for yourselves treasures in heaven, where
neither rust nor moth consumes, nor thieves
21 break in and steal. For where thy treasure is,
there also will thy heart be."

Trust in God

NECESSITY of a RIGHT MOTIVE

JAN. 8 or July 9

"THE LAMP of the body is the eye. If thy Matt. 6
eye be sound, thy whole body will be 22-34
full of light. But if thy eye be evil, thy whole 23
body will be full of darkness. Therefore if the
light that is in thee is darkness, how great is
the darkness itself!

Serve only One Master

"No man can serve two masters; for either he 24
will hate the one and love the other, or else
he will stand by the one and despise the other.
You cannot serve God and mammon.

25 "Therefore I say to you, do not be anxious
for your life, what you shall eat; nor yet for
your body, what you shall put on. Is not the
life a greater thing than the food, and the
body than the clothing?

Work, yet Trust in Divine Providence

26 "Look at the birds of the air: they do not sow,
or reap, or gather into barns; yet your heavenly Father feeds them. Are not you of much
27 more value than they? But which of you by
being anxious about it can add to his stature
a single cubit?
28 "And as for clothing, why are you anxious?
Consider how the lilies of the field grow; they
29 neither toil nor spin, yet I say to you that not
even Solomon in all his glory was arrayed like
30 one of these. But if God so clothes the grass of
the field, which flourishes today but tomorrow is thrown into the oven, how much more
you, O you of little faith!
31 "Therefore do not be anxious, saying,
'What shall we eat?' or, 'What shall we drink?'
32 or, 'What are we to put on?' (for after all these
things the Gentiles seek); for your Father
33 knows that you need all these things. But seek

first the kingdom of God and his justice, and all these things shall be given you besides.
Therefore do not be anxious about tomorrow; 34
for tomorrow will have anxieties of its own. Sufficient for the day is its own trouble.

The Rules of Charity

"Do not judge, and you shall not be judged; Luke 6
do not condemn, and you shall not be con- 37
demned. For with what judgment you judge, Matt. 7
you shall be judged. Forgive, and you shall 2 Luke 6
be forgiven; give, and it shall be given to 37-38 38
you; good measure, pressed down, shaken together, running over, shall they pour into your lap. For with what measure you measure, it shall be measured to you."

SELF-EXAMINATION

JAN. 9 or July 10

Luke 6 39-42 AND HE SPOKE a parable also to them, "Can
a blind man guide a blind man? Will not
40 both fall into a pit? No disciple is above his

teacher, but when perfected, everyone will
be like his teacher. But why dost thou see the 41
speck in thy brother's eye, and yet dost not
consider the beam in thy own eye? And how 42
canst thou say to thy brother, 'Brother, let me
cast out the speck from thy eye,' while thou
thyself dost not see the beam in thy own eye?
Thou hypocrite, first cast out the beam from
thy own eye, and then thou wilt see clearly
to cast out the speck from thy brother's eye.

Do Not Profane Holy Things

"Do not give to dogs what is holy, neither cast Matt. 7
your pearls before swine, or they will trample 6-14
them under their feet and turn and tear you.

Confidence in Prayer

"Ask, and it shall be given you; seek, and you 7
shall find; knock, and it shall be opened to
you. For everyone who asks, receives; and he 8
who seeks, finds; and to him who knocks, it
shall be opened. Or what man is there among 9
you, who, if his son asks him for a loaf, will
hand him a stone; or if he asks for a fish, will 10
hand him a serpent? Therefore, if you, evil as 11
you are, know how to give good gifts to your

children, how much more will your Father
in heaven give good things to those who ask
him!
12 "Therefore all that you wish men to do to
you, even so do you also to them; for this is
the Law and the Prophets.

Twofold Gate, Twofold Way

13 "Enter by the narrow gate. For wide is the gate
and broad is the way that leads to destruction,
14 and many there are who enter that way. How
narrow the gate and close the way that leads
to life! And few there are who find it."

BEWARE of FALSE LEADERS

JAN. 10 or July 11

"BEWARE of false prophets, who come to Matt. 7
you in sheep's clothing, but inwardly 15-20
are ravenous wolves. By their fruits you will 16
know them. Do men gather grapes from
thorns, or figs from thistles? Even so, every 17
good tree bears good fruit, but the bad tree
bears bad fruit. A good tree cannot bear bad 18
fruit, nor can a bad tree bear good fruit.

19 Every tree that does not bear good fruit is
20 cut down and thrown into the fire. Therefore,
by their fruits you will know them.

Luke 6 45-46 "The good man from the good treasure
of his heart brings forth that which is good;
and the evil man from the evil treasure brings
forth that which is evil. For out of the abun-
46 dance of the heart the mouth speaks. But why
do you call me, 'Lord, Lord,' and not practise
the things that I say?

Works, Not Words

Matt. 7 21-23 "Not everyone who says to me, 'Lord, Lord,'
shall enter the kingdom of heaven; but he
who does the will of my Father in heaven shall
22 enter the kingdom of heaven. Many will say
to me in that day, 'Lord, Lord, did we not
prophesy in thy name, and cast out devils in
thy name, and work many miracles in thy
23 name?' And then I will declare to them, 'I
never knew you. Depart from me, you workers of iniquity!'

Be as a House Built on Rock

Luke 6 47 "Everyone who comes to me and hears my
words and acts upon them, shall be likened

to a wise man who built his house on rock. Matt. 7
And the rain fell, and the floods came, and the 24-26 25
winds blew and beat against that house, but it
did not fall, because it was founded on rock.
And everyone who hears these my words and 26
does not act upon them, shall be likened to
a foolish man who built his house on sand, Luke 6
without a foundation. 49

"And the rain fell, and the floods came, and Matt. 7
the winds blew and beat against that house, 27-29
and it fell, and was utterly ruined."

And it came to pass when Jesus had finished 28
these words, that the crowds were astonished 29
at his teaching; for he was teaching them as
one having authority, and not as their Scribes
and Pharisees.

The CENTURION'S SERVANT

JAN. 11 or July 12

Luke 7 1-3 WHEN HE had finished all his discourse in
the hearing of the people, he entered
2 Capharnaum. Now a servant of a certain
centurion, to whom he was dear, was sick to
3 the point of death. And the centurion, hearing of Jesus, sent to him elders of the Jews,

beseeching him to come and save his servant,
saying, "Lord, my servant is lying sick in the Matt. 8
house, paralyzed, and is grievously afflicted." 6
And when they came to Jesus, they entreated Luke 7
him earnestly, saying to him, "He is worthy that 4-5
thou shouldst do this for him, for he loves our 5
nation and himself has built us our synagogue."
Jesus said to him, "I will come and cure him." Matt. 8
7

The Centurion's Humility and Faith

So Jesus went with them. And when he was Luke 7
now not far from the house, the centurion 6-9
sent friends to say to him, "Lord, do not
trouble thyself, for I am not worthy that thou
shouldst come under my roof; this is why I did 7
not think myself worthy to come to thee. But
say the word, and my servant will be healed.
For I too am a man subject to authority, and 8
have soldiers subject to me; and I say to one,
'Go,' and he goes; and to another, 'Come,'
and he comes; and to my servant, 'Do this,'
and he does it."
Now when Jesus heard this, he marvelled, 9
and turning to the crowd that followed him,
said, "Amen I say to you, not even in Israel
have I found such great faith.

Jesus Rebukes Unbelief

Matt. 8 11-13 "And I tell you that many will come from the
east and from the west, and will feast with
Abraham and Isaac and Jacob in the kingdom
12 of heaven, but the children of the kingdom
will be put forth into the darkness outside;
there will be the weeping, and the gnashing
of teeth."
13 Then Jesus said to the centurion, "Go thy
way; as thou hast believed, so be it done to
Luke 7 10 thee." And when the messengers returned
to the house, they found the servant in good
health who had been ill.

RAISES WIDOW'S SON to LIFE

JAN. 12 or July 13

AND IT CAME to pass soon afterwards, that he went to a town called Naim; and his disciples and a large crowd went with him. Luke 7 11-18

12 And as he drew near the gate of the town,
behold, a dead man was being carried out,
the only son of his mother, and she was a
widow; and a large gathering from the town
was with her.

13 And the Lord, seeing her, had compassion
14 on her, and said to her, "Do not weep." And
he went up and touched the stretcher; and the
bearers stood still. And he said, "Young man,
15 I say to thee, arise." And he who was dead, sat
up, and began to speak. And he gave him to
his mother.

16 But fear seized upon all, and they began
to glorify God, saying, "A great prophet has
risen among us," and "God has visited his peo-
17 ple." And this report concerning him went
forth throughout the whole of Judea, and all
18 the country roundabout. And John's disciples
brought him word of all these things.

Miracles a Proof of His Divinity

Matt. 11 2-3 But when John had heard in prison of the
works of Christ, he sent two of his disciples
3 to say to him, [1]"Art thou he who is to come,
or shall we look for another?"

---

1. The Baptist asked this question for the benefit of his disciples and the people. He wished to convince them fully that Jesus was the Messias.

And when the men had come to him, they Luke 7 20-21
said, "John the Baptist has sent us to thee, saying, 'Art thou he who is to come, or shall we
look for another?'" In that very hour he cured 21
many of diseases, afflictions and evil spirits,
and to many who were blind he granted sight.

And Jesus answering said to them, "Go Matt. 11 4-6
and report to John what you have heard and
seen: the blind see, the lame walk, the lepers 5
are cleansed, the deaf hear, the dead rise, the
poor have the gospel preached to them. And 6
blessed is he who is not scandalized in me."

JESUS PRAISES JOHN

JAN. 13 or July 14

Luke 7 24-26 THEN, AS the messengers of John left, he
began to say to the crowds concerning
John, "What did you go out to the desert to
see? A reed shaken by the wind?
25 "But what did you go out to see? A man
clothed in soft garments? Behold, those who
wear fine clothes and live in luxury are in the
26 houses of kings. But what did you go out to

see? A prophet? Yes, I tell you, and more than
a prophet.

"This is he of whom it is written, 'Behold, Matt. 11
I send my messenger before thy face, who 10
shall make ready thy way before thee.' I say Luke 7
to you among those born of women there is 28-30
not a greater prophet than John the Baptist;
yet the least in the kingdom of God is greater
than he."

People Accepted, Rulers Rejected John

And when they had heard him, all the people 29
and the publicans [1]justified God, having been
baptized with the baptism of John. But the 30
Pharisees and the lawyers, not having been
baptized by him, brought to naught God's
purpose concerning themselves.

"But from the days of John the Baptist until Matt. 11
now the kingdom of heaven has been endur- 12-15
ing violent assault, and the violent have been
seizing it by force. For all the Prophets and the 13
Law have prophesied until John. And if you 14
are willing to receive it, he is Elias who was to
come. He who has ears to hear, let him hear. 15

1. *Justified God:* acknowledged in their baptism the mercy of God manifest in the Baptist's preaching.

The Stubborn Children

Luke 7 31-35 "To what then shall I liken the men of this
32 generation? And what are they like? They
are like children sitting in the market place,
calling to one another and saying, 'We have
piped to you, and you have not danced; we
have sung dirges, and you have not wept.'
33 "For John the Baptist came neither eating
bread nor drinking wine, and you say, 'He
34 has a devil.' The Son of Man came eating and
drinking, and you say, 'Behold a man who is a
glutton, and a wine-drinker, a friend of pub-
35 licans and sinners!' And wisdom is justified by
all her children."

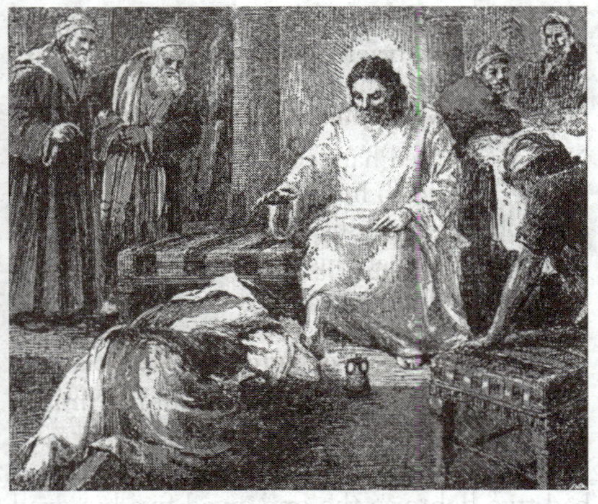

The PENITENT WOMAN

JAN. 14 or July 15

NOW ONE of the Pharisees asked him to Luke 7
dine with him; so he went into the 36-50
house of the Pharisee and reclined at table.
And behold, a woman in the town who was 37
a sinner, upon learning that he was at table
in the Pharisee's house, brought an alabas- 38
ter jar of ointment; and standing behind him
at his feet, she began to bathe his feet with
her tears, and wiped them with the hair of

her head, and kissed his feet, and anointed
them with ointment.

The Impenitent Pharisee

39 Now when the Pharisee, who had invited him,
saw it, he said to himself, "This man, were he
a prophet, would surely know who and what
manner of woman this is who is touching him,
for she is a sinner."

Penitent's Gratitude for Pardon

40 And Jesus answered and said to him, "Simon,
I have something to say to thee." And he said,
41 "Master, speak." "A certain money-lender
had two debtors; the one owed five hundred
42 denarii, the other fifty. As they had no means
of paying, he forgave them both. Which of
them, therefore, will love him more?" Simon
43 answered and said, "He, I suppose, to whom
he forgave more." And he said to him, "Thou
hast judged rightly."

Jesus Forgives Her Repented Sins

44 And turning to the woman, he said to Simon,
"Dost thou see this woman? I came into thy
house; thou gavest me no water for my feet;

but she has bathed my feet with tears, and has
wiped them with her hair. Thou gavest me no 45
kiss; but she, from the moment she entered,
has not ceased to kiss my feet. Thou didst not 46
anoint my head with oil; but she has anointed
my feet with ointment.

"Wherefore I say to thee, her sins, many as 47
they are, shall be forgiven her, because she has
loved much. But he to whom little is forgiven,
loves little." And he said to her, "Thy sins are 48
forgiven." And they who were at table with 49
him began to say within themselves, "Who is
this man, who even forgives sins?" But he said 50
to the woman, "Thy faith has saved thee; go
in peace."

Jesus drives out an evil spirit

In the SERVICE of CHRIST

JAN. 15 or July 16

Luke 8 1-3 AND IT CAME to pass afterwards, that he
was journeying through towns and villages, preaching and proclaiming the good
news of the kingdom of God. And with him
2 were the Twelve, and certain women who
had been cured of evil spirits and infirmities:

Mary, who is called the Magdalene, from
whom seven devils had gone out, and Joanna, 3
the wife of Chuza, Herod's steward, and
Susanna, and many others, who used to pro-
vide for them out of their means.

Christ's Friends Try to Restrain Him

And they came to the house, and again a Mark 3 20-21
crowd gathered so that they could not so
much as take their food. But when his own 21
people had heard of it, they went out to lay
hold of him, for they said, "He has gone mad."

He Drives Out an Evil Spirit

Then there was brought to him a possessed man Matt. 12 22-24
who was blind and dumb; and he cured him so
that he spoke and saw. And all the crowds were 23
amazed, and they said, "Can this be the Son
of David?" But the Pharisees, and the Scribes 24
who had come down from Jerusalem hearing Matt. 3 22
this, said, "This man does not cast out devils Matt. 12 24-30
except by Beelzebub, the prince of devils."

Then Refutes Calumnies of Pharisees

And knowing their thoughts Jesus said to 25
them, "Every kingdom divided against itself

is brought to desolation, and every city or
house divided against itself will not stand.
26 And if Satan casts out Satan, he is divided
against himself; how then shall his kingdom
27 stand? And if I cast out devils by Beelzebub, by
whom do your children cast them out? Therefore they shall be your judges.
28 "But if I cast out devils by the Spirit of
God, then the kingdom of God has come
29 upon you. Or, how can anyone enter the
strong man's house, and plunder his goods,
unless he first binds the strong man? Then he
30 will plunder his house. He who is not with
me is against me, and he who does not gather
with me scatters."

The true brethren of Jesus

SINS against HOLY SPIRIT

JAN. 16 or July 17

"THEREFORE I say to you, that every kind Matt. 12
of sin and blasphemy shall be forgiven 31-37
to men; but the blasphemy against the Spirit
will not be forgiven. And whoever speaks a 32
word against the Son of Man, it shall be forgiven him; [1]but whoever speaks against the
Holy Spirit, it will not be forgiven him, either
in this world or in the world to come.

1. The sin against the Holy Spirit is to ascribe to the devil the works of the Holy Spirit. One who thus attacks directly this source of all grace, rejects the source of salvation. It is morally impossible that he should ever meet the conditions for absolution.

33 “Either make the tree good and its fruit
good, or make the tree bad and its fruit bad;
34 for by the fruit the tree is known. You brood
of vipers, how can you speak good things,
when you are evil? For out of the abundance
of the heart the mouth speaks.
35 “The good man from his good treasure
brings forth good things; and the evil man
from his evil treasure brings forth evil things.
36 But I tell you, that of every [1]idle word men
speak, they shall give account on the day
37 of judgment. For by thy words thou wilt
be justified, and by thy words thou wilt be
condemned.”

The True Brethren of Jesus

Matt. 12 While he was still speaking to the crowds,
46 his mother and his brethren †came to him,
‡seeking to speak to him. *And they could not
Mark 3 get to him because of the crowd; and standing
31-32 32 outside, they sent to him, calling him. Now a
crowd was sitting about him, and they said to

1. An idle word is one which profits neither the speaker nor the hearer. If the word is merely useless, its utterance is not seriously wrong.

† Luke 8, 19

‡ Matt. 12, 46

* Luke 8, 19

him, "Behold, thy mother and thy [1]brethren
are outside, seeking thee."

But he answered and said to him who Matt. 12
told him, "Who is my mother and who are 48-50
my brethren?" And stretching forth his hand 49
towards his disciples, he said, "Behold my
mother and my brethren! For whoever does 50
the will of my Father in heaven, he is my
brother and sister and mother."

1. *Brethren:* relatives of Jesus, not blood brothers. This wider use of the term was common among the Jews. Jesus does not disclaim the bonds of physical relationship, but He seizes the opportunity to give a lesson on the greater dignity of spiritual relationship. St. Augustine says that Mary was more blessed in that she believed in Christ than in that she had given Him birth.

PARABLE of the SOWER

JAN. 17 or July 18

Matt. 13 ON THAT DAY Jesus left house and was sit-
1 Luke 8 ting by the water's edge. Now when
4 a very great crowd was gathering together
Matt. 13 and men from every town were resorting to
2 him, he got into a boat and sat down. And all
Mark 4 the crowd stood on the shore. And he taught
2-3 them many things in parables, and he said to
3 them in his instruction, "Hear! Behold, the
sower went out to sow.

What Happened to the Seed

Luke 8 "And as he sowed, some seed fell by the way-
5 Matt. 13 side and was trodden under foot, and the
4 Mark 4 birds came and ate them up. And other seed
5-10 fell upon rocky ground, where it had not
much earth, and it sprang up at once, because
6 it had no depth of earth, but when the sun
rose it was scorched, and because it had no

root it withered away. And other seed fell 7
among thorns; and the thorns grew up and
choked it, and it yielded no fruit.
"And other seed fell upon good ground, 8
and yielded fruit that grew up, made increase
and produced, one thirty, another sixty, and
another a hundredfold." Then he said, "He 9
who has ears to hear, let him hear."

Why Jesus Speaks in Parables

And when he was alone, †the disciples came 10
up and said to him, "Why dost thou speak to
them in parables?" And he said to them, "To Mark 4
you it is given to know the mystery of the 11
kingdom of God; but to those outside, all
things are treated in parables.
[1]"For to him who has shall be given, and he Matt. 13
shall have abundance; but from him who does 12-17
not have, even that which he has shall be taken
away. This is why I speak to them in parables, 13
because seeing they do not see, and hearing
they do not hear, neither do they understand.

† Matt. 13, 10

1. One grace prepares for another; one who fails to correspond with grace will lose what he has.

14 In them is being fulfilled the prophecy of Isaias, who says,

Some Hear but Do Not Heed

"'Hearing you will hear, but not understand;
15 and seeing you will see, but not perceive. For
the heart of this people has been hardened,
and with their ears they have been hard of
hearing, and their eyes they have closed; lest
at any time they see with their eyes, and hear
with their ears, and understand with their
mind, and be converted, and I heal them.'
16 "But blessed are your eyes, for they see;
17 and your ears, for they hear. For amen I say to
you, many prophets and just men have longed
to see what you see, and they have not seen
it; and to hear what you hear, and they have
not heard it."

EXPLAINS PARABLE of SOWER

JAN. 18 or July 19

AND HE SAID to them, "Do you not know Matt. 4
this parable? How then will you under- 13
stand all the parables?

Matt. 13 19-23 [†]"Hear, therefore, the parable of the
sower. [‡]The sower sows the word. When
anyone hears the word of the kingdom,
but does not understand it, the wicked one
comes and snatches away what has been sown
in his heart. This is he who was sown by the
wayside.
20 "And the one sown on rocky ground, that
is he who hears the word and receives it
21 immediately with joy; yet he has no root in
himself, but continues only for a time, and
when trouble and persecution come because
of the word, he at once falls away.
22 "And the one sown among the thorns,
that is he who listens to the word; but the
care of this world and the deceitfulness
of riches choke the word, and it is made
fruitless.
23 "And the one sown upon good ground,
that is he who hears the word and under-
stands it; he bears fruit and yields in one case
a hundredfold, in another sixtyfold, and in
another thirtyfold.

---

† Matt. 13, 18
‡ Mark 4, 14

Heed What You Hear

"Now no one, when he has lighted a lamp, Luke 8 16-17
covers it with a vessel, or puts it under a
couch, but he puts it upon a lamp-stand, that
they who enter may see the light. For there is 17
nothing hidden that will not be made manifest; nor anything concealed that will not be
known and come to light. If anyone has ears Mark 4 23
to hear, let him hear.

"Take heed, therefore, how you hear; for Luke 8 18
to him who has shall be given; and from him
who does not have, even what he thinks he has
shall be taken away."

"The kingdom of heaven is like a man who sowed good seed in his field; but while men were asleep, his enemy came and sowed weeds among the wheat, and went away."

SEED THAT GREW by ITSELF

JAN. 19 or July 20

AND HE SAID, "Thus is the kingdom of God, Mark 4 26-29
as though a man should cast seed into 27
the earth, then sleep and rise, night and day,
and the seed should sprout and grow without
his knowing it. For of itself the earth bears 28
the crop, first the blade, then the ear, then the
full grain in the ear. But when the fruit is ripe, 29
immediately he puts in the sickle because the
harvest has come."

Weeds amongst the Grain

Another parable he set before them, saying, Matt. 13 24-30
"The kingdom of heaven is like a man who
sowed good seed in his field; but while men 25
were asleep, his enemy came and sowed
weeds among the wheat, and went away.

"And when the blade sprang up and brought 26
forth fruit, then the weeds appeared as well.
And the servants of the householder came and 27
said to him, 'Sir, didst thou not sow good seed
in thy field? How then does it have weeds?' He 28
said to them, 'An enemy has done this.'

"And the servants said to him, 'Wilt thou 29
have us go and gather them up?' 'No,' he

said, 'lest in gathering the weeds you root up
30 the wheat along with them. Let both grow
together until the harvest; and at harvest time
I will say to the reapers, Gather up the weeds
first and bind them in bundles to burn; but
gather the wheat into my barn.'"

EXPLAINS PRESENCE of WEEDS

JAN. 20 or July 21

THEN HE LEFT the crowds and went into the Matt. 13 36-46
house. And his disciples came to him,

saying, "Explain to us the parable of the weeds
37 in the field." So answering them he said, "He
who sows the good seed is the Son of Man.
38 The field is the world; the good seed, the sons
of the kingdom; the weeds, the sons of the
39 wicked one; and the enemy who sowed them
is the devil.

"But the harvest is the end of the world,
40 and the reapers are the angels. Therefore,
just as the weeds are gathered up and burnt
with fire, so will it be at the end of the world.
41 The Son of Man will send forth his angels,
and they will gather out of his kingdom all
42 scandals and those who work iniquity, and
cast them into the furnace of fire, where
there will be the weeping, and the gnashing
43 of teeth. Then the just will shine forth like
the sun in the kingdom of their Father. He
who has ears to hear, let him hear.

The Treasure and the Pearl

44 "The kingdom of heaven is like a treasure hidden in a field; he who finds it hides it, and in
his joy goes and sells all that he has and buys
45 that field. Again, the kingdom of heaven is like
46 a merchant in search of fine pearls. When he

finds a single pearl of great price, he goes and sells all that he has and buys it."

He Teaches by Parables

All these things Jesus spoke to the crowds in Matt. 13
parables. And in many such parables he spoke 34 Mark 4
the word to them, according as they were 33
able to understand it. And without parables Matt. 13
he did not speak to them; that what was spo- 35
ken through the prophet might be fulfilled, "I
will open my mouth in parables, I will utter
things hidden since the foundation of the
world." But privately he explained all things Mark 4
to his disciples. 34

Jesus calms the storm

GOOD and BAD in CHURCH

JAN. 21 or July 22

Matt. 13 47-52 AGAIN, the kingdom of heaven is like a net cast into the sea that gathered in

fish of every kind. When it was filled, they 48
hauled it out, and sitting down on the beach,
they gathered the good fish into vessels, but
threw away the bad. So will it be at the end 49
of the world. The angels will go out and separate the wicked from among the just, and
will cast them into the furnace of fire, where 50
there will be the weeping, and the gnashing
of teeth.

The Wise Scribe

"Have you understood all these things?" They 51
said to him, "Yes." And he said to them, "So 52
then, every Scribe instructed in the kingdom
of heaven is like a householder who brings
forth from his storeroom things new and old."

Jesus Tests Faith of His Disciples

And he said to them on that day, when eve- Mark 4 35
ning had come, "Let us cross over to the other Luke 8 22
side of the lake." And sending away the crowd, Mark 4
they took him just as he was, in the boat; and 36
there were other boats with him. But as they Luke 8
were sailing, there arose a great squall, and 23
the waves were beating into the boat, so that Mark 4 37
the boat was now filling and *they* were in peril. Luke 8 23

Mark 4 And he himself was in the stern of the boat,
38 on the cushion, asleep. And they woke him
and said to him, "Master, does it not concern
Matt. 8 thee that we are perishing? Lord, save us! we
25-26 26 are perishing!" But he said to them, "Why are
you fearful, O you of little faith?"

And Calms the Storm

Mark 4 Then rising up, he rebuked the wind, and said
39-40 to the sea, "Peace, be still!" And the wind fell
40 and there came a great calm . . . And they
feared exceedingly and said to one another,
"Who, then, is this, that even the wind and
the sea obey him?"

The MAN with an EVIL SPIRIT
JAN. 22 or July 23

AND THEY CAME to the other side of the Mark 5 1
sea, to the country of the Gerasenes,
†which is opposite Galilee. ‡And as soon as he
stepped out of the boat, there met him from
the tombs a man with an unclean spirit, who Luke 8 27
for a long time was possessed by a devil, and
wore no clothes, and lived in the tombs, not
in a house.

And no one could any longer bind him, Mark 5 3-9
even with chains, for often he had been bound 4
with fetters and chains, and he had rent the
chains asunder and broken the fetters into
pieces. And no one was able to control him.
And constantly, night and day, he was in the 5
tombs and on the mountains, howling and
gashing himself with stones.

The Evil Spirit Pleads with Jesus

And when he saw Jesus from afar, he ran and 6
worshipped him, and crying out with a loud 7
voice, he said, "What have I to do with thee,
Jesus, Son of the most high God? I adjure

† Luke 8, 26
‡ Mark 5, 2

8 thee by God, do not torment me!" For he
was saying to him, "Go out of the man, thou
unclean spirit."

9 And he asked him, "What is thy name?" And
he said to him, "My name is Legion, for we
Luke 8 are many," because many devils had entered
30 Mark 6 into him. And he entreated him earnestly not
10 to drive them out of the country.

Evil Spirits Cast into Herd of Swine

Matt. 8 Now not far from them there was a herd
30-31 31 of many swine, feeding. And the devils kept
entreating him, saying, "If thou cast us out,
Mark 5 send us into the herd of swine, that we may
12-16 13 enter into them." [1]And Jesus immediately
gave them leave. And the unclean spirits came
out and entered into the swine; and the herd,
in number about two thousand, rushed down
with great violence into the sea, and were
drowned in the sea.

14 But the swineherds fled and reported it
in the town and in the country; and people
15 came out to see what had happened. And they

1. He granted the devils permission to enter the swine, thereby showing His Apostles the reality of demoniac possession and expulsion, the power of Satan as well as the dependence of the devil upon the permissive will of God and upon His own superior power.

came to Jesus, and saw the man who had been
afflicted by the devil, sitting clothed and in his
right mind, and they were afraid. And those 16
who had seen it reported to them how it had
happened to the possessed man, and about
the swine.

And all the people of the Gerasene district Luke 8
besought him to depart from them; for they 37
were seized with great fear.

Victim, Now Freed, Spreads Good News

And as Jesus was getting into the boat, the Mark 5
man who had been afflicted by the devil began 18-20
to entreat him that he might remain with him.
And he did not allow him, but said to him,
"Go home to thy relatives, and tell them all 19
that the Lord has done for thee, and how he
has had mercy on thee." And he departed, and 20
began to publish in the Decapolis all that Jesus
had done for him. And all marvelled.

Sick Woman Touches Cloak

JAIRUS PRAYS for HIS DAUGHTER

JAN. 23 or July 24

Mark 5 21-22 AND WHEN Jesus had again crossed over in
the boat to the other side, a great crowd
22 gathered together to him, and he was at the
water's edge. And there came one of the rulers of the synagogue named Jairus. And seeing
Luke 8 41-42 Jesus, he fell at his feet, †and worshipped him,

† Matt. 9, 18

and entreated him to come to his house, for 42
he had an only daughter about twelve years of
age, and she was dying.
“My daughter is at the point of death; Mark 5
come, lay thy hands upon her, that she may be 23
saved and live.” And Jesus arose and followed Matt. 9
him, and so did his disciples. A great crowd 19 Mark 5
was following him and pressing upon him. 24-27

Woman Healed of Her Affliction

And there was a woman who for twelve 25
years had had a hemorrhage, and had suffered 26
much at the hands of many physicians, and
had spent all that she had, and found no benefit, but rather grew worse. Hearing about 27
Jesus, she came up behind him in the crowd
and touched his cloak, saying to herself, “If I Matt. 9
touch but his cloak I shall be saved.” 21

And at once the flow of her blood was Mark 5
dried up, and she felt in her body that she was 29-30
healed of her affliction. And Jesus, instantly 30
perceiving in himself that power had gone
forth from him, turned to the crowd, and
said, “Who touched my cloak?” But as all Luke 8
were denying it, Peter, and those who were 45 Mark 5
with him, said, “Master, thou seest the crowd 31

Luke 8 pressing upon thee, and dost thou say, 'Who
46 touched me?'" But Jesus said, "Someone
touched me; for I perceived that power had
Mark 5 gone forth from me." And he was looking
32-33 round to see her who had done this.

She Declares Herself Cured

33 But the woman, fearing and trembling, knowing what had happened within her, came and
fell down before him, . . . told him all the
Luke 8 truth, *and* declared in the presence of all
47 the people why she had touched him, and how
she had been healed instantly. [‡]But he said to
her, [*]"Take courage, daughter; thy faith has
Mark 5 saved thee. Go in peace, and be thou healed of
34 Mark 9 thy affliction." And the woman was restored
22 to health from that moment.

---

‡ Mark 5, 34
* Matt. 9, 22

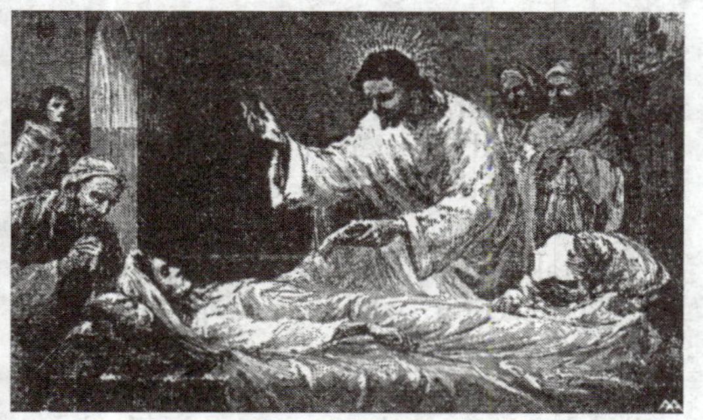

RAISES DEAD GIRL to LIFE

JAN. 24 or July 25

WHILE HE was yet speaking, there came Mark 5
some from the house of the ruler of 35
the synagogue, saying, "Thy daughter is dead.
Why dost thou trouble the Master further?"
But Jesus on hearing this word answered the Luke 8
father of the girl, "Do not be afraid; only have 50-51
faith and she shall be saved."

And when he came to the house, he allowed 51
no one to enter with him, except Peter and
James and John, and the girl's father and
mother. And he saw a tumult, people weeping Mark 5
and wailing greatly. And going in he said to 38-39
them "Why do you make this din, and weep? 39

Luke 8 Do not weep; she is asleep, not dead." And
52-53 they laughed him to scorn, knowing that she
Mark 5 was dead. But he, putting them all out, took
40-41 the father and mother of the girl and those
who were with him, and entered in where
the girl was lying.
41 And taking the girl by the hand, he said to
her, "Talitha cumi," which is interpreted, "Girl,
Luke 8 I say to thee, arise." And her spirit returned,
55 and she rose up immediately †and began to
walk; she was twelve years old. ‡And her
Mark 5 parents were amazed. And he charged them
43 strictly that no one should know of it, and
directed that something be given her to eat.

Restores Sight to Two Blind Men

Matt. 9 And the report of this spread throughout all
26-34
27 that district. Now as Jesus was passing on
from there, two blind men followed him, crying out and saying, "Have pity on us, Son of
28 David!" And when he had reached the house,
the blind men came to him.
And Jesus said to them, "Do you believe
that I can do this to you?" They answered him,

---

† Mark 5, 42
‡ Luke 8, 56

"Yes, Lord." Then he touched their eyes, saying "Let it be done to you according to your 29
faith." And their eyes were opened. And Jesus
strictly charged them, saying, "See that no one 30
knows of this!" But they went out and spread 31
his fame abroad throughout all that district.

Heals Dumb Man Possessed by Devil

Now as they were going out, behold, there 32
was brought to him a dumb man possessed
by a devil. And when the devil had been cast 33
out, the dumb man spoke; and the crowds
marvelled, saying, "Never has the like been
seen in Israel." But the Pharisees said, "By the 34
prince of devils he casts out devils."

TEACHES in HIS HOME TOWN

JAN. 25 or July 26

Mark 6 1 AND LEAVING that place, he went into his
Luke 4 own country, and his disciples followed
16-22 him. And he came to Nazareth, where he had
been brought up; and according to his custom, he entered the synagogue on the Sabbath
17 and stood up to read. And the volume of Isaias
the prophet was handed to him.

And after he opened the volume, he found
18 the place where it was written, "The Spirit
of the Lord is upon me because he has
anointed me; to bring good news to the
19 poor he has sent me, to proclaim to the captives release, and sight to the blind; to set
at liberty the oppressed, to proclaim the
acceptable year of the Lord, and the day of
recompense."

20 And closing the volume, he gave it back to
the attendant and sat down. And the eyes of
21 all in the synagogue were gazing on him. But
he began to say to them, "Today this Scrip-
22 ture has been fulfilled in your hearing." And
all bore him witness, and marvelled at the
words of grace that came from his mouth.
And they said,

Scoffed at by His Own Townsmen

“Where did he get all this?” and, “What is this Mark 6
wisdom that is given to him?” and, “What 2
mean such miracles wrought by his hands? †Is Mark 6
not this Joseph’s son? Is not this the carpenter, 3
the son of Mary, the brother of James, Joseph,
Jude, and Simon? And are not also his sisters Matt. 13 56-57
here with us? Then where did he get all this?” 57
And they took offense at him.

And he said to them, “You will surely Luke 4
quote me this proverb, ‘Physician, cure thy- 23
self! Whatever things we have heard of as
done in Capharnaum, do here also in thy own
country!’” And Jesus said to them, “A prophet Mark 6
is not without honor except in his own coun- 4
try, and among his own kindred, and in his
own house.

“In truth I say to you, there were many Luke 4
widows in Israel in the days of Elias, when 25-30
heaven was shut up for three years and six
months, and a great famine came over all the
land; and to none of them was Elias sent, but 26
rather to a widowed woman in Sarepta of
Sidon. And there were many lepers in Israel 27

† Luke 4, 22

in the time of Eliseus the prophet; and not
one of them was cleansed, but only Naaman
the Syrian."

Thrust Out of His Own Town

28 And all in the synagogue, as they heard these
29 things, were filled with wrath. And they rose
up and put him forth out of the town, and
led him to the brow of the hill, on which
their town was built, that they might throw
30 him down headlong. But he, passing through
Matt. 13 their midst, went his way. And because of
58 Mark 6 their unbelief, he did not work many mira-
5-6 cles there, beyond curing a few sick people by
6 laying his hands upon them. And he marvelled
because of their unbelief. And he made a cir-
cuit of the villages, teaching.

PLEADS for SPIRITUAL LABORERS

JAN. 26 or July 27

AND JESUS was going about all the towns Matt. 9
and villages, teaching in their syn- 35-38
agogues, and preaching the gospel of the
kingdom, and curing every kind of disease
and infirmity. But seeing the crowds, he was 36
moved with compassion for them, because

they were bewildered and dejected, like
sheep without a shepherd.
37 Then he said to his disciples, "The harvest indeed is great, but the laborers are
38 few. Pray therefore the Lord of the harvest
Matt. 10 to send forth laborers into his harvest." Then
1 having summoned his twelve disciples, he
gave them power over unclean spirits, to cast
them out, and to cure every kind of disease
and infirmity.

Directions for Apostles

Mark 6 And *he* began to send them forth two by two,
7 Luke 9 to preach the kingdom of God, and to heal
2 Matt. 10 the sick. These twelve Jesus sent forth, hav-
5-13 ing instructed them thus: "Do not go in the
direction of the Gentiles, nor enter the towns
6 of Samaritans; but go rather to the lost sheep
of the house of Israel.
7 "And as you go, preach the message, 'The
8 kingdom of heaven is at hand!' Cure the sick,
raise the dead, cleanse the lepers, cast out
devils. Freely you have received, freely give.
9 Do not keep gold, or silver, or money in your
10 girdles, no wallet for your journey, nor two

tunics, nor sandals, nor staff; for the laborer deserves his living.

Duty of Hospitality

"And whatever town or village you enter, 11
inquire who in it is worthy; and stay there
until you leave. As you enter the house, salute 12
it. If then that house be worthy, your peace 13
will come upon it; but if it be not worthy, let
your peace return to you. And whoever does Mark 6
not receive you, or listen to you—go forth 11
from there, and shake off the dust from your
feet for a witness against them.

"Amen I say to you, it will be more toler- Matt. 10
able for the land of Sodom and Gomorrah in 15
the day of judgment than for that town."

EXPECT PERSECUTION

JAN. 27 or July 28

Matt. 10 16-27 BEHOLD, I am sending you forth like sheep in the midst of wolves. Be therefore

wise as serpents, and guileless as doves. But 17
beware of men; for they will deliver you up
to councils, and scourge you in their syna- 18
gogues, and you will be brought before governors and kings for my sake, for a witness to
them and to the Gentiles.

Holy Spirit Will Inspire Your Message

"But when they deliver you up, do not be anx- 19
ious how or what you are to speak; for what
you are to speak will be given you in that hour.
For it is not you who are speaking, but the 20
Spirit of your Father who speaks through you.
"And brother will hand over brother to 21
death, and the father his child; children will
rise up against parents and put them to death.
And you will be hated by all for my name's 22
sake; but he who has persevered to the end
will be saved. When they persecute you in 23
one town, flee to another. Amen I say to you,
you will not have gone through the towns of
Israel before the Son of Man comes.

In Step with Christ

"No disciple is above his teacher, nor is the 24
servant above his master. It is enough for the 25

disciple to be like his teacher, and for the servant to be like his master. If they have called the master of the house Beelzebub, how much more those of his household!

Preach Courageously

26 “Therefore do not be afraid of them. For
there is nothing concealed that will not be
disclosed, and nothing hidden that will not
27 be made known. What I tell you in darkness,
speak it in the light; and what you hear whispered, preach it on the housetops.”

"He who receives you, receives me"

DO NOT BE AFRAID

JAN. 28 or July 29

"AND DO NOT be afraid of those who kill the Matt. 10
body but cannot kill the soul. But rather 28-42

be afraid of him who is able to destroy both soul
29 and body in hell. Are not two sparrows sold for
a farthing? And yet not one of them will fall
30 to the ground without your Father's leave. But
as for you, the very hairs of your head are all
31 numbered. Therefore do not be afraid; you are
of more value than many sparrows.
32 "Therefore, everyone who acknowledges
me before men, I also will acknowledge him
33 before my Father in heaven. But whoever dis-
owns me before men, I in turn will disown
him before my Father in heaven.

Enemies in Own Household

34 "Do not think that I have come to send peace
upon the earth; I have come to bring a sword,
35 not peace. For I have come to set a man at
variance with his father, and a daughter with
her mother, and a daughter-in-law with her
36 mother-in-law; and a man's enemies will be
those of his own household.
37 "He who loves father or mother more than
me is not worthy of me; and he who loves
son or daughter more than me is not worthy
38 of me. And he who does not take up his cross
39 and follow me, is not worthy of me. He who

finds his life will lose it, and he who loses his life for my sake, will find it.

Receiving Christ's Messengers

"He who receives you, receives me; and he 40
who receives me, receives him who sent me.
He who receives a prophet because he is a 41
prophet, shall receive a prophet's reward; and
he who receives a just man because he is a just
man, shall receive a just man's reward.
"And whoever gives to one of these little 42
ones but a cup of cold water to drink because
he is a disciple, amen I say to you, he shall not
lose his reward."

JOHN the BAPTIST BEHEADED

JAN. 29 or July 30

Mark 6 17-29 FOR Herod himself had sent and taken John, and bound him in prison, because of Herodias, his brother Philip's wife, whom

he had married. For John had said to Herod, 18
"It is not lawful for thee to have thy brother's
wife." But Herodias laid snares for him, and 19
would have liked to put him to death, but she
could not.
For Herod feared John, knowing that he 20
was a just and holy man, and protected him;
and when he heard him talk, he did many
things, and he liked to hear him.

Influence of Evil Person

And a favorable day came when Herod on his 21
birthday gave a banquet to the officials, tri-
bunes and chief men of Galilee. And Herodias' 22
own daughter having come in and danced, she
pleased Herod and his guests. And the king
said to the girl, "Ask of me what thou willest,
and I will give it to thee." And he swore to 23
her, "Whatever thou dost ask, I will give thee,
even though it be the half of my kingdom."
Then she went out and said to her mother, 24
"What am I to ask for?" And she said, "The
head of John the Baptist." And she came in at 25
once with haste to the king, and asked, saying,
"I want thee right away to give me on a dish
the head of John the Baptist."

Rash Oath and Evil Counsel

26 And grieved as he was, the king, because
of his oath and his guests, was unwilling to
27 displease her. But sending an executioner,
he commanded that his head be brought on
a dish. Then he beheaded him in the prison,
28 and brought his head on a dish, and gave it to
29 the girl; and the girl gave it to her mother. His
disciples, hearing of it, came and took away
his body, and laid it in a tomb.

Jesus invites His Apostles to a retreat

TEACHING, PREACHING, HEALING

JAN. 30 or July 31

NOW IT CAME to pass when Jesus had fin- Matt. 11
ished giving instructions to his twelve 1
disciples, that he Passed on from there to

Luke 9 teach and preach in their towns. And going
6 Mark 6 forth, they went about from village to village,
12-13 13 preaching the gospel that men should repent,
and they cast out many devils, and anointed
with oil many sick people, and healed them.

Herod Is Informed; He Fears

Luke 9 Now Herod the tetrarch heard of all that was
7 Mark 6 being done by him, for his name had become
14 Matt. 14 well known; and he said to his servants,
2 "This is John the Baptist; he has risen from
the dead, and that is why miraculous powers
Luke 9 are working through him." *He* was much per-
7-9 8 plexed, because it was said by some, "John
has risen from the dead"; and by some, "Elias
has appeared"; and by others, "One of the
9 prophets of old has risen again." But Herod
said, "John I beheaded; but who is this about
whom I hear such things?" And he endeavored
to see him.

Jesus Invites His Apostles to a Retreat

Mark 6 And the apostles came together to meet Jesus
30-32 and reported to him all that they had done
31 and taught. And he said to them, "Come apart
into a desert place and rest a while." For there

were many coming and going, and they had
no leisure even to eat. And they got into the 32
boat and went off to a desert place apart.

Great Multitudes Follow Jesus

And there followed him a great crowd, John 6
because they witnessed the signs he worked 2 Mark 6
on those who were sick. And from all the 33
towns they hurried on foot to the place, and
got there ahead of them. Jesus therefore went John 6
up the mountain, and sat there with his disci- 3-4
ples. Now the Passover, the feast of the Jews, 4
was near.

JESUS FEEDS FIVE THOUSAND

JAN. 31 or Aug. 1

John 6 WHEN, therefore, Jesus had lifted up his
5 eyes and seen that a very great crowd
had come to him, he had compassion on
Mark 6 them, because they were like sheep without
34 Luke 9 a shepherd. And he began to teach them many
11 things, and spoke to them of the kingdom of
God, and those in need of cure he healed.

Not Enough Food for All

Mark 6 Now when the day was far spent, his disciples
35 came, saying, "This is a desert place and the
Matt. 14 hour is already late." But Jesus said to them,
16 "They do not need to go away; you yourselves
Mark 6 give them some food." And they said to him,
37 "Are we to go and buy two hundred denarii
worth of bread and give them to eat?"

He said to Philip, "Whence shall we buy John 6 5-7
bread that these may eat?" But he said this to try 6
him, for he himself knew what he would do.
Philip answered him, "Two hundred dena- 7
rii worth of bread is not enough for them,
that each one may receive a little." And he said Mark 6 38
to them, "How many loaves have you? Go and John 6 8-9
see." When they had found out, one of his disciples, Andrew, the brother of Simon Peter,
said to him, "There is a young boy here who 9
has five barley loaves and two fishes; but what
are these among so many?" He said to them, Matt. 14 18
"Bring them here to me."

Jesus Multiplies Loaves and Fishes

And he ordered them to make all the people Mark 6 39-40
recline in groups on the green grass. And they 40
reclined in groups of hundreds and of fifties. 41
And he took the five loaves and the two fishes
and, looking up to heaven, blessed and broke
the loaves, and gave them to his disciples to
set before the people; and the two fishes he
divided among them all. And all ate and were 42
satisfied.

Teaches Respect for Food

John 6 But when they were filled, he said to his disci-
12-13 ples, "Gather the fragments that are left over,
13 lest they be wasted." They therefore gathered
them up; and they filled twelve baskets with
the fragments of the five barley loaves left
Matt. 14 over by those who had eaten. Now the num-
21 ber of those who had eaten was five thousand
men, without counting women and children.

John 6 When the people, therefore, had seen the
14-15 sign which Jesus had worked, they said, "This
is indeed the Prophet who is to come into
15 the world." So when Jesus perceived that they
would come to take him by force and make
Mark 6 him king, immediately afterwards he made
45-46 his disciples get into the boat and cross the
sea ahead of him to Bethsaida, while he him-
46 self dismissed the crowd. And when he had
dismissed them, he went away to the mountain to pray.

Jesus walks upon the sea

The STORM

FEB. 1 or Aug. 2

AND GETTING into a boat, they went across John 6
the sea towards Capharnaum. And it 17-18
was already dark, but Jesus had not come

18 to them. Now the sea was rising, because a
Matt. 14 strong wind was blowing. But the boat was in
24 the midst of the sea, buffeter by the waves, for
the wind was against them.

Mark 6 And seeing them straining at the oars, for
48 the wind was against them, about the fourth
watch of the night he came to them, walking
upon the sea, and he would have passed by
them.

Jesus Walks upon the Sea

Matt. 14 And they, seeing him walking upon the sea,
26-33 were greatly alarmed, and exclaimed, "It is a
27 ghost!" And they cried out for fear. Then Jesus
immediately spoke to them, saying, "Take
courage; it is I, do not be afraid."

28 But Peter answered him and said, "Lord,
if it is thou, bid me come to thee over the
29 water." And he said, "Come." Then Peter got
out of the boat and walked on the water
30 to come to Jesus. But seeing the wind was
strong, he was afraid; and as he began to sink
31 he cried out, saying, "Lord, save me!" And
Jesus at once stretched forth his hand and
took hold of him, saying to him, "O thou of
little faith, why didst thou doubt?"

Jesus Calms the Storm

And when they got into the boat, the wind 32
fell. But they who were in the boat came and 33
worshipped him, saying, "Truly thou art the
Son of God." And they were utterly beside Mark 6 51-52
themselves with astonishment, for they had 52
not understood about the loaves, because
their heart was blinded. And immediately John 6 21
the boat was at the land towards which they
were going.

The PEOPLE SEEK JESUS

FEB. 2 or Aug. 3

Mark 6 53-56 AND CROSSING OVER, they came to the land
at Genesareth and moored the boat.
54 And when they had gotten out of the boat, the
55 people at once recognized him; and they hurried through that whole country, and began
to bring the sick on their pallets, wherever
56 they heard he was. And wherever he went,
into village or hamlet or town, they laid the
sick in the market places, and entreated him
to let them touch but the tassel of his cloak;
John 6 22-33 and as many as touched him were saved.

The next day, the crowd which had remained on the other side of the sea observed that there

had been but one boat at that place, and that
Jesus had not gone into the boat with his disciples, but that his disciples had departed alone.
But other boats from Tiberias came near the 23
place where they had eaten the bread, when
the Lord gave thanks. When therefore the 24
crowd perceived that Jesus was not there, nor
his disciples, they themselves got into the boats
and came to Capharnaum, seeking Jesus.

Seek and Labor for Eternal Food

And when they had found him on the other 25
side of the sea, they said to him, "Rabbi, when
didst thou come here?"

Jesus answered them and said, "Amen, 26
amen, I say to you, you seek me, not because
you have seen signs, but because you have
eaten of the loaves and have been filled. Do 27
not labor for the food that perishes, but for
that which endures unto life everlasting,
which the Son of Man will give you. For upon
him the Father, God himself, has set his seal."

They said therefore to him, "What are we 28
to do that we may perform the works of God?"
In answer Jesus said to them, "This is the work 29
of God, that you believe in him whom he has

30 sent." They said therefore to him, "What sign,
then, dost thou, that we may see and believe
31 thee? What work dost thou perform? Our
fathers ate the manna in the desert, even as it
is written, 'Bread from heaven he gave them
to eat.'"

32 Jesus then said to them, "Amen, amen, I
say to you, Moses did not give you the bread
from heaven, but my Father gives you the true
33 bread from heaven. For the bread of God is
that which comes down from heaven and
gives life to the world."

"I AM the BREAD of LIFE"

FEB. 3 or Aug. 4

THEY SAID therefore to him, "Lord, give us John 6 34-47
always this bread."
But Jesus said to them, "I am the bread of 35
life. He who comes to me shall not hunger,

and he who believes in me shall never thirst.
36 But I have told you that you have seen me and
37 you do not believe. All that the Father gives
to me shall come to me, and him who comes
to me I will not cast out.

38 "For I have come down from heaven, not to
do my own will, but the will of him who sent
39 me. Now this is the will of him who sent me,
the Father, that I should lose nothing of what
he has given me, but that I should raise it up
40 on the last day. For this is the will of my Father
who sent me, that whoever beholds the Son,
and believes in him, shall have everlasting life,
and I will raise him up on the last day."

His Words and Divinity Challenged

41 The Jews therefore murmured about him
because he had said, "I am the bread that has
42 come down from heaven." And they kept saying, "Is this not Jesus the son of Joseph, whose
father and mother we know? How, then, does
he say, 'I have come down from heaven'?"
43 In answer therefore Jesus said to them,
44 "Do not murmur among yourselves. No one
can come to me unless the Father who sent
me draw him, and I will raise him up on the

last day. It is written in the Prophets, 'And 45
they all shall be taught of God.'
"Everyone who has listened to the Father,
and has learned, comes to me; not that any- 46
one has seen the Father except him who is
from God, he has seen the Father. Amen, 47
amen, I say to you, he who believes in me has
life everlasting."

"If anyone eat of this bread he shall live forever; and the bread that I will give is my flesh for the life of the world."

HOLY EUCHARIST PROMISED

FEB. 4 or Aug. 5

"I AM the bread of life. †Your fathers ate John 6 48-59
the manna in the desert, and have died.
This is the bread that so comes down from 50
heaven, so that if anyone eat of it he will not
die. I am the living bread that has come down 51
from heaven.

"If anyone eat of this bread he shall live for- 52
ever; and the bread that I will give is my flesh
for the life of the world."

The Jews on that account argued with one 53
another, saying, "How can this man give us his
flesh to eat?"

Jesus therefore said to them, "Amen, 54
amen, I say to you, unless you eat the flesh of
the Son of Man, and drink his blood, you shall
not have life in you.

A Pledge of Our Resurrection

"He who eats my flesh and drinks my blood 55
has life everlasting and I will raise him up on
the last day. For my flesh is food indeed, and 56
my blood is drink indeed. He who eats my 57

† 49

flesh, and drinks my blood, abides in me and
I in him.

58 "As the living Father has sent me, and as I
live because of the Father, so he who eats me,
59 he also shall live because of me. This is the
bread that has come down from heaven; not
as your fathers ate the manna, and died. He
who eats this bread shall live forever."

UNBELIEF

FEB. 5 or Aug. 6

THESE THINGS he said when teaching in the synagogue at Capharnaum. John 6 60-72

61 Many of his disciples therefore, when they
heard this, said, "This is a hard saying. Who
62 can listen to it?" But Jesus, knowing in himself
that his disciples were murmuring at this, said
63 to them, "Does this scandalize you? What then
if you should see the Son of Man ascending
64 where he was before? It is the spirit that gives
life; the flesh profits nothing.
"The words that I have spoken to you are
65 spirit and life. But there are some among you
who do not believe." For Jesus knew from the
beginning who they were who did not believe,
and who it was who should betray him.
66 And he said, "This is why I have said to you,
'No one can come to me unless he is enabled
67 to do so by my Father.'" From this time many
of his disciples turned back and no longer
went about with him.

Belief

68 Jesus therefore said to the Twelve, "Do you
69 also wish to go away?" Simon Peter therefore
answered, "Lord, to whom shall we go? Thou
70 hast words of everlasting life, and we have
come to believe and to know that thou art
the Christ, the Son of God."

Jesus answered them, "Have I not chosen 71
you, the Twelve? Yet one of you is a devil." Now 72
he was speaking of Judas Iscariot, the son of
Simon; for he it was, though one of the Twelve,
who would betray him.

Now after these things Jesus went about John 7
in Galilee, for he did not wish to go about in 1
Judea because the Jews were seeking to put
him to death.

JESUS EXPOSES HYPOCRISY

FEB. 6 or Aug. 7

Mark 7 1-13 AND THE Pharisees and some of the Scribes
who had come from Jerusalem gathered
2 about him. And when they saw that some of
his disciples were eating bread with defiled
(that is, unwashed) hands, they found fault.
3 For the Pharisees and all the Jews do not eat

without frequent washing of hands, holding the tradition of the ancients. And when 4
they come from the market, they do not eat
without washing first. And there have been
handed down to them many other things to
observe: washing of cups and pots, and bra-
zen vessels and beds.

Nullifying God's Commandment

So the Pharisees and Scribes asked him, "Why 5
do not thy disciples walk according to the tradition of the ancients, instead of eating bread
with defiled hands?" But answering he said to 6
them, "Well did Isaias prophesy of you hypocrites, as it is written, 'This people honors
me with their lips, but their heart is far from
me; and in vain do they worship me, teaching 7
as doctrine the precepts of men.'

"For, letting go the commandment of God, 8
you hold fast the tradition of men, the washing of pots and of cups; and many other things
you do like to these."

And he said to them, "Well do you nul- 9
lify the commandment of God, that you may
keep your own tradition! For Moses said, 10
'Honor thy father and thy mother'; and, 'Let

him who curses father or mother be put to
11 death.' But you say, 'Let a man say to his father
or his mother, "Any support thou mightest
have had from me is [1]Corban"' (that is, given
12 to God). And you do not allow him to do
13 anything further for his father or mother. You
make void the commandment of God by your
tradition, which you have handed down; and
many suchlike things you do."

1. *Corban:* a gift to God which could be put to no other use. A son could evade giving support to his parents by declaring Corban what might have been given them. Jesus here illustrates how the Pharisees' teaching frustrated the Law of Moses.

"Out of the heart of men, come evil thoughts . . . murders, thefts . . . wickedness."

WHAT DEFILES a MAN

FEB. 7 or Aug. 8

Mark 7 14-17 THEN HE CALLED the crowd to him again,
and said to them, "Hear me, all of you,
15 and understand. There is nothing outside a
man that, entering into him, can defile him;
but the things that come out of a man, these
16 are what defile a man. If anyone has ears to
hear, let him hear."

17 And when he had entered the house away
Matt. 15 12-18 from the crowd, his disciples said to him, "Dost
thou know that the Pharisees have taken offense
13 at hearing this saying?" But he answered and
said, "Every plant that my heavenly Father has
14 not planted will be rooted up. Let them alone;
they are blind guides of blind men. But if a blind
man guide a blind man, both fall into a pit."

15 But Peter spoke to him, saying, "Explain
16 to us this parable." And he said, "Are you also
17 even yet without understanding? Do you not
realize that whatever enters the mouth passes
into the belly and is cast out into the drain?

An Evil Heart Defiles

18 "But the things that proceed out of the mouth
come from the heart, and it is they that defile a

man. For from within, out of the heart of men, Mark 7
come evil thoughts, adulteries, immorality, 21-22
murders, thefts, covetousness, wickedness, 22
deceit, shamelessness, jealousy, blasphemy,
pride, foolishness. These are the things that Matt. 15
defile a man; but to eat with unwashed hands 20
does not defile a man."

A MOTHER'S PRAYER

FEB. 8 or Aug. 9

Matt. 15 21-24 AND LEAVING THERE, Jesus retired to the
22 district of Tyre and Sidon. And behold,
a Canaanite woman came out of that territory and cried out to him, saying, "Have pity
on me, O Lord, Son of David! My daughter
23 is sorely beset by a devil." He answered her
not a word. And his disciples came up and
besought him, saying, "Send her away, for she
24 is crying after us." But he answered and said,
"I was not sent except to the lost sheep of the
house of Israel."

Mark 7 24 And he entered a house, and wanted no one to know it, but he could not keep it secret.

Answered by Jesus

But she came and worshipped him, saying, Matt. 15 25
"Lord!" And she besought him to cast the devil Mark 7
out of her daughter. But he said to her, [1]"Let 26-27 27
the children first have their fill, for it is not
fair to take the children's bread and to cast it
to the dogs."

But she said, "Yes, Lord; for even the dogs Matt. 15
eat of the crumbs that fall from their masters' 27-28
table." Then Jesus answered and said to her, 28
"O woman, great is thy faith! Let it be done
to thee as thou wilt. Go thy way; the devil has Mark 7
gone out of thy daughter." †And her daughter 29
was healed from that moment. And when she Mark 7
went to her house, she found the girl lying 30-37
upon the bed, and the devil gone.

Jesus Heals a Deaf-mute

And departing again from the district of Tyre, 31
he came by way of Sidon to the sea of Galilee,
through the midst of the district of Decapolis. And they brought to him one deaf and 32
dumb, and entreated him to lay his hand upon

1. Jesus repeatedly pointed out that the Messias had come to bring the kingdom of God first to the children of Israel.

† Matt 15, 28

33 him. And taking him aside from the crowd, he
put his fingers into the man's ears, and spit-
34 ting, he touched his tongue. And looking up
to heaven, he sighed, and said to him, "Eph-
pheta," that is, "Be thou opened."
35 And his ears were at once opened, and the
bond of his tongue was loosed, and he began
36 to speak correctly. And he charged them to
tell no one. But the more he charged them, so
much the more did they continue to publish it.
37 And so much the more did they wonder, saying, "He has done all things well. He has made
both the deaf to hear and the dumb to speak."

"Great crowds came to him, bringing with them the dumb, the blind, the lame . . . and he cured them."

JESUS CURES the SICK

FEB. 9 or Aug. 10

Matt. 15 29-39 AND WHEN Jesus had departed from there,
he went along the sea of Galilee; and he
30 went up the mountain and sat there. And great
crowds came to him, bringing with them the
dumb, the blind, the lame, the maimed, and
many others; and they set them down at his
31 feet, and he cured them; so that the crowds
marvelled to see the dumb speak, the lame
walk, and the blind see. And they glorified
the God of Israel.

Again Feeds the Crowd

32 Then Jesus called together his disciples and
said, "I have compassion on the crowd, for
they have now been with me three days, and
have nothing to eat; and I am unwilling to send
them away fasting, lest they faint on the way."
33 And the disciples said to him, "But in a
desert, where are we to get enough loaves to
34 satisfy so great a crowd?" Jesus said to them,
"How many loaves have you?" And they said,
"Seven, and a few little fishes."
35 And he bade the crowd recline on the
36 ground. Then taking the seven loaves and

the fishes, he gave thanks, broke them and
gave them to his disciples, and the disciples
gave them to the crowd. And they all ate 37
and were satisfied; and they took up what
was left of the fragments, seven full baskets.
Now those who had eaten were four thou- 38
sand men, apart from children and women.
When he had dismissed the crowd, he got 39
into the boat, and came into the district of
Magedan.

ASKING a SIGN from JESUS
FEB. 10 or Aug. 11

Matt. 16 1-4 AND THE Pharisees and Sadducees came to
him to test him, and they asked him to
2 show them a sign from heaven. But answering them he said, "When it is evening you say,
'The weather will be fair, for the sky is red.'
3 And in the morning you say, 'It will be stormy
4 today, for the sky is red and lowering.' You
know then how to read the face of the sky,
but cannot read the signs of the times!"

Matt. 12 39-42 †And sighing deeply in spirit, he said, "An
evil and adulterous generation demands a
sign, and no sign shall be given it but the sign
40 of Jonas the prophet. For even as Jonas was
in the belly of the fish three days and three

† Mark 8, 12

nights, so will the Son of Man be three days
and three nights in the heart of the earth.
"The men of Nineve will rise up in the 41
judgment with this generation and will condemn it; for they repented at the preaching
of Jonas, and behold, a greater than Jonas is
here. The queen of the South will rise up in 42
the judgment with this generation and will
condemn it; for she came from the ends of
the earth to hear the wisdom of Solomon, and
behold, a greater than Solomon is here."

Jesus Cautions against Pharisees

And he left them, and getting back into the Mark 8
boat, crossed the sea. And when his disciples 13 Matt. 16
crossed the sea, they found that they had 5
forgotten to bring bread. And he began to Mark 8
charge them, saying, "Take heed; beware of 15-21
the leaven of the Pharisees, and of the leaven
of Herod!" And they began to argue among 16
themselves, saying, "We have no bread."
But Jesus knowing this, said to them, "Why 17
do you argue because you have no bread? Do
you not yet perceive, nor understand? Is your
heart still blinded? Though you have eyes do 18
you not see, and though you have ears do you

19 not hear? And do you not remember? When
I broke the five loaves among five thousand,
how many baskets full of fragments did you
take up?" They said to him, "Twelve."
20 "And when I broke the seven loaves
among four thousand, how many large baskets of fragments did you take up?" They said,
21 "Seven." And he said to them, "How is it that
Matt. 16 11-12 you do not yet understand that it was not
of bread I said to you, 'Beware of the leaven
12 of the Pharisees and Sadducees'?" Then they
understood that he bade them beware not of
the leaven of bread, but of the teaching of the
Pharisees and Sadducees.

RESTORES SIGHT to BLIND MAN

FEB. 11 or Aug. 12

AND they came to Bethsaida and they Mark 8
brought him a blind man and entreated 22-27
him to touch him. And taking the blind man 23
by the hand, he led him forth outside the village; and applying spittle to his eyes, he laid
his hands upon him, and asked him if he saw
anything. And the man looked up, and said, "I 24
see men as though they were trees, but walking about."

25 Then again he laid his hands upon the man's
eyes, and he began to see, and was restored so
26 that he saw all things plainly. And he sent him
to his house, saying, "Go to thy house, and if
thou enter the village, tell nobody."

Peter Recognizes Jesus to Be God

27 And Jesus and his disciples went out into the
villages of Cæsarea Philippi; and on the way
he asked his disciples, saying to them, "Who
Matt. 16 do men say that I am?" But they said, "Some
14-20 say, John the Baptist; and others, Elias; and
15 others, Jeremias, or one of the prophets." He
said to them, "But who do you say that I am?"
16 Simon Peter answered and said, "Thou art
17 the Christ, the Son of the living God." Then
Jesus answered and said, "Blessed art thou,
Simon Bar-Jona, for flesh and blood has not
revealed this to thee, but my Father in heaven.

Peter to Be Head of His Church

18 "And I say to thee, thou art Peter, and upon
is this rock I will build my Church, and [1]the

1. *The gates of hell:* hostile, evil powers. Their aggressive force will struggle in vain against the Church. She shall never be overcome; she is indefectible. And since she has the office of teacher, and since she would be overcome if error prevailed, she is infallible.

gates of hell shall not prevail against it. And 19
I will give thee the [1]keys of the kingdom of
heaven; and whatever thou shalt bind on earth
shall be bound in heaven, and whatever thou
shalt loose on earth shall be loosed in heaven."
Then he strictly charged his disciples to tell 20
no one that he was Jesus the Christ.

1. *Keys:* a symbol of authority. Peter has the power to admit into the Church and to exclude therefrom. Nor is he merely the porter; he has complete power within the Church. "To bind and loose" seems to have been used by the Jews in the sense of to forbid or to permit; but 18, 18 as well as the present context requires a more comprehensive meaning. In heaven God ratifies the decisions which Peter makes on earth, in the name of Christ.

JESUS FORETELLS HIS DEATH

FEB. 12 or Aug. 13

Matt. 16 21 FROM THAT TIME Jesus began to show his
disciples that he must go to Jerusalem

and suffer many things from the elders and
Scribes and chief priests, and be put to death,
and on the third day rise again.

And what he said he spoke openly. And Mark 8
Peter taking him aside, began to chide him, 32 Matt. 16
saying, "Far be it from thee, O Lord; this 22
will never happen to thee." But he, turning Mark 8
and seeing his disciples, rebuked Peter, say- 33-38
ing, "Get behind me, satan, for thou dost not
mind the things of God, but those of men."

The Doctrine of the Cross

And calling the crowd together with his dis- 34
ciples, he said to them, "If anyone wishes to
come after me, let him deny himself, and take
up his cross, and follow me. For he who would 35
save his life will lose it; but he who loses his
life for my sake and for the gospel's sake will
save it. For what does it profit a man, if he gain 36
the whole world, but suffer the loss of his own
soul? Or what will a man give in exchange for 37
his soul?

"For whoever is ashamed of me and of 38
my words in this adulterous and sinful generation, of him will the Son of Man also be
ashamed when he comes with the holy angels

Matt. 16 in the glory of his Father. For the Son of Man
27 is to come with his angels in the glory of his
Father, and then he will render to everyone
according to his conduct."

Mark 8 And he said to them, "Amen I say to you
39 there are some of those standing here [1]who
will not taste death, till they have seen the
kingdom of God coming in power."

---

1. *Who will not taste death*: i.e., even in the lifetime of some of His listeners He will manifest the power of His kingdom.

JESUS TRANSFIGURED

FEB. 13 or Aug. 14

NOW AFTER six days Jesus took Peter, Mark 9
James and John, and led them up a high 1
mountain off by themselves, and was trans- Luke 9
figured before them. And as he prayed, the 29
appearance of his countenance was changed, Mark 9
and his raiment became a radiant white as 29
snow, as no fuller on earth can whiten. And Luke 9
behold, two men were talking with him. 30-33
And these were Moses and Elias, who, 31
appearing in glory, spoke of his death, which
he was about to fulfill in Jerusalem.

Now Peter and his companions were heavy 32
with sleep. But when they were fully awake,
they saw his glory and the two men who were
standing with him. And it came to pass as 33
they were parting from him, that Peter said
to Jesus, "Master, it is good for us to be here.
And let us set up three tents, one for thee,
and one for Moses, and one for Elias."

Mark 9 For he did not know what to say, for they
5 were struck with fear.

Jesus Is the Son of God

Matt. 17 As he was still speaking, behold, a bright cloud
5-9 overshadowed them, and behold, a voice out
of the cloud said, "This is my beloved Son, in
6 whom I am well pleased; hear him." And on
hearing it the disciples fell on their faces and
7 were exceedingly afraid. And Jesus came near
and touched them, and said to them, "Arise,
8 and do not be afraid." But lifting up their eyes,
they saw no one but Jesus only.

9 And as they were coming down from the
mountain, Jesus cautioned them, saying, "Tell
the vision to no one, till the Son of Man has
Luke 9 risen from the dead." And they kept silence
36 and told no one at that time any of these
things that they had seen.

Mark 9 And they kept what he said to themselves,
9 discussing with one another what the words,
"When he shall have risen from the dead,"
might mean.

John the Baptist Is "Elias to Come"

And the disciples asked him, saying, "Why Matt. 17 10-13
then do the Scribes say that Elias must come
first?" But he answered and said, [1]"Elias 11
indeed is to come and will restore all things.
But I say to you that Elias has come already, 12
and they did not know him, but did to him
whatever they wished. So also shall the Son
of Man suffer at their hands." Then the disci- 13
ples understood that he had spoken to them
of John the Baptist.

1. Jesus refers to the Jewish tradition that Elias was to come as precursor of the messianic age, and explains that he has come in the person of the Baptist.

LUNATIC BROUGHT to JESUS

FEB. 14 or Aug. 15

Mark 9 13-17 AND ON COMING to his disciples, he saw
a great crowd around them, and the
14 Scribes arguing with them. And immediately
all the crowd, on seeing him, were amazed
and struck with fear, and is running up, began
15 to greet him. And he asked them, "What are
you arguing about among yourselves?"

16 And one of the crowd answering, said,
"Master, I have brought to thee my son, who
17 has a dumb spirit; and wherever it seizes him
it throws him down, and he foams and grinds
his teeth; and he is wasting away. And I told
thy disciples to cast it out, but they could not.

The Father Pleads for His Child

Luke 9 38 "Master, I pray thee to look at my son, for he
Matt. 17 is my only child. Lord, have pity on my son,
14 for he is a lunatic, and suffers severely; for
often he falls into the fire, and often into the

water." Jesus answered and said, "O unbeliev- Matt. 17
ing and perverse generation, how long shall 16
I be with you? How long shall I put up with
you? Bring him here to me." And they brought Mark 9
him to him; and the spirit, when it saw Jesus, 19-26
immediately threw the boy into convulsions,
and he fell down on the ground, and rolled
about foaming at the mouth.

So he asked his father, "How long is it since 20
this has come upon him?" And he said, "From
his infancy. Oftentimes it has thrown him into 21
the fire and into the waters to destroy him.
But if thou canst do anything, have compassion on us and help us." But Jesus said to him, 22
"If thou canst believe, all things are possible
to him who believes." At once the father of 23
the boy cried out, and said with tears, "I do
believe; help my unbelief."

Jesus Frees Boy from Evil Spirit

Now when Jesus saw that a crowd was rapidly 24
gathering, he rebuked the unclean spirit, saying to it, "Thou deaf and dumb spirit, I command thee, go out of him and enter him no
more." And crying out and violently convuls- 25
ing him, it went out of him, and he became

like one dead, so that many said, "He is dead."
26 But Jesus took him by the hand, and raised
him and he stood up.

Luke 9 43 And Jesus restored him to his father. And
Matt. 17 17 from that moment the boy was cured.

Power of Prayer and Fasting

Mark 9 27 And when he had come into the house, his
disciples asked him privately, "Why could not
Matt. 7 19-20 we cast it out?" He said to them, "Because of
your little faith; for amen I say to you, if you
have faith like a mustard seed, you will say
to this mountain, 'Remove from here'; and it
will remove. And nothing will be impossible
20 to you. But this kind can be cast out only by
prayer and fasting."

Jesus goes up to Jerusalem "But as soon as his brethren had gone up to the feast, then he also went up."

JESUS DENIED by HIS OWN

FEB. 15 or Aug. 16

John 7 2-10 NOW THE JEWISH FEAST of Tabernacles was
at hand. His brethren therefore said to
3 him, "Leave here and go into Judea that thy
4 disciples also may see the works that thou
dost; for no one does a thing in secret if he
wants to be publicly known. If thou dost these
5 things, manifest thyself to the world." For not
even his brethren believed in him.

6 Jesus therefore said to them, "My time has
not yet come, but your time is always at hand.
7 The world cannot hate you, but it hates me
because I bear witness concerning it, that its
8 works are evil. As for you, go up to the feast,
but I do not go up to this feast, for my time is
not yet fulfilled."

Jesus Goes up to Jerusalem

9 When he had said these things he stayed on in
10 Galilee. But as soon as his brethren had gone
up to the feast, then he also went up, not pub-
Mark 9 29 licly, but as it were privately. And leaving that
place, they were passing through Galilee, and
he did not wish anyone to know it.

The Jews therefore were looking for him John 7
at the feast, and were saying, "Where is he?" 11-14
And there was much whispered comment 12
among the crowd concerning him. For some
were saying, "He is a good man." But others were saying, "No, rather he seduces the
crowd." Yet for fear of the Jews no one spoke 13
openly of him.

When, however, the feast was already half 14
over, Jesus went up into the temple and began
to teach.

The SOURCE of CHRIST'S TEACHINGS

FEB. 16 or Aug. 17

John 7 15-36 AND THE Jews marvelled, saying, "How
does this man come by learning, since
he has not studied?"
16 Jesus answered them and said, "My teach-
17 ing is not my own, but his who sent me. If
anyone desires to do his will, he will know
of the teaching whether it is from God, or
18 whether I speak on my own authority. He
who speaks on his own authority seeks his
own glory. But he who seeks the glory of the
one who sent him is truthful, and there is no
19 injustice in him. Did not Moses give you the
Law, and none of you observes the Law?

Men Would Kill Him

20 "Why do you seek to put me to death?" The
crowd answered and said, "Thou hast a devil.
Who seeks to put thee to death?"
21 Jesus answered and said to them, [1]"One
22 work I did and you all wonder. [2]For this reason

---

1. *One work:* the cure of the sick man at the pool of Bethsaida.

2. Circumcision was established as a sign of the covenant made with Abraham. Moses, however, provided the laws which governed it. When the recipient was a Jew, the Jews interpreted these laws as permitting circumcision, and all things necessary thereto, on the Sabbath.

Moses gave you the circumcision"—not that
it is from Moses, but from the fathers—"and
on a Sabbath you circumcise a man. If a man 23
receives circumcision on a Sabbath, that the
Law of Moses may not be broken, are you
indignant with me because I made a whole
man well on a Sabbath? Judge not by appear- 24
ances but give just judgment."

Some therefore of the people of Jerusalem 25
were saying, "Is not this the man they seek to
kill? And behold, he speaks openly and they 26
say nothing to him. Can it be that the rulers have really come to know that this is the
Christ? Yet we know where this man is from; 27
but when the Christ comes, no one will know
where he is from."

Jesus therefore, while teaching in the tem- 28
ple, cried out and said, "You both know me,
and know where I am from. Yet I have not
come of myself, but he is true who has sent
me, whom you do not know. I know him 29
because I am from him, and he has sent me."

They Try to Arrest Christ

They wanted therefore to seize him, but no 30
one laid hands on him because his hour had

31 not yet come. Many of the people, however,
believed in him, and they kept saying, "When
the Christ comes will he work more signs
32 than this man works?" The Pharisees heard
the crowd whispering these things about him,
and the rulers and Pharisees sent attendants
to seize him.

33 Jesus then said, "Yet a little while I am with
34 you, and then I go to him who sent me. You
will seek me and will not find me; and where
35 I am you cannot come." The Jews therefore
said among themselves, "Where is he going
that we shall not find him? Will he go to those
dispersed among the Gentiles, and teach the
36 Gentiles? What is this statement that he has
made, 'You will seek me and will not find me,
and where I am you cannot come'?"

Only GOD CAN SATISFY MAN

FEB. 17 or Aug. 18

NOW ON the last, the great day of the feast, John 7
Jesus stood and cried out, saying, "If 37-53
anyone thirst, let him come to me and drink.

38 He who believes in me, as the Scripture says,
'From within him there shall flow rivers of
39 living water.'" He said this, however, of the
Spirit whom they who believed in him were
to receive; for the Spirit had not yet been
given, since Jesus had not yet been glorified.
40 Some of the crowd, therefore, when they
had heard these words, said, "This is truly the
Prophet."

Disagreement Concerning Christ

41 Others said, "This is the Christ." Some, how-
42 ever said, "Can the Christ come from Galilee? Does not the Scripture say that it is of
the offspring of David, and from Bethlehem,
the village where David lived, that the Christ
43 is to come?" So there arose a division among
44 the crowd because of him. And some of them
wanted to seize him, but no one laid hands
on him.
45 The attendants therefore came to the chief
priests and Pharisees; and these said to them,
46 "Why have you not brought him?" The attendants answered, "Never has man spoken as
47 this man." The Pharisees then answered them,
48 "Have you also been led astray? Has any one of

the rulers believed in him, or any of the Pharisees? But this crowd, which does not know 49
the Law, is accursed."

Nicodemus Defends Christ

Nicodemus, he who had come to him at 50
night, so who was one of them, said to them,
"Does our Law judge a man unless it first give 51
him a hearing, and know what he does?" They 52
answered and said to him, "Art thou also a
Galilean? Search the Scriptures and see that
out of Galilee arises no prophet."

And they returned each one to his own 53
house.

ABSOLVES an ADULTERESS
FEB. 18 or Aug. 19

John 8 1-20 BUT JESUS went to the Mount of Olives.
And at daybreak he came again into the
2 temple, and all the people came to him; and
sitting down he began to teach them.
3 Now the Scribes and Pharisees brought a
woman caught in adultery, and setting her in
4 the midst, said to him, "Master, this woman
5 has just now been caught in adultery. And in
the Law Moses commanded us to stone such
6 persons. What, therefore, dost thou say?"
Now they were saying this to test him, in
order that they might be able to accuse him.
But Jesus, stooping down, began to write
with his finger on the ground.

But when they continued asking him, he 7
raised himself and said to them, "Let him who
is without sin among you be the first to cast
a stone at her." And again stooping down, he 8
began to write on the ground. But hearing 9
this, they went away, one by one, beginning
with the eldest. And Jesus remained alone,
with the woman standing in the midst.

And Jesus, raising himself, said to her, 10
"Woman, where are they? Has no one condemned thee?" She said, "No one, Lord." Then 11
Jesus said, "Neither will I condemn thee. Go
thy way, and from now on sin no more."

Jesus Is Light of the World

Again, therefore, Jesus spoke to them, saying, 12
"I am the light of the world. He who follows
me does not walk in the darkness, but will
have the light of life." The Pharisees therefore 13
said to him, "Thou bearest witness to thyself.
Thy witness is not true."

Jesus answered and said to them, "Even if 14
I bear witness to myself, my witness is true,
because I know where I came from and where
I go. But you do not know where I came from
or where I go. You judge according to the 15

16 flesh; I judge no one. And even if I do judge,
my judgment is true, because I am not alone,
but with me is he who sent me, the Father.
17 And in your Law it is written that the witness
18 of two persons is true. It is I who bear witness
to myself, and he who sent me, the Father,
bears witness to me."

19 They therefore said to him, "Where is
thy father?" Jesus answered, "You know neither me nor my Father. If you knew me, you
would then know my Father also."

20 Jesus spoke these words in the treasury,
while teaching in the temple. And no one
seized him, because his hour had not yet
come.

WORLDLINESS PULLS DOWN

FEB. 19 or Aug. 20

AGAIN, THEREFORE, Jesus said to them, "I John 8
go, and you will seek me, and in your 21-36
sin you will die. Where I go you cannot 22
come." The Jews therefore kept saying, "Will
he kill himself, since he says, 'Where I go you
cannot come'?"

23 And he said to them, "You are from below,
I am from above. You are of this world, I am
24 not of this world. Therefore I said to you that
you will die in your sins; for if you do not
believe that [1]I am he, you will die in your sin."
25 They therefore said to him, "Who art
thou?" Jesus said to them, "Why do I speak
26 to you at all! I have many things to speak and
to judge concerning you; but he who sent
me is true, and the things that I heard from
27 him, these I speak in the world." And they did
not understand that he was speaking to them
about the Father.

Other-worldliness Lifts Up

28 Jesus therefore said to them, "When you
have lifted up the Son of Man, then you will
know that I am he, and that of myself I do
nothing: but that I preach only what the
29 Father has taught me. And he who sent me
is with me; he has not left me alone, because
I do always the things that are pleasing to
30 him." When he was speaking these things,
many believed in him.

---

1. *I am he:* i.e., the Messias.

Jesus therefore said to the Jews who had 31
come to believe in him, "If you abide in my
word, you shall be my disciples indeed, and 32
you shall know the truth, and the truth shall
make you free."

Slavery versus True Liberty

They answered him, "We are the children of 33
Abraham, and we have never yet been slaves to
anyone. How sayest thou, 'You shall be free'?"
Jesus answered them, "Amen, amen, I say 34
to you, everyone who commits sin is a slave
of sin. But the slave does nct abide in the 35
house forever; the son abides there forever. 36
If therefore the Son makes you free, you will
be free indeed."

If GOD WERE YOUR FATHER

FEB. 20 or Aug. 21

John 8
37-47 I KNOW that you are the children of Abraham; but you seek to kill me because my

word takes no hold among you. I speak what 38
I have seen with the Father; and you do what
you have seen with your father."
They answered and said to him, "Abra- 39
ham is our father." Jesus said to them, "If you
are the children of Abraham, do the works
of Abraham. But as it is, you are seeking to 40
kill me, one who has spoken the truth to you
which I have heard from God. That is not
what Abraham did. You are doing the works 41
of your father." They therefore said to him,
"We have not been born of fornication; we
have one Father, God."
Jesus therefore said to them, "If God were 42
your Father, you would surely love me. For
from God I came forth and have come; for
neither have I come of myself, but he sent
me. Why do you not understand my speech?
Because you cannot listen to my word. 43

But You Have Made the Devil Your Father

"The father from whom you are is the devil, 44
and the desires of your father it is your will to
do. He was a murderer from the beginning,
and has not stood in the truth because there is
no truth in him. When he tells a lie he speaks

from his very nature, for he is a liar and the
father of lies.

45 "But because I speak the truth you do
46 not believe me. Which of you can convict
me of sin? If I speak the truth, why do you
47 not believe me? He who is of God hears the
words of God. The reason why you do not
hear is that you are not of God."

LIFE ETERNAL

FEB. 21 or Aug. 22

THE JEWS therefore in answer said to him, John 8 48-59
"Are we not right in saying that thou art

49 a Samaritan, and hast a devil?" Jesus answered,
"I have not a devil, but I honor my Father, and
50 you dishonor me. Yet I do not seek my own
51 glory; there is one who seeks and who judges.
Amen, amen, I say to you, if anyone keep my
word, he will never see death."

52 The Jews therefore said, "Now we know
that thou hast a devil. Abraham is dead, and
the prophets, and thou sayest, 'If anyone
53 keep my word he will never taste death.' Art
thou greater than our father Abraham, who
is dead? And the prophets are dead. Whom
dost thou make thyself?"

Before Abraham Came to Be, I Am

54 Jesus answered, "If I glorify myself, my glory
is nothing. It is my Father who glorifies me, of
55 whom you say that he is your God. And you
do not know him, but I know him. And if I
say that I do not know him, I shall be like you,
a liar. But I know him, and I keep his word.
56 Abraham your father rejoiced that he was to
see my day. [1]He saw it and was glad."

1. *He saw it:* Abraham can be said to have seen Christ's day either in faith and prophetic vision, or from his place in limbo when Christ was born.

The Jews therefore said to him, "Thou art 57
not yet fifty years old, and hast thou seen
Abraham?" Jesus said to them, "Amen, amen, 58
I say to you, before Abraham came to be,
[1]I am." They therefore took up stones to cast 59
at him; but Jesus hid himself, and went out
from the temple.

1. *I am*: the use of the present emphasizes His eternal existence.

CURES a BLIND MAN

FEB. 22 or Aug. 23

John 9 1-17
2 AND AS he was passing by, he saw a man
blind from birth. And his disciples asked
him, "Rabbi, who has sinned, this man or his
3 parents, that he should be born blind?" Jesus
answered, "Neither has this man sinned, nor
his parents, but the works of God were to be
4 made manifest in him. I must do the works
of him who sent me while it is day; night is

coming, when no one can work. As long as I 5
am in the world I am the light of the world."
When he had said these things, he spat on 6
the ground and made clay with the spittle,
and spread the clay over his eyes, and said to 7
him, "Go, wash in the pool of Siloe (which
is interpreted 'sent')." So he went away, and
washed, and returned seeing.

Blind Man's Neighbors Astonished

The neighbors therefore and they who were 8
wont to see him before as a beggar, began saying, "Is not this he who used to sit and beg?"
Some said, "It is he." But others said, "By no 9
means, he only resembles him." Yet the man
declared, "I am he."
They therefore said to him, "How were thy 10
eyes opened?" He answered, "The man who is 11
called Jesus made clay and anointed my eyes,
and said to me, 'Go to the pool of Siloe and
wash.' And I went and washed, and I see." And
they said to him, "Where is he?" He said, "I do 12
not know."

Pharisees Question Blind Man

They took him who had been blind to the 13
Pharisees. Now it was a Sabbath on which 14

Jesus made the clay and opened his eyes.
15 Again, therefore, the Pharisees asked him
how he received his sight. But he said to them,
"He put clay upon my eyes, and I washed, and
I see."

16 Therefore some of the Pharisees said, "This
man is not from God, for he does not keep
the Sabbath." But others said, "How can a man
who is a sinner work these signs?" And there
17 was a division among them. Again therefore
they said to the blind man, "What dost thou
say of him who opened thy eyes?" But he said,
"He is a prophet."

PARENTS TESTIFY to CURE

FEB. 23 or Aug. 24

THE JEWS therefore did not believe of him John 9
that he had been blind and had got his 18-41
sight, until they called the parents of the one
who had gained his sight, and questioned
them, saying, "Is this your son, of whom you 19
say that he was born blind? How then does 20
he now see?" His parents answered them and
said, "We know that this is our son, and that 21
he was born blind; but how he now sees we
do not know, or who opened his eyes we ourselves do not know. Ask him; he is of age, let
him speak for himself."

These things his parents said because they 22
feared the Jews. For already the Jews had
agreed that if anyone were to confess him to
be the Christ, he should be put out of the
synagogue. This is why his parents said, "He 23
is of age; question him."

Blind Man Confesses That Jesus Is God

They therefore called a second time the man 24
who had been blind, and said to him, "Give
glory to God! We ourselves know that this
man is a sinner." He therefore said, "Whether 25

he is a sinner, I do not know. One thing I do
know, that whereas I was blind, now I see."
26 They therefore said to him, "What did he
27 do to thee? How did he open thy eyes?" He
answered them, "I have told you already, and
you have heard. Why would you hear again?
28 Would you also become his disciples?" They
heaped abuse on him therefore, and said,
"Thou art his disciple, but we are disciples of
29 Moses. We know that God spoke to Moses;
but as for this man, we do not know where
he is from."
30 In answer the man said to them, "Why,
herein is the marvel, that you do not know
where he is from, and yet he opened my eyes.
31 Now we know that God does not hear sinners; but if anyone is a worshipper of God,
32 and does his will, him he hears. Not from the
beginning of the world has it been heard that
anyone opened the eyes of a man born blind.
33 If this man were not from God, he could do
34 nothing." They answered and said to him,
"Thou wast altogether born in sins, and dost
thou teach us?" And they turned him out.
35 Jesus heard that they had turned him out,
and when he had found him, said to him,

"Dost thou believe in the Son of God?" He 36
answered and said, "Who is he, Lord, that I
may believe in him?" And Jesus said to him,
"Thou hast both seen him, and he it is who 37
speaks with thee." And he said, "I believe,
Lord." And falling down, he worshipped him. 38

Those Who Refuse to See

And Jesus said, "For judgment have I come 39
into this world, that they who do not see may
see, and they who see may become blind."
And some of the Pharisees who were with 40
him heard this, and they said to him, "Are we
also blind?" Jesus said to them, "If you were 41
blind, you would not have sin. But now that
you say, 'We see,' your sin remains."

The GOOD SHEPHERD

FEB. 24 or Aug. 25

John 10 1-21 "AMEN, AMEN, I say to you, he who enters
not by the door into the sheepfold, but
climbs up another way, is a thief and a robber.
2 But he who enters by the door is shepherd of
3 the sheep. To this man the gatekeeper opens,
and the sheep hear his voice, and he calls his
own sheep by name and leads them forth.

4 "And when he has let out his own sheep, he
goes before them; and the sheep follow him
5 because they know his voice. But a stranger
they will not follow, but will flee from him,
because they do not know the voice of
strangers."

6 This parable Jesus spoke to them, but they
did not understand what he was saying to
them.

Hirelings Care Not for the Sheep

Again, therefore, Jesus said to them, "Amen, 7
amen, I say to you, I am the door of the sheep.
[1]All whoever have come are thieves and rob- 8
bers; but the sheep have not heard them. I 9
am the door. If anyone enter by me he shall
be safe, and shall go in and out, and shall find
pastures. The thief comes only to steal, and 10
slay, and destroy. I came that they may have
life, and have it more abundantly.
"I am the good shepherd. The good shep- 11
herd lays down his life for his sheep. But 12
the hireling , who is not a shepherd, whose
own the sheep are not, sees the wolf coming
and leaves the sheep and flees. And the wolf
snatches and scatters the sheep; but the hire- 13
ling flees because he is a hireling, and has no
concern for the sheep.

Jesus Ready to Lay Down His Life

"I am the good shepherd, and I know mine 14
and mine know me, even as the Father knows 15
me and I know the Father; and I lay down my

---

1. The Greek text reads, "all who have come before me." This can refer to pretenders, e.g., Judas the Galilean, or to the Scribes and Pharisees, who taught largely their own doctrine.

16 life for my sheep. And other sheep I have that
are not of this fold. Them also I must bring,
and they shall hear my voice, and there shall
17 be one fold and one shepherd. For this reason the Father loves me, because I lay down
18 my life that I may take it up again. No one
takes it from me, but I lay it down of myself.
I have the power to lay it down, and I have the
power to take it up again. Such is the command I have received from my Father."

19 Again there arose a division among the
20 Jews because of these words. Many of them
were saying, "He has a devil and is mad. Why
21 do you listen to him?" Others were saying,
"These are not the words of one who has a
devil. Can a devil open the eyes of the blind?"

Be humble as a child

AGAIN FORETELLS HIS DEATH

FEB. 25 or Aug. 26

NOW WHILE they were together in Galilee, Matt. 17
[†]and all were astounded at the majesty 21
of God, he was teaching his disciples, and say- Mark 9
ing to them, [‡]"Store up these words in your 30
minds: The Son of Man is to be betrayed into Mark 9
the hands of men, and they will kill him; and 30
having been killed, he will rise again on the
third day."

† Luke 9, 44
‡ Luke 9, 44

Luke 9 45 *And they were exceedingly sorry. But they did not understand this saying, and it was hidden from them, that they might not perceive it; and they were afraid to ask him about this saying.

Matt. 17 25-26 And when they had come to Capharnaum,
those who were collecting the didrachma
came to Peter, and said, "Does your Master
24 not pay the didrachma?" He said, "Yes." But
when he had entered the house, Jesus spoke
first, saying, "What dost thou think, Simon?
From whom do the kings of the earth receive
tribute or customs; from their own sons, or
25 from others?" And he said, "From others."
Jesus said to him, "The sons then are
26 exempt. But that we may not give offense to
them, go to the sea and cast a hook, and take
the first fish that comes up. And opening its
mouth thou wilt find a stater; take that and
give it to them for me and for thee."

Corrects Secret Ambition of Apostles

Mark 9 32-34 And they came to Capharnaum. When he was at home, he asked them, "What were

* Matt. 17, 22

you arguing about on the way?" But they kept 33
silence, for on the way they had discussed with
one another which of them was the greatest.
And sitting down, he called the Twelve and 34
said to them, "If any man wishes to be first,
he shall be last of all, for he who is the least Luke 9 48
among you, he is the greatest."

Be Humble as a Child

But Jesus, knowing the reasoning of their Luke 9 47
heart, took a little child ** and set him in their
midst, and taking him into his arms, he said
to them, "Amen I say to you, unless you turn Matt. 18 3-4
and become like little children, you will not
enter into the kingdom of heaven. Whoever, 4
therefore, humbles himself as this little child,
he is the greatest in the kingdom of heaven.
"Whoever receives one such little child for Mark 9 36
my sake, receives me; and whoever receives
me, receives not me but him who sent me."

** Mark 9, 35

THOSE WHO WORK for CHRIST

FEB. 26 or Aug. 27

Luke 9 49 BUT JOHN answered and said, "Master,
we saw a man casting out devils in thy
name, and we forbade him, because he does
Mark 9 38-41 not follow with us." But Jesus said, "Do not
forbid him, because there is no one who shall
work a miracle in my name, and forthwith
39 be able to speak ill of me. For he who is not
40 against you is for you. For whoever gives you
a cup of water to drink in my name, because
you are Christ's, amen I say to you, he shall
not lose his reward.

Woe to Those Who Scandalize

41 "And whoever causes one of these little ones
who believe in me to sin, it were better for
him if a great millstone were hung about his
neck, and he were thrown into the sea.

Matt. 18 7 "Woe to the world because of scandals! For
it must needs be that scandals come, but woe
to the man through whom scandal does come!

Parable of the Lost Sheep

Matt. 18 10-14 "See that you do not despise one of these little ones; for I tell you, their angels in heaven

always behold the face of my Father in heaven.
For the Son of Man came to save what was 11
lost. What do you think? If a man have a hun- 12
dred sheep, and one of them stray, will he not
leave the ninety-nine in the mountains, and
go in search of the one that has strayed?
"And if he happen to find it, amen I say to 13
you, he rejoices over it more than over the
ninety-nine that did not go astray. Even so, it 14
is not the will of your Father in heaven that a
single one of these little ones should perish.

Cut Off All Sinful Influence

"If thy hand is an occasion of sin to thee, [1]cut Mark 9
if off! It is better for thee to enter into life 42-49
maimed, than, having two hands, to go into
hell, into the unquenchable fire, 'Where their 43
worm dies not, and the fire is not quenched.'
"And if thy foot is an occasion of sin to 44
thee, cut it off! It is better for thee to enter
into life everlasting lame, than, having two
feet, to be cast into the hell of unquenchable
fire, 'Where their worm dies not, and the fire 45
is not quenched.'

---

1. . . . *cut it off:* no sacrifice, however painful it may be, is too great if one may save his soul thereby.

46 "And if thy eye is an occasion of sin to thee,
pluck it out! It is better for thee to enter into
the kingdom of God with one eye, than, hav-
47 ing two eyes, to be cast into hell-fire, 'Where
their worm dies not, and the fire is not
48 quenched.' For everyone shall be salted with
fire, and every victim shall be salted.

Parable of the Salt

49 "Salt is good; but if the salt becomes insipid,
what shall you season it with? Have salt in
yourselves, and be at peace with one another."

Duty of being merciful

POWER of FORGIVING SIN

FEB. 27 or Aug. 28

BUT IF thy brother sin against thee, go and Matt. 18
show him his fault, between thee and 15-35

him alone. If he listen to thee, thou hast won
16 thy brother. But if he do not listen to thee,
take with thee one or two more so that on the
word of two or three witnesses every word
17 may be confirmed. And if he refuse to hear
them, appeal to the Church, but if he refuse
to hear even the Church, let him be to thee
as the heathen and the publican.

18 "Amen I say to you, whatever you bind on
earth shall be bound also in heaven; and whatever you loose on earth shall be loosed also
in heaven.[1]

The Power of United Prayer

19 "I say to you further, that if two of you shall
agree on earth about anything at all for which
they ask, it shall be done for them by my
20 Father in heaven. For where two or three are
gathered together for my sake, there am I in
the midst of them."

Duty of Being Merciful

21 Then Peter came up to him and said, "Lord,
how often shall my brother sin against me,

1. To the Apostles as a body is given a part of the power granted to Peter. There will be no conflict of authority, since Peter is the head of the Church, including the Apostles, he alone having received "the keys of the kingdom of heaven."

and I forgive him? Up to seven times?" [1]Jesus 22
said to him, "I do not say to thee seven times,
but seventy times seven.

"This is why the kingdom of heaven is lik- 23
ened to a king who desired to settle accounts
with his servants. And when he had begun 24
the settlement, one was brought to him who
owed him ten thousand talents. And as he had 25
no means of paying, his master ordered him
to be sold, with his wife and children and all
that he had, and payment to be made.

"But the servant fell down and besought 26
him, saying, 'Have patience with me and I will
pay thee all!' And moved with compassion, 27
the master of that servant released him, and
forgave him the debt.

The Unmerciful Servant

"But as that servant went out, he met one of 28
his fellow-servants who owed him a hundred
denarii, and he laid hold of him and throt-
tled him, saying, 'Pay what thou owest.' His 29
fellow-servant therefore fell down and began
to entreat him, saying, 'Have patience with

1. A sinner must be forgiven as often as he repents. The expression "seventy times seven" is for an indefinite number.

30 me and I will pay thee all.' But he would not;
but went away and cast him into prison until
he should pay what was due.

Unmercifulness Rebuked

31 "His fellow-servants therefore, seeing
what had happened, were very much saddened, and they went and informed their
32 master of what had taken place. Then his
master called him, and said to him, 'Wicked
servant! I forgave thee all the debt, because
33 thou didst entreat me. Shouldst not thou also
have had pity on thy fellow-servant, even as I
had pity on thee?'
34 "And his master, being angry, handed him
over to the torturers until he should pay all
35 that was due to him. So also my heavenly
Father will do to you, if you do not each forgive your brothers from your hearts."

To SAVE, NOT to DESTROY
FEB. 28 or Aug. 29

NOW IT CAME TO PASS, when the days had Luke 9
come for him to be taken up, that he 51-57
steadfastly set his face to go to Jerusalem, 52
and sent messengers before him. And they
went and entered a Samaritan town to make
ready for him; and they did not receive 53
him, because his face was set for Jerusalem.
But when his disciples James and John saw 54
this, they said, "Lord, wilt thou that we bid
fire come down from heaven and consume
them?"

But he turned and rebuked them, saying, 55
"You do not know of what manner of spirit
you are; for the Son of Man did not come to 56
destroy men's lives, but to save them." And
they went to another village.

Conditions Necessary to Follow Christ

And it came to pass as they went on their 57
journey, a Scribe came and said to him, "Mas- Matt. 8 19-20
ter, I will follow thee wherever thou goest."
But Jesus said to him, "The foxes have dens, 20
and the birds of the air have nests; but the Son
of Man has nowhere to lay his head."

Luke 9 59-62 And he said to another, "Follow me." But
he said, "Lord, let me first go and bury my
60 father." But Jesus said to him, "Let the dead
bury their dead, but do thou go and proclaim
61 the kingdom of God." And another said, "I
will follow thee, Lord, but let me first bid
farewell to those at home." Jesus said to him,
62 [1]"No one, having put his hand to the plow and
looking back, is fit for the kingdom of God."

1. Undivided attention is required of the disciples.

A lamb in the midst of wolves

INSTRUCTING HIS LABORERS

FEB. 29 or Aug. 30

Now After this the Lord appointed Luke 10 1-12
seventy-two others, and sent them
forth two by two before him into every

town and place where he himself was about
2 to come. And he said to them, "The harvest
indeed is great, but the laborers are few. Pray
therefore the Lord of the harvest to send
forth laborers into his harvest.

3 "Go. Behold, I send you forth as lambs in
4 the midst of wolves. Carry neither purse,
nor wallet, nor sandals, [1]and greet no one on
5 the way. Whatever house you enter, first say,
6 'Peace to this house!' And if a son of peace be
there, your peace will rest upon him; but if
not, it will return to you.

7 "And remain in the same house, eating
and drinking what they have; for the laborer
deserves his wages. Do not go from house to
8 house. And whatever town you enter, and they
9 receive you, eat what is set before you, and
cure the sick who are there, and say to them,
'The kingdom of God is at hand for you.'

Woe to Those Who Receive You Not

10 "But whatever town you enter, and they do
not receive you—go out into its streets and

1. The disciples are not to spend much unnecessary time in long oriental salutations, but are rather to devote themselves without delay and distraction to their higher calling.

say, 'Even the dust from your town that cleaves 11
to us we shake off against you; yet know this,
that the kingdom of God is at hand.' I say to 12
you, that it will be more tolerable for Sodom
in that day than for that town."

"Come to me"

The IMPENITENT TOWNS

MAR. 1 or Aug. 31

Matt. 11 20-24 THEN HE BEGAN to reproach the towns in
which most of his miracles were worked,
21 because they had not repented. "Woe to thee,
Corozain! woe to thee, Bethsaida! For if in
Tyre and Sidon had been worked the miracles that have been worked in you, they would
have repented long ago in sackcloth and ashes.
22 But I tell you, it will be more tolerable for
Tyre and Sidon on the day of judgment than
for you.

nothing? Behold, the entire world has gone
after him!"

And some of the Pharisees from the crowds Luke 19
said to him, "Master, rebuke thy disciples." 39-44
He said to them, "I tell you that if these keep 40
silence, the stones will cry out."

Jesus Weeps over Jerusalem

And when he drew near and saw the city, he 41
wept over it, saying, "If thou hadst known, in 42
this thy day, even thou, the things that are for
thy peace! But now they are hidden from thy
eyes. For days will come upon thee when thy 43
enemies will throw up a rampart about thee,
and surround thee and shut thee in on every
side, and will dash thee to the ground and 44
thy children within thee, and will not leave
in thee one stone upon another, because thou
hast not known the time of thy visitation."

EXERCISES HEALING MINISTRY

APR. 6 or Oct. 6

Matt. 21 10-11 AND WHEN he entered Jerusalem, all the
city was thrown into commotion, say-
11 ing, "Who is this?" But the crowds kept on
saying, "This is Jesus the prophet from Nazareth of Galilee."

Matt. 21 14-17 And the blind and the lame came to him in
15 the temple, and he healed them. But the chief
priests and the Scribes, seeing the wonderful deeds that he did, and the children crying
out in the temple, and saying, "Hosanna to
16 the Son of David," were indignant, and said

to him, "Dost thou hear what these are saying?" And Jesus said to them, "Yes; have you
never read, 'Out of the mouth of infants and
sucklings thou hast perfected praise'?" And 17
leaving them, he went out of the city to Bethany and he stayed there.

The Fig Tree Is Cursed

[†]And the next day, [‡]in the morning, [*]after they Matt. 21 18
had left Bethany, on his way back to the city, Mark 11 13-14
he felt hungry. And seeing in the distance a
fig tree in leaf, he went to see if he might
find anything on it. But when he came up to
it, he found nothing but leaves; for it was not
the season for figs. Then he spoke to it saying, 14
"May no one ever eat fruit of thee hencefor-
ward forever." And his disciples heard. And Matt. 21 19
immediately the fig tree withered up.

Drives Money-changers from Temple

And they came to Jerusalem. And he entered Mark 11 15-17
the temple, and began to cast out those who
were selling and buying in the temple; and

† Mark 11, 12
‡ Matt. 21, 18
* Mark 11, 12

he overturned the tables of the money-
changers and the seats of those who sold the
16 doves. He would not allow anyone to carry a
17 vessel through the temple. And he began to
teach, saying to them, "Is it not written, 'My
house shall be called a house of prayer for all
the nations'? But you have made it a den of
thieves."

Luke 19 47 The chief priests and the Scribes and the
Mark 11 18 leading men of the people heard it, and they
sought a way to destroy him; for they were
afraid of him, because all the crowd were
Luke 19 48 astonished at his teaching. But they found
nothing that they could do to him, for all the
Mark 11 19 people hung upon his words. And when it was
evening he went out of the city.

HIS LIFE-GIVING DEATH

APR. 7 or Oct. 7

NOW THERE were certain Gentiles among John 12 20-36
those who had gone up to worship on
the feast. These therefore approached Philip, 21
who was from Bethsaida of Galilee, and asked
him, saying, "Sir, we wish to see Jesus." Philip 22
came and told Andrew; again, Andrew and
Philip spoke to Jesus.

But Jesus answered them, "The hour has 23
come for the Son of Man to be glorified. 24
Amen, amen, I say to you, unless the grain
of wheat falls into the ground and dies, it 25

remains alone. But if it dies, it brings forth
much fruit. He who loves his life, loses it; and
26 he who hates his life in this world, keeps it
unto life everlasting. If anyone serves me, let
him follow me; and where I am there also
shall my servant be. If anyone serves me, my
Father will honor him.

The Eternal Father Testifies to His Son

27 [1]"Now my soul is troubled. And what shall I
say? Father, save me from this hour! No, this
28 is why I came to this hour. Father, glorify thy
name!" There came therefore a voice from
heaven, "I have both glorified it, and I will
29 glorify it again." Then the crowd which was
standing round and had heard, said that it had
thundered. Others said, "An angel has spoken
30 to him." Jesus answered and said, "Not for me
did this voice come, but for you.
31 "Now is the judgment of the world; now
32 will the prince of the world be cast out. And
I, if I be lifted up from the earth, will draw all

1. *Troubled:* this emotion is human fear and sadness, occasioned by the impending Passion. St. Thomas calls this scene a brief anticipation of the Agony in the Garden.

things to myself." Now he said this signifying 33
by what death he was to die.

World Continues to Challenge

The crowd answered him, "We have heard 34
from the Law that the Christ abides forever.
And how canst thou say, 'The Son of Man
must be lifted up'? Who is this Son of Man?" 35
Jesus therefore said to them, "Yet a little
while the light is among you. Walk while you
have the light, that darkness may not overtake you. He who walks in the darkness does
not know where he goes. While you have 36
the light, believe in the light, that you may
become sons of light."

These things Jesus spoke, and he went away and hid himself from them.

The POWER of FAITH

APR. 8 or Oct. 8

Mark 11 AND AS THEY passed by in the morning,
20 they saw the fig tree withered from the
Matt. 21 roots. And upon seeing this the disciples mar-
20 Mark 11 velled, saying, "How did it come to wither
21-22 up immediately?" And Peter, remembering,
said to him, "Rabbi, behold, the fig tree that
22 thou didst curse is withered up." But Jesus
Matt. 21 21 answered and said to them, "Have faith in
God. Amen I say to you, if you have faith and
do not waver, not only will you do what I have
done to the fig tree, but even if you shall say
to this mountain, 'Arise, and hurl thyself into
the sea,' it shall be done.

The Power of Prayer

Mark 11 "Therefore I say to you, all things whatever
24-27 you ask for in prayer, believe that you shall
25 receive, and they shall come to you. And

when you stand up to pray, forgive whatever
you have against anyone, that your Father in
heaven may also forgive you your offenses.
But if you do not forgive, neither will your 26
Father in heaven forgive you your offenses."

"By What Authority?"

And they came back to Jerusalem. †And when 27
he had come into the temple, the chief priests
and elders of the people came to him as he
was teaching, and said, "By what authority
dost thou do these things? And who gave thee
this authority?" Jesus answered and said to 24
them, "I also will ask you one question, and
if you answer me this, I in turn will tell you
by what authority I do these things. Was the Mark 11 30-31
baptism of John from heaven, or from men?
Answer me."

But they began to argue among them- 31
selves, saying, "If we say, 'From heaven,' he
will say, 'Why then did you not believe him?' Matt. 21 26-32
But if we say, 'From men,' we fear the people,
for all regard John as a prophet." And they 27
answered Jesus and said, "We do not know."

† Matt. 21, 23-24

Then he in turn said to them, "Neither do I tell you by what authority I do these things.

Parable of the Two Sons

28 "But what do you think? A man had two
sons; and he came to the first and said, 'Son,
29 go and work today in my vineyard.' But he
answered and said, 'I will not'; but afterwards
30 he regretted it and went. And he came to the
other and spoke in the same manner. And this
one answered, 'I go, sir'; but he did not go.
31 Which of the two did the father's will?" They
said, "The first." Jesus said to them, "Amen
I say to you, the publicans and harlots are
32 entering the kingdom of God before you. For
John came to you in the way of justice, and
you did not believe him. But the publicans
and the harlots believed him; whereas you,
seeing it, did not even repent afterwards, that
you might believe him."

The VINEYARD WORKERS

APR. 9 or Oct. 9

1 AND HE began to speak to them in par- Mark 12 1-4
ables. "A man planted a vineyard, and
put a hedge about it, and dug a wine vat,
and built a tower; then he let it out to vine-
dressers, and went abroad. And at the proper 2
time he sent a servant to the vine-dressers to
receive from the vine-dressers some of the
fruit of the vineyard; but they seized him, and 3
beat him, and sent him away empty-handed.

---

1. God is the landowner of the parable. He had sent His prophets, and lastly His Son, to the vine-dressers, the Jews.

Servant Killed, Then the Son

4 "And again he sent another servant to them;
but this one they wounded in the head and
Luke 20 treated shamefully. And he sent yet a third;
12 Matt. 21 but him also they wounded and cast out. And
35 the vine-dressers seized his servants, and beat
one, killed another, and stoned another.
Mark 12 "Now he still had one left, a beloved son.
6 Luke 20 But the owner of the vineyard said, 'What
12 shall I do? I will send my beloved son; perhaps
when they see him, they will respect him.'
Matt. 21 But the vine-dressers, on seeing the son, said
38-40 among themselves, 'This is the heir; come, let
us kill him, and we shall have his inheritance.'
39 So they seized him, cast him out of the vineyard, and killed him.
40 "When, therefore, the owner of the vineyard comes, what will he do to those vine-
Mark 12 dressers? He will come and destroy the
9 Matt. 21 vine-dressers, and will give the vineyard to
41 Luke 20 others, who will render to him the fruits in
16-17 their seasons." Upon hearing this, they said to
him, "By no means." But he looked on them
17 and said, "What then is this that is written;
Mark 12 have you not read this Scripture: 'The stone
10-11 which the builders rejected, has become the

corner stone; By the Lord this has been done, 11
and it is wonderful in our eyes'?

"Therefore I say to you, that the kingdom Matt. 21
of God will be taken away from you and will 43-46
be given to a people yielding its fruits. And 44
he who falls on this stone will be broken to
pieces; but upon whomever it falls, it will
grind him to powder."

And when the chief priests and Pharisees 45
had heard his parables, they knew that he was
speaking about them. And though they sought 46
to lay hands on him, they feared the people,
because they regarded him as a prophet. And Mark 12
leaving him, they went their way. 12

PARABLE of ROYAL MARRIAGE

APR. 10 or Oct. 10

Matt. 22 1-14 2 AND JESUS addressed them, and spoke to
them again in parables, saying, "The

kingdom of heaven is like a king who made a
marriage feast for his son. And he sent his ser- 3
vants to call in those invited to the marriage
feast, but they would not come.

"Again he sent out other servants, saying, 4
'Tell those who are invited, Behold, I have
prepared my dinner; my oxen and fatlings
are killed, and everything is ready; come to
the marriage feast.' But they made light of it, 5
and went off, one to his farm, and another
to his business; and the rest laid hold of his 6
servants, treated them shamefully, and killed
them.

"But when the king heard of it, he was 7
angry; and he sent his armies, destroyed those
murderers, and burnt their city.

Invitation Refused, Invites Others

"Then he said to his servants, 'The marriage 8
feast indeed is ready, but those who were
invited were not worthy; go therefore to the 9
crossroads, and invite to the marriage feast
whomever you shall find.' And his servants 10
went out into the roads, and gathered all
whom they found, both good and bad; and
the marriage feast was filled with guests.

11 "Now the king went in to see the guests,
and he saw there a man who had not on a wed-
12 ding garment. And he said to him, 'Friend,
how didst thou come in here without a wed-
13 ding garment?' But he was speechless. Then
the king said to the attendants, 'Bind his hands
and feet and cast him forth into the darkness
outside, where there will be the weeping, and
14 the gnashing of teeth.' For many are called,
but few are chosen."

"Render, therefore, to Cæsar the things that are Cæsar's, and to God the things that are God's.

TRYING to ENSNARE JESUS

APR. 11 or Oct. 11

Matt. 22 15 THEN THE PHARISEES went and took counsel how they might trap him in his talk.
Luke 20 20-21 So watching their opportunity, they sent
forth spies, who should pretend to be just
men, that they might trap him in his talk and
deliver him up to the ruling power and to the
authority of the procurator.

21 And they asked him, saying, "Master, we
know that thou speakest and teachest rightly.
Matt. 22 16-18 We know that thou art truthful, and that thou
teachest the way of God in truth and that thou
carest naught for any man; for thou dost not
regard the person of men.

Concerning Tribute to Caesar

17 "Tell us, therefore, what dost thou think: Is
18 it lawful to give tribute to Cæsar, or not?"
Luke 20 23 But Jesus, knowing their wickedness, know-
Matt. 22 18-22 ing their craftiness, said, "Why do you test
19 me, you hypocrites? Show me the coin of
the tribute." So they offered him a denarius.
20 Then Jesus said to them, "Whose are this
21 image and the inscription?"They said to him,
"Cæsar's."

Then he said to them, "Render, therefore,
to Cæsar the things that are Cæsar's, and to
God the things that are God's." And hearing 22
this they marvelled. And they could not take Luke 20 26
hold of what he said before the people; and
marvelling at his answer, they kept silence Matt. 22 22
and leaving him went off.

SADDUCEES CHALLENGE JESUS on the RESURRECTION

APR. 12 or Oct. 12

Luke 20 27-33 NOW THERE CAME to him certain of the
Saddducees, who say that there is no

resurrection, and they questioned him, say- 28
ing, "Master, Moses has written for us: 'If a
man's brother die, having a wife, and he be
childless, his brother shall take the widow and
raise up issue to his brother.' Now there were 29
seven brothers.

"And the first took a wife and died childless. And the next took her and he also died 30
childless. Then the third took her; and in like 31
manner all seven, and they died without leaving children. Last of all the woman also died. 32
At the resurrection, therefore, of which of 33
them will she be wife? For the seven had her
as wife."

No Bodily Necessities in Heaven

And Jesus answered and said to them, "Is not Mark 12
this why you err—because you know neither 24
the Scriptures nor the power of God? The Luke 20
children of this world marry and are given in 34-40 35
marriage. But those who shall be accounted
worthy of that world and of the resurrection
from the dead, neither marry nor take wives.
For neither shall they be able to die any more, 36
for they are equal to the angels, and are sons
of God, being sons of the resurrection.

37 "But that the dead rise, even Moses showed
in the passage about the Bush, when he calls
the Lord the God of Abraham, and the God
38 of Isaac, and the God of Jacob. Now he is not
the God of the dead, but of the living, for all
live to him."

39 And certain of the Scribes answered and
40 said, "Master, thou hast said well." And they
did not dare to question him any further.

LOVE of GOD and NEIGHBOR

APR. 13 or Oct. 13

BUT THE PHARISEES, hearing that he had Matt. 22
silenced the Saducees, gathered together. 34
And one of the Scribes came forward who had Mark 12
heard them disputing together; and seeing 28-30
that he had answered them well, he asked him
which was the first commandment of all.

But Jesus answered him, "The first com- 29
mandment of all is, 'Hear, O Israel! The Lord
our God is one God; and thou shalt love the 30

Lord thy God with thy whole heart, and with
thy whole soul, and with thy whole mind, and
Matt. 22 with thy whole strength.' This is the greatest
38 and the first commandment.

Inseparable from Love of Neighbor

Mark 12 "And the second is like it, 'Thou shalt love thy
31 neighbor as thyself.' There is no other com-
Matt. 22 mandment greater than these. On these two
40 commandments depend the whole Law and
the Prophets."

Mark 12 And the Scribe said to him, "Well answered,
32-34 Master, thou hast said truly that he is one and
33 that there is no other besides him; and that
he should be loved with the whole heart, and
with the whole understanding, and with the
whole soul, and with one's whole strength;
and that to love one's neighbor as oneself is
a greater thing than all holocausts and sacri-
34 fices." And Jesus, seeing that he had answered
wisely, said to him, "Thou art not far from
the kingdom of God." And no one after that
ventured to ask him questions.

Christ Both Human and Divine

Matt. 22 Now while the Pharisees were gathered
41-43 together, Jesus questioned them, saying,
42 "What do you think of the Christ? Whose son

is he?"They said to him, "David's." He said to 43
them, "How then does David in the Spirit call
him Lord, saying in the Book of Psalms, 'The Luke 20
Lord said to my Lord: Sit at my right hand, till 42-43 43
I make thy enemies thy footstool'?

[1]"If David, therefore, calls him 'Lord,' how Matt. 22
is he his son?" And no one could answer him a 45-46 46
word; neither did anyone dare from that day
forth to ask him any more questions. And the Mark 12
mass of the common people liked to hear him. 37

1. David's son is David's Lord: there is implied a claim to divinity.

BAD EXAMPLE of RULERS

APR. 14 or Oct. 14

Matt. 23 1-23 THEN JESUS spoke to the crowds and to his
2 disciples, saying, "The Scribes and the
3 Pharisees have sat on the chair of Moses. All
things, therefore, that they command you,
observe and do. But do not act according
to their works; for they talk but do nothing.
4 And they bind together heavy and oppressive
burdens, and lay them on men's shoulders;
but not with one finger of their own do they
choose to move them.

They Are Actuated by Vanity

5 "In fact, all their works they do in order to
be seen by men; for they widen their [1]phylac-
6 teries, and enlarge their tassels, and love the
first places at suppers and the front seats in
7 the synagogues, and greetings in the market
8 place, and to be called by men [2]'Rabbi.' But

1. *Phylacteries:* little boxes containing Scripture texts which were bound to the forehead and left arm when the Jews were saying their prayers. A misinterpretation of the Law made them think they were obliged to wear them. The fringes, tassels attached to the cloak, were prescribed by Num. 15, 37-41; Deut. 22, 12.

2. *Rabbi:* means "my master."

do not you be called 'Rabbi'; [1]for one is your
Master, and all you are brothers. And call 9
no one on earth your father; for one is your
Father, who is in heaven. Neither be called 10
masters; for one only is your Master, the 11
Christ. He who is greatest among you shall 12
be your servant. And whoever exalts himself shall be humbled, and whoever humbles himself shall be exalted.

Eight Woes: 1st, Stumbling-blocks

"But woe to you, Scribes and Pharisees, hyp- 13
ocrites! because you shut the kingdom of heaven against men. For you yourselves do not go in, nor do you allow those going in to enter.

2nd, Hypocrisy

["Woe to you, Scribes and Pharisees, hypo- 14
crites! because you devour the houses of widows, praying long prayers. For this you shall receive a greater judgment.]

---

1. It would be blameworthy for Christians to give or receive such titles as "master," "father," "doctor," without recognizing that one is "father in Christ," that is, in union with and subordination to our Lord and to the Father.

3rd, Perverting

15 "Woe to you, Scribes and Pharisees, hypocrites! because you traverse sea and land to
make one convert; and when he has become
one, you make him twofold more a son of hell
than yourselves.

4th, Trifling with Sacred Oaths

16 "Woe to you, blind guides, who say. 'Whoever
swears by the temple, it is nothing; but whoever swears by the gold of the temple, he is
17 bound.' You blind fools! for which is greater,
18 the gold, or the temple which sanctifies the
gold? 'And whoever swears by the altar, it is
nothing; but whoever swears by the gift that
19 is upon it, he is bound.' Blind ones! for which
is greater, the gift, or the altar which sancti-
20 fies the gift? Therefore he who swears by the
21 altar swears by it, and by all things that are on
it; and he who swears by the temple swears
22 by it, and by him who dwells in it. And he
who swears by heaven swears by the throne of
God, and by him who sits upon it."

The EIGHT WOES (Cont'd)

5th, Trifles versus Important Duties

APR. 15 or Oct. 15

WOE TO YOU, Scribes and Pharisees, hyp- Matt. 23
ocrites! because you pay tithes on mint 23-39
and anise and cummin, and have left undone
the weightier matters of the Law, right judgment and mercy and faith. These things you
ought to have done, while not leaving the others undone. Blind guides, who strain out the 24
gnat but swallow the camel!

6th, Neglecting Interior Piety

"Woe to you, Scribes and Pharisees, hypo- 25
crites! because you clean the outside of the
cup and the dish, but within they are full of
robbery and uncleanness. Thou blind Phari- 26
see! clean first the inside of the cup and of the
dish, that the outside too may be clean.

7th, Mere External Respectability

"Woe to you, Scribes and Pharisees, hyp-
27 ocrites! because you are like whited sepulchres, which outwardly appear to men
beautiful, but within are full of dead men's
28 bones and of all uncleanness. So you also outwardly appear just to men, but within you are
full of hypocrisy and iniquity.

8th, Arrogance and Presumption

29 "Woe to you, Scribes and Pharisees, hypocrites! you who build the sepulchres of the
30 prophets, and adorn the tombs of the just,
and say, 'If we had lived in the days of our
fathers, we would not have been their accom-
31 plices in the blood of the prophets.' Thus you
are witnesses against yourselves that you are
the sons of those who killed the prophets.
32 "You also fill up the measure of your
33 fathers. Serpents, brood of vipers, how are
you to escape the judgment of hell?

Retribution, Desolation, Their Final Lot

34 "Therefore, behold, I send you prophets, and
wise men, and scribes; and some of them
you will put to death, and crucify, and some

you will scourge in your synagogues, and
persecute from town to town; that upon you 35
may come all the just blood that has been
shed on the earth, from the blood of Abel
the just unto the blood of Zacharias the son
of Barachias, whom you killed between the
temple and the altar. Amen I say to you, all 36
these things will come upon this generation.

"Jerusalem, Jerusalem! thou who killest 37
the prophets, and stonest those who are sent
to thee! How often would I have gathered thy
children together, as a hen gathers her young
under her wings, but thou wouldst not!
Behold, your house is left to you desolate. For 38
I say to you, you shall not see me henceforth 39
until you shall say, 'Blessed is he who comes
in the name of the Lord!'"

WIDOW'S MITE IS GREAT

APR. 16 or Oct. 16

Mark 12 41-44 AND JESUS Sat down opposite the treasury, and observed how the crowd were
putting money into the treasury; and many
42 rich people were putting in large sums. And
there came one poor widow, and she put in
43 two mites, which make a quadrans. And he
called his disciples together, and said to them,
"Amen I say to you, this poor widow has put
in more than all those who have been putting
44 money into the treasury. For they all have put
in out of their abundance; but she out of her
want has put in all that she had—all that she
had to live on."

Jesus Rebukes Obstinate Unbelief

Now though he had worked so many signs in John 12 37-50
their presence, they did not believe in him;
that the word which the prophet Isaias spoke 38
might be fulfilled, "Lord, who has believed
our report, and to whom has the arm of the
Lord been revealed?" This is why [1]they could 39
not believe, because Isaias said again, "He has 40
blinded their eyes, and hardened their hearts;
lest they see with their eyes, and understand
with their mind, and be converted, and I heal
them." Isaias said these things when he saw his 41
glory and spoke of him.

Belief without Courage

And yet, even among the rulers, many 42
believed in him; but because of the Pharisees
they did not acknowledge it, lest they should
be put out of the synagogue. For they loved 43
the glory of men more than the glory of God.

But Jesus cried out, and said, "He who 44
believed in me, believes not in me but in
him who sent me. And he who sees me, sees 45

1. *They could not believe:* faith is a gift of God which often cannot be received because of an obstacle which man puts in its way. The obstacle here is their obstinacy. Isaias had foretold this.

46 him who sent me. I have come a light into
the world, that whoever believes in me may
not remain in the darkness.

We Condemn Ourselves

47 "And if anyone hears my words, and does not
keep them, it is not I who judge him; for I
have not come to judge the world, but to save
48 the world. He who rejects me, and does not
accept my words, has one to condemn him.
The word that I have spoken will condemn
49 him on the last day. For I have not spoken on
my own authority, but he who sent me, the
Father, has commanded me what I should say,
50 and what I should declare. And I know that his
commandment is everlasting life. The things,
therefore, that I speak, I speak as the Father
has bidden me."

TEMPLE to BE DESTROYED

APR. 17 or Oct. 17

AND AS HE was going out of the temple, Mark 13 1
some were saying of the temple that it Luke 21 5
was adorned with beautiful stones and offer-
ings. One of his disciples said to him, "Master, Mark 13 1-4
look, what wonderful stones and buildings!"
[1]And Jesus answered and said to him, "Dost 2
thou see all these great buildings? There will
not be left one stone upon another that will
not be thrown down."

Antichrists Will Try to Deceive

And as he was sitting on the Mount of Olives, 3
opposite the temple, Peter and James and

1. This long prophecy deals with both the destruction of Jerusalem and the end of the world. The elements of the prophecy are so intermingled that it is difficult at times to determine to which cataclysm Jesus refers.

4 John and Andrew asked him privately, "Tell
us, when are these things to happen, and
what will be the sign when all these things
Matt. 24 will begin to come to pass, and what will be
3 Mark 13 the sign of thy coming and of the end of the
5 world?" And in answer Jesus began to say to
them, "Take care that no one leads you astray.
Matt. 24 For many will come in my name, saying, 'I am
5 the Christ,' [†]and, 'The time is at hand;' [‡]and
Luke 21 they will lead many astray. Do not, therefore,
8 go after them.

Fear Not Wars

Mark 13 "But when you hear of wars and rumors of
7 Mark 13 wars, [*]and insurrections, do not be alarmed;
7-8 for they must come to pass, but the end is not
8 yet. For nation will rise against nation, ands
kingdom against kingdom; and there will be
Luke 21 earthquakes in various places, and pestilences
11 and famines, and there will be terrors and
Matt. 24 great signs from heaven. But all these things
8 are the beginnings of sorrows.

† Luke 21, 8
‡ Mark 13, 6
* Luke 21, 9

Final Victory over Persecution

**"But be on your guard. But before all these Luke 21 12-14
things they will arrest you and persecute you,
delivering you up to the synagogues and pris-
ons, dragging you before kings and governors
for my name's sake. It shall lead to your bear- 13
ing witness.
"Resolve therefore in your hearts not to 14
meditate beforehand how you are to make
your defense. And when they lead you away Mark 13 11
to deliver you up, do not be anxious beforehand what you are to speak; but speak whatever is given you in that hour. For I myself Luke 21 15
will give you utterance and wisdom, which
all your adversaries will not be able to resist
or gainsay. For it is not you who are speaking, Mark 13 11
but the Holy Spirit."

** Mark 13, 9

Destruction foretold

RELATIVES, FRIENDS WILL BETRAY

APR. 18 or Oct. 18

Luke 21 16-19 BUT YOU will be delivered up by your
parents and brothers and relatives and
17 friends; and some of you they will put to
18 death. And you will be hated by all for my
19 Matt. 24 name's sake; yet not a hair of your head shall
10 perish. By your patience you will win your
souls. And then many will fall away, and
will betray one another, and will hate one
Mark 13 another. And brother will hand over brother
12 to death, and the father his child; children
will rise up against parents and put them
to death.

"And many false prophets will arise, and Matt. 24
will lead many astray. And because iniquity 11-14 12
will abound, the charity of the many will
grow cold. But whoever perseveres to the 13
end, he shall be saved. And this gospel of 14
the kingdom shall be preached in the whole
world, for a witness to all nations; and then
will come the end.

How to Act during Persecution

"And when you see Jerusalem being sur- Luke 21
rounded by an army, then know that her des- 20
olation is at hand. Therefore when you see the Matt. 24
abomination of desolation, which was spoken 15
of by Daniel the prophet, standing in the holy Mark 13
place, where it ought not—let him who reads 14
understand—then let those who are in Judea
flee to the mountains; and let those who are Luke 21
in her midst go out; and let him who is on 21 Mark 13
the housetop not go down and enter to take 15 Matt. 24
anything from his house; and let him who is 18-20
in the field not turn back to take his cloak.
But woe to those who are with child, or have 19
infants at the breast in those days! But pray 20
that your flight may not be in the winter, or
on the Sabbath.

Prophecy of Destruction

Luke 21 "For these are days of vengeance, that all
22 Mark 13 things that are written may be fulfilled. For
19 in those days will be tribulations, such as have
not been from the beginning of the creation
which God created until now, nor will be.

Luke 21 "For there will be great distress over the
23-24 24 land, and wrath upon this people. And they
will fall by the edge of the sword, and will
Mark 13 be led away as captives to all the nations. And
20 unless the Lord had shortened the days, no
living creature would be saved. But for the
sake of the elect whom he has chosen, he has
Luke 21 shortened the days. And Jerusalem will be
24 trodden down by the Gentiles, until the times
of the nations be fulfilled."

The end of the world

COMING of ANTICHRISTS

APR. 19 or Oct. 19

Matt. 24 23-29 "THEN IF anyone say to you, 'Behold, here
is the Christ,' or, 'There he is,' do not
24 believe it. For false christs and false prophets
will arise, and will show great signs and wonders, so as to lead astray, if possible, even the
25 elect. Behold, I have told it to you beforehand.
26 "If therefore they say to you, 'Behold, he
is in the desert,' do not go forth; 'Behold,
he is in the inner chambers,' do not believe
27 it. For as the lightning comes forth from the
east and shines even to the west, so also will
28 the coming of the Son of Man be. Wherever
the body is, there will the eagles be gathered
together.

29 "But immediately after the tribulation of
Luke 21 25 those days, there will be signs in the sun and
Mark 13 24-25 moon and stars. The sun will be darkened,
Luke 21 25-26 and the moon will not give her light, and the
stars of heaven will be falling, and upon the
earth distress of nations bewildered by the
26 roaring of sea and waves; men fainting for
fear and for expectation of the things that
are coming on the world; for the powers of
heaven will be shaken.

The Coming of Christ

"And then will appear the sign of the Son of Matt. 24 30-31
Man in heaven; and then will all tribes of the
earth mourn, and they will see the Son of
Man coming upon the clouds of heaven with
great power and majesty. And he will send 31
forth his angels with a trumpet and a great
sound, and they will gather his elect from the
four winds, from one end of the heavens to
the other."

TIME of DESTRUCTION of JERUSALEM

APR. 20 or Oct. 20

Luke 21 "BUT WHEN these things begin to come to
28 pass, look up, and lift up your heads,
Mark 13 because your redemption is at hand. [1]Now
28 Luke 21 from the fig tree learn this parable. When its
29-33 branch is now tender, and the leaves break
30 forth and all the trees . . . now put forth their
31 buds, you know that summer is near. Even
so, when you see these things coming to pass,
32 know that the kingdom of God is near. Amen

1. This passage seems at first sight, on account of its immediately preceding context, to refer to the Second Coming as well as to the destruction of Jerusalem; and so the words of our Lord, *This generation will not pass away till all things have been accomplished,* would promise the Second Coming before the death of many of those then living. But He does not actually make this promise, for He says explicitly that no one knows, not even Himself (with a knowledge He may communicate), when it will come. *That day:* in the Bible, this predicted day always refers to the day of judgment. *This generation:* may mean that the Jewish nation would survive to the end of the world. The expression does not always necessarily refer to contemporaries. And despite their position, the words may be referred to the destruction of Jerusalem. The signs announcing it would enable the Christians to flee, whereas the end of the world was to come suddenly and there would be no escape from the calamities which preceded it.

I say to you, this generation will not pass away
till all things have been accomplished. Heaven 33
and earth will pass away, but my words will
not pass away.

Time of the End of the World

"But of that day and hour no one knows, not Matt. 24 36-41
even the angels of heaven, but the Father only.
And as it was in the days of Noe, even so will 37
be the coming of the Son of Man. For as in 38
the days before the flood they were eating and
drinking, marrying and giving in marriage,
until the day when Noe entered the ark, and 39
they did not understand until the flood came
and swept them all away; even so will be the
coming of the Son of Man.

"Then two men will be in the field; one 40
will be taken, and one will be left. Two 41
women will be grinding at the millstone; one
will be taken, and one will be left.

Take Heed, Therefore

"But take heed to yourselves, lest your hearts Luke 21 34-35
be overburdened with self-indulgence and
drunkenness and the cares of this life, and that
day come upon you suddenly as a snare. For 35

come it will upon all who dwell on the face of all the earth.

Watch and Pray

Matt. 24 “Watch therefore, for you do not know at
42-44 43 what hour your Lord is to come. But of this
be assured, that if the householder had known
at what hour the thief was coming, he would
certainly have watched, and not have let his
44 house be broken into. Therefore you also
must be ready, because at an hour that you do
not expect, the Son of Man will come.”

"I SAY to ALL, WATCH"

APR. 21 or Oct. 21

"WATCH, THEN, praying all times, that you Luke 21
may be accounted worthy to escape all 36
these things that are to be, and to stand before
the Son of Man: just as a man, when he leaves Mark 13
home to journey abroad, puts his servants in 34-37
charge, to each his work, and gives orders to
the porter to keep watch. Watch, therefore, 35
for you do not know when the master of the
house is coming, in the evening, or at midnight, or at cockcrow, or early in the morn- 36
ing; lest coming suddenly he find you sleeping. 37
And what I say to you, I say to all, 'Watch.'"

Necessity of Preparedness

"Who, dost thou think, is the faithful and pru- Matt. 24
dent servant whom his master has set over 45-51

his household to give them their food in due
46 time? Blessed is that servant whom his mas-
47 ter, when he comes, shall find so doing. Amen
I say to you, he will set him over all his goods.

48 "But if that wicked servant says to himself,
49 'My master delays his coming,' and begins to
beat his fellow-servants, and to eat and drink
50 with drunkards, the master of that servant
will come on a day he does not expect, and
51 in an hour he does not know, and will cut him
asunder and make him share the lot of the
hypocrites. There will be the weeping, and
the gnashing of teeth.

Wise and Foolish Virgins

Matt. 25 1-13 "Then will the kingdom of heaven be like ten
virgins who took their lamps and went forth
to meet the bridegroom and the bride. Five
2-3 of them were foolish and five wise. But the
five foolish, when they took their lamps, took
4 no oil with them, while the wise did take oil
5 in their vessels with the lamps. Then as the
bridegroom was long in coming, they all
became drowsy and slept.

6 "And at midnight a cry arose, 'Behold, the
bridegroom is coming, go forth to meet him!'

Then all those virgins arose and trimmed 7
their lamps. And the foolish said to the wise,
'Give us some of your oil, for our lamps are 8
going out.' The wise answered, saying, 'Lest 9
there may not be enough for us and for you,
go rather to those who sell it, and buy some
for yourselves.'

"Now while they were gone to buy it, the 10
bridegroom came; and those who were ready
went in with him to the marriage feast, and
the door was shut. Finally there came also the 11
other virgins, who said, 'Sir, sir, open the door
for us!' But he answered and said, 'Amen I say 12
to you, I do not know you.' Watch therefore, 13
for you know neither the day nor the hour."

PARABLE of the TALENTS

APR. 22 or Oct. 22

Matt. 25 14-30 "FOR IT IS like a man going abroad, who
called his servants and handed over his
15 goods to them. And to one he gave five talents, to another two, and to another one,
to each according to his particular ability,
16 and then he went on his journey. And he
who had received the five talents went and
17 traded with them, and gained five more. In
18 like manner, he who had received the two
gained two more. But he who had received
the one went away and dug in the earth and
hid his master's money.

Good Servants Are Rewarded

"Then after a long time the master of those 19
servants came and settled accounts with
them. And he who had received the five tal- 20
ents came and brought five other talents, saying, 'Master, thou didst hand over to me five
talents; behold, I have gained five others in 21
addition.' His master said to him, 'Well done,
good and faithful servant; because thou hast
been faithful over a few things, I will set thee
over many; enter into the joy of thy master.'

"And he also who had received the two tal- 22
ents came and said, 'Master, thou didst hand
over to me two talents; behold, I have gained
two more.' His master said to him, 'Well done, 23
good and faithful servant; because thou hast
been faithful over a few things, I will set thee
over many; enter into the joy of thy master.'

Lazy Servant Is Punished

"But he who had received the one talent 24
came and said, 'Master, I know that thou art
a stern man; thou reapest where thou hast
not sowed and gatherest where thou hast not
winnowed; and as I was afraid, I went away 25
and hid thy talent in the earth; behold, thou

26 hast what is thine.' But his master answered
and said to him, 'Wicked and slothful servant!
thou didst know that I reap where I do not
sow, and gather where I have not winnowed?
27 Thou shouldst therefore have entrusted my
money to the bankers, and on my return I
should have got back my own with interest.
28 Take away therefore the talent from him, and
give it to him who has the ten talents.

29 "'For to everyone who has shall be given,
and he shall have abundance; but from him
who does not have, even that which he seems
30 to have shall be taken away. But as for the
unprofitable servant, cast him forth into the
darkness outside, where there will be the
weeping, and the gnashing of teeth.'"

The LAST JUDGMENT

APR. 23 or Oct. 23

"BUT WHEN the Son of Man shall come Matt. 25 31-46
in his majesty, and all the angels with
him, then he will sit on the throne of his
glory; and before him will be gathered all the 32
nations, and he will separate them one from
another, as the shepherd separates the sheep

33 from the goats; and he will set the sheep on
his right hand, but the goats on the left.

Social Justice and Charity Rewarded

34 "Then the king will say to those on his right
hand, 'Come, blessed of my Father, take possession of the kingdom prepared for you from
35 the foundation of the world; for I was hungry
and you gave me to eat; I was thirsty and you
gave me to drink; I was a stranger and you
36 took me in; naked and you covered me; sick
and you visited me; I was in prison and you
37 came to me.' Then the just will answer him,
saying, 'Lord, when did we see thee hungry,
and feed thee; or thirsty, and give thee drink?
38 And when did we see thee a stranger, and take
39 thee in; or naked, and clothe thee? Or when
did we see thee sick, or in prison, and come
40 to thee?' And answering the king will say to
them, 'Amen I say to you, as long as you did
it for one of these, the least of my brethren,
you did it for me.'

Omission of Works of Mercy Punished

41 "Then he will say to those on his left hand,
'Depart from me, accursed ones, into the

everlasting fire which was prepared for the
devil and his angels. For I was hungry, and you 42
did not give me to eat; I was thirsty and
you gave me no drink; I was a stranger and you 43
did not take me in; naked, and you did not
clothe me; sick, and in prison, and you did
not visit me.' Then they also will answer and 44
say, 'Lord, when did we see thee hungry, or
thirsty, or a stranger, or naked, or sick, or in
prison, and did not minister to thee?' Then he 45
will answer them, saying, 'Amen I say to you,
as long as you did not do it for one of these
least ones, you did not do it for me.' And 46
these will go into everlasting punishment, but
the just into everlasting life."

Judas Betrays Jesus

RULERS PLOT to KILL JESUS

APR. 24 or Oct. 24

Luke 21 37-38 NOW IN the daytime he was teaching in
the temple; but as for the nights, he
38 would go out and pass them on the mountain
called Olivet. And all the people came to him
early in the morning in the temple, to hear
him.

Matt. 26 1-5 And it came to pass when Jesus had finished all these words, that he said to his dis-
2 ciples, "You know that after two days the
Passover will be here; and the Son of Man
will be delivered up to be crucified."

Then the chief priests and the elders of the 3
people gathered together in the court of the
high priest, who was called Caiphas, and they 4
took counsel together how they might seize
Jesus by stealth and put him to death. But they 5
said, "Not on the feast, or there might be a riot Luke 22
among the people," for they feared the people. 2-4

Judas Betrays Jesus

But Satan entered into Judas, surnamed Iscar- 3
iot, one of the Twelve. And he went away and 4
discussed with the chief priests and the captains, how he might betray him to them, and
said to them, "What are you willing to give Matt. 26
me for delivering him to you?" And they were 15 Luke 22
glad, and agreed to give him money. They 5 Matt. 26
assigned him thirty pieces of silver. He accord- 15 Luke 22
ingly promised, and sought out an opportu- 6
nity to betray him without a disturbance.

Jesus Prepares for Last Supper

And on the first day of the Unleavened Bread, Mark 14
when it was customary for them to sacrifice 12-13
the passover, the disciples said to him, "Where dost thou want us to go and prepare for thee to eat the passover?"

13 And he sent two of his disciples, †Peter and
John, ‡and said to them, "Go into the city, and
Luke 22 there will meet you a man carrying a pitcher
10-11 Matt. 26 of water; follow him into the house into
18 Luke 22 which he goes. And you shall say to the mas-
11 Mark 14 ter of the house, 'The Master says, My time
15-16 is near at hand; where is the guest chamber,
that I may eat the passover there with my disciples?' And he will show you a large upper
room furnished; there make ready for us."
16 And his disciples went forth, and came into
the city, and found just as he had told them;
Matt. 26 and . . . did as Jesus bade them, and prepared
19 the passover.

---

† Luke 22, 8
‡ Mark 14, 13

"I have greatly desired to eat this passover with you before I suffer."

LAST SUPPER BEGINS

APR. 25 or Oct. 25

Mark 14 NOW WHEN evening arrived, he came
17 with the Twelve. And when the hour
Luke 22 14-18 had come, he reclined at table, and the twelve
15 apostles with him. And he said to them, "I
have greatly desired to eat this passover with
16 you before I suffer; for I say to you that I will
eat of it no more, until it has been fulfilled in
the kingdom of God."

17 And having taken a cup, he gave thanks and
18 said, "Take this and share it among you; for I
say to you that I will not drink of the fruit of
the vine, until the kingdom of God comes."

Jesus Settles a Strife

Luke 22 Now there arose also a dispute among them,
24-30 which of them was reputed to be the greatest.
25 But he said to them, "The kings of the Gentiles lord it over them, and they who exercise
26 authority over them are called Benefactors. But
not so with you. On the contrary, let him who
is greatest among you become as the youngest,
and him who is the chief as the servant.

27 "For which is the greater, he who reclines
at table, or he who serves? Is it not he who

reclines? But I am in your midst as he who
serves. But you are they who have continued 28
with me in my trials. And I appoint to you a 29
kingdom, even as my Father has appointed to 30
me, that you may eat and drink at my table in
my kingdom; and you shall sit upon thrones,
judging the twelve tribes of Israel."

WASHES FEET of APOSTLES

APR. 26 or Oct. 26

John 13 1-17 BEFORE THE FEAST of the Passover, Jesus,
knowing that the hour had come for him
to pass out of this world to the Father, having
loved his own who were in the world, loved
them to the end.
2 And during the supper, the devil having
already put it into the heart of Judas Iscar-
3 iot, the son of Simon, to betray him, Jesus,
knowing that the Father had given all things
into his hands, and that he had come forth

from God and was going to God, rose from
the supper and laid aside his garments, and 4
taking a towel girded himself. Then he poured 5
water into the basin and began to wash the
feet of the disciples, and to dry them with the
towel with which he was girded.

Peter Protests

He came, then, to Simon Peter. And Peter 6
said to him, "Lord, dost thou wash my feet?"
Jesus answered and said to him, "What I do 7
thou knowest not now; but thou shalt know
hereafter." Peter said to him, "Thou shalt 8
never wash my feet!" Jesus answered him, "If
I do not wash thee, thou shalt have no part
with me." Simon Peter said to him, "Lord, not 9
my feet only, but also my hands and my head!"
Jesus said to him, "He who has bathed [1]needs 10
only to wash, and he is clean all over. And you
are clean, but not all." For he knew who it was 11
that would betray him. This is why he said,
"You are not all clean."

---

1. *Needs only to wash:* the words "his feet" are added here in some manuscripts. If we retain them, the sense is: He who has bathed, on returning home needs only to wash the dust from his feet. Or it might also mean that the liturgical and social requirements are satisfied with this partial bathing.

Imitate Jesus' Humble Service

12 Now after he had washed their feet and put on
his garments, when he had reclined again, he
said to them, "Do you know what I have done
13 to you? You call me Master and Lord, and you
14 say well, for so I am. If, therefore, I the Lord
and Master have washed your feet, you also
15 ought to wash the feet of one another. For
I have given you an example, that as I have
16 done to you, so you also should do. Amen,
amen, I say to you, no servant is greater than
his master, nor is one who is sent greater than
17 he who sent him. If you know these things,
blessed shall you be if you do them."

JESUS GRIEVED by BETRAYAL

APR. 27 or Oct. 27

John 13 18-21
"I DO NOT SPEAK of you all. I know whom I
have chosen; but that the Scripture may
be fulfilled, 'He who eats bread with me has
lifted up his heel against me.' I tell you now 19
before it comes to pass, that when it has come
to pass you may believe that I am he. Amen, 20
amen, I say to you, he who receives anyone I
send, receives me; and he who receives me,
receives him who sent me."

When Jesus had said these things he was 21
troubled in spirit, and said solemnly, "Amen,
amen, I say to you, one of you will betray me.
But behold, the hand of him who betrays me Luke 22 21
is with me on the table."

The Apostles Also Grieve

Matt. 26 22-23 And being very much saddened they began
23 each to say, "Is it I, Lord?" But he answered
and said, †"One of the Twelve; ‡he who dips
his hand into the dish with me, he will betray
me. *For the Son of Man indeed goes his way,
Matt. 26 as it has been determined, as it is written of
24 him; but woe to that man by whom the Son of
Man is betrayed! It were better for that man
if he had not been born."

John 13 The disciples therefore looked at one
22 Luke 22 another, uncertain of whom he was speaking.
23 And they began to inquire among themselves
which of them it might be that was about to
do this.

John 13 Now one of his disciples, he whom Jesus
23-27 24 loved, was reclining at Jesus' bosom. Simon
Peter therefore beckoned to him, and said
25 to him, "Who is it of whom he speaks?" He
therefore, leaning back upon the bosom of
Jesus, said to him, "Lord, who is it?"

---

† Mark 14, 20
‡ Matt. 26, 23
* Luke 22, 22

The Traitor Is Revealed

Jesus answered, "It is he for whom I shall 26
dip the bread, and give it to him." And when
he had dipped the bread, he gave it to Judas
Iscariot, the son of Simon. And after the 27
morsel, [1]Satan entered into him. And Judas Matt. 26 25
who betrayed him answered and said, "Is it
I, Rabbi?" He said to him, "Thou hast said it."
And Jesus said to him, "What thou dost, John 13 27-30
do quickly." But none of those at the table 28
understood why he said this to him. For 29
some thought that because Judas held the
purse, Jesus had said to him, "Buy the things
we need for the feast"; or that he should give
something to the poor. When, therefore, he 30
had received the morsel, he went out quickly.
Now it was night.

---

1. *Satan entered into him:* Judas now gave himself entirely into the power of Satan (St. Thomas). It probably marks a definite decision on the part of Judas to carry out the betrayal of his Master at once.

"Take and eat; this is my body." "All of you drink of this; for this is my blood."

INSTITUTES HOLY EUCHARIST

APR. 28 or Oct. 28

AND WHILE they were eating, Jesus took Mark 14
bread, †gave thanks and blessed and 22
broke, and gave it to his disciples, and said, Matt. 26
"Take and eat; this is my body, which is being 26 Luke 22
given for you; do this in remembrance of me." 19-20
In like manner ‡taking a cup *after the sup- 20 Matt. 26
per, he gave thanks and gave it to them, say- 27-29
ing, "All of you drink of this; for this is my 28
blood of the new covenant, which is being
shed for many unto the forgiveness of sins.
But I say to you, I will not drink henceforth 29
of this fruit of the vine, until that day when I
shall drink it new with you in the kingdom of
my Father." And they all drank of it. Mark 14 23

A New Commandment

When, therefore, Judas had gone out, John 13
Jesus said, "Now is the Son of Man glorified, 31-35
and God is glorified in him. If God is glorified 32
in him, God will also glorify him in himself,
and will glorify him at once.

---

† Luke 22, 19
‡ Matt. 26, 27
* Luke 22, 20

33 "Little children, yet a little while I am with
you. You will seek me, and, as I said to the
Jews, 'Where I go you cannot come,' so to
34 you also I say it now. A new commandment I
give you, that you love one another: that as
35 I have loved you, you also love one another.
By this will all men know that you are my
disciples, if you have love for one another."

PREDICTS PETER'S DENIALS

APR. 29 or Oct. 29

SIMON PETER said to him, "Lord, where art John 13
thou going?" Jesus answered, "Where I 36-38

am going thou canst not follow me now, but
37 thou shalt follow later." Peter said to him,
"Why can I not follow thee now? I will lay
down my life for thee."

38 Jesus answered him, "Wilt thou lay down
Mark 14 27-30 thy life for me? Amen, amen, I say to thee,
you will all be scandalized this night; for it is
written, 'I will smite the shepherd, and the
sheep will be scattered.'

28 "But after I have risen, I will go before you
29 into Galilee." But Peter said to him, "Even
though all shall be scandalized, yet not I."
30 Jesus said to him, "Amen I say to thee, today,
this very night, before a cock crows twice,
thou wilt deny me three times.

Jesus Prays for Peter

Luke 22 31-32 "Simon, Simon, behold, Satan has desired to
32 have you, that he may sift you as wheat. But
I have prayed for thee, that thy faith may not
fail; and do thou, when once thou hast turned
Mark 14 31 again, strengthen thy brethren." But *Peter* went
Luke 22 on speaking more vehemently, "Lord, with thee
33 I am ready to go both to prison and to death!
Mark 14 Even if I should have to die with thee, I will not
31 deny thee!" And they all said the same thing.

Apostles Will Be Tested

And *Jesus* said to them, †"When I sent you Luke 22
forth without purse or wallet or sandals, did 34-38
you lack anything?" And they said, "Nothing." 36
Then he said to them, "But now, let him who
has a purse take it, and likewise a wallet; and
let him who has no sword sell his tunic and buy
one. For I say to you that this which is written 37
must yet be fulfilled in me, 'And he was reckoned among the wicked.' For that which con-
cerns me is at its end." And they said, "Lord, 38
behold, here are two swords." And he said to
them, "Enough."

† 35

JESUS CONSOLES DISCIPLES

APR. 30 or Oct. 30

John 14
1-14
"LET NOT your heart be troubled. You believe in God, believe also in me. In

my Father's house there are many mansions. 2
Were it not so, I should have told you, because
I go to prepare a place for you. And if I go and 3
prepare a place for you, I am coming again,
and I will take you to myself; that where I am,
there you also may be. And where I go you 4
know, and the way you know."
Thomas said to him, "Lord, we do not 5
know where thou art going, and how can
we know the way?" Jesus said to him, "I am 6
the way, and the truth, and the life. No one
comes to the Father but through me. If you 7
had known me, you would also have known
my Father. And henceforth you do know him,
and you have seen him."

Jesus Affirms He Is Divine

Philip said to him, "Lord, show us the Father 8
and it is enough for us." Jesus said to him, 9
"Have I been so long a time with you, and
you have not known me? Philip, he who sees
me sees also the Father. How canst thou say,
'Show us the Father'? Dost thou not believe 10
that I am in the Father and the Father in me?
The words that I speak to you I speak not on
my own authority. But the Father dwelling

11 in me, it is he who does the works. Do you
believe that I am in the Father and the Father
in me?

12 "Otherwise believe because of the works
themselves. Amen, amen, I say to you, he who
believes in me, the works that I do he also
shall do, and greater than these he shall do,
13 because I am going to the Father. And whatever you ask in my name, that I will do, in
order that the Father may be glorified in the
14 Son. If you ask me anything in my name, I
will do it."

HOLY SPIRIT WILL COME

MAY 1 or Oct. 31

“IF YOU love me, keep my commandments. John 14 15-31
And I will ask the Father and he will give 16
you another [1]Advocate to dwell with you for- 17
ever, the Spirit of truth whom the world cannot receive, because it neither sees him nor
knows him. But you shall know him, because
he will dwell with you, and be in you.

He Will Live in You

“I will not leave you orphans; I will come to 18
you. Yet a little while and the world no longer 19
sees me. [2]But you see me, for I live and you
shall live. In that day you will know that I am 20
in my Father, and you in me, and I in you. He 21
who has my commandments and keeps them,

---

1. *Advocate:* or Paraclete. The latter is a Greek term which is better rendered into English by Advocate or Intercessor. Cf. 1 John 2, 1. The function of the One thus designated is protection, assistance, defense. The thought of Consoler is not wanting from the context (St. Thomas, St. Jerome, St. Augustine).

2. *But you see me:* i.e., the world will not see me, but you will see me.

he it is who loves me. But he who loves me
will be loved by my Father, and I will love him
and manifest myself to him."

He Will Teach You

22 Judas, not the Iscariot, said to him, "Lord, how
is it that thou art about to manifest thyself to
23 us, and not to the world?" Jesus answered and
said to him, "If anyone love me, he will keep
my word, and my Father will love him, and we
will come to him and make our abode with
24 him. He who does not love me does not keep
my words. And the word that you have heard
is not mine, but the Father's who sent me.
25 "These things I have spoken to you while
26 yet dwelling with you. But the Advocate, the
Holy Spirit, whom the Father will send in my
name, he will teach you all things, and bring
to your mind whatever I have said to you.

Jesus Bestows His Peace

27 "Peace I leave with you, my peace I give
to you; not as the world gives do I give to
you. Do not let your heart be troubled, or
28 be afraid. You have heard me say to you, 'I go
away and I am coming to you.' If you loved

me, you would indeed rejoice that I am going
to the Father, for the Father is greater than I.
"And now I have told you before it comes 29
to pass, that when it has come to pass you
may believe. I will no longer speak much with 30
you, for the prince of the world is coming,
and [1]in me he has nothing. But he comes that 31
the world may know that I love the Father,
and that I do as the Father has commanded
me. Arise, let us go from here."

1. *In me he has nothing:* i.e., he has no claim on me or power over me. The success of the powers of darkness in the death of Christ was only apparent. This was permitted to show Christ's perfect correspondence with the will of the Father. On this rested His triumph over sin and death.

UNION with JESUS

MAY 2 or Nov. 1

John 15 1-17 2 "I AM THE true vine, and my Father is the
vine-dresser. Every branch in me that
bears no fruit he will take away; and every
branch that bears fruit he will cleanse, that
3 it may bear more fruit. You are already clean
because of the word that I have spoken to you.
4 Abide in me, and I in you. As the branch cannot
bear fruit of itself unless it remain on the vine,
so neither can you unless you abide in me.

"Without Me You Can Do Nothing"

"I am the vine, you are the branches. He who 5
abides in me, and I in him, he bears much
fruit; for without me you can do nothing. If 6
anyone does not abide in me, he shall be cast
outside as the branch and wither; and they
shall gather them up and cast them into the
fire, and they shall burn.

True Joy through Union with Jesus

"If you abide in me, and if my words abide in 7
you, ask whatever you will and it shall be done
to you. In this is my Father glorified, that you 8
may bear very much fruit, and become my disciples. As the Father has loved me, I also have 9
loved you. Abide in my love.

"If you keep my commandments you 10
will abide in my love, as I also have kept my
Father's commandments, and abide in his
love. These things I have spoken to you that 11
my joy may be in you, and that your joy may
be made full.

Sacrifice and Service

"This is my commandment, that you love one 12
another as I have loved you. Greater love than 13

this no one has, that one lay down his life for
14 his friends. You are my friends if you do the
15 things I command you. No longer do I call you
servants, because the servant does not know
what his master does. But I have called you
friends, because all things that I have heard
from my Father I have made known to you.
16 "You have not chosen me, but I have chosen you, and have appointed you that you
should go and bear fruit, and that your fruit
should remain; that whatever you ask the
17 Father in my name he may give you. These
things I command you, that you may love one
another."

HATRED for CHRISTIANS

MAY 3 or Nov. 2

“IF THE world hates you, know that it has John 15 18-27
hated me before you. If you were of the 19

world, the world would love what is its own.
But because you are not of the world, but I
have chosen you out of the world, therefore
the world hates you.
20 "Remember the word that I have spoken to
you: No servant is greater than his master. If
they have persecuted me, they will persecute
you also; if they have kept my word, they will
21 keep yours also. But all these things they will do
to you for my name's sake, because they do not
22 know him who sent me. If I had not come and
spoken to them, they would have no sin. But
now they have no excuse for their sin.
23 "He who hates me hates my Father also. If
24 I had not done among them works such as no
one else has done, they would have no sin. But
now they have seen, and have hated both me
25 and my Father; but that the word written in
their Law may be fulfilled, 'They have hated
me without cause.'

As Witnesses, We Must Testify

26 "But when the Advocate has come, whom I
will send you from the Father, the Spirit of
truth who proceeds from the Father, he will
27 bear witness concerning me. And you also

bear witness, because from the beginning you are with me.

"These things I have spoken to you that you John 16 1-4
may not be scandalized. They will expel you 2
from the synagogues. Yes, the hour is coming
for everyone who kills you to think that he
is offering worship to God. And these things 3
they will do because they have not known the
Father nor me. But these things I have spoken 4
to you, that when the time for them has come
you may remember that I told you. These
things, however, I did not tell you from the
beginning, because I was with you."

"You . . . have sorrow now; but I will see you again, and your heart shall rejoice."

SIN of UNBELIEF

MAY 4 or Nov. 3

John 16 5-22 6 AND NOW I am going to him who sent me,
and no one or you asks me, 'Where art
thou going?' But because I have spoken to you
7 these things, sorrow has filled your heart. But
I speak the truth to you; it is expedient for
you that I depart. For if I do not go, the Advocate will not come to you; but if I go, I will
send him to you.

8 "And when he has come he will [1]convict
9 the world of sin, and of justice, and of judg-
10 ment: of sin, because they do not believe in
me; of justice, because I go to the Father, and

1. *Convict:* bring conviction relative to these truths. Elsewhere the term is rendered "expose."

you will see me no more; and of judgment, 11
because the prince of this world has already
been judged.

"Many things yet I have to say to you, but you 12
cannot bear them now. But when he, the Spirit 13
of truth, has come, he will teach you all the
truth. For he will not speak on his own authority, but whatever he will hear he will speak, and
the things that are to come he will declare to
you. He will glorify me, because he will receive 14
of what is mine and declare it to you. All things 15
that the Father has are mine. That is why I have
said that he will receive of what is mine, and
will declare it to you.

Belief Is the Source of Joy

"A little while and you shall see me no longer; 16
and again a little while and you shall see me,
because I go to the Father."

Some of his disciples therefore said to one 17
another, "What is this he says to us, 'A little
while and you shall not see me, and again a
little while and you shall see me'; and, 'I go
to the Father'?" They kept saying therefore, 18
"What is this 'little while' of which he speaks?
We do not know what he is saying."

19 But Jesus knew that they wanted to ask
him, and he said to them, "You inquire about
this among yourselves because I said, 'A little
while and you shall not see me, and again a
little while and you shall see me.'

Counsels against Discouragement

20 "Amen, amen, I say to you, that you shall weep
and lament, but the world shall rejoice; and
you shall be sorrowful, but your sorrow shall
21 be turned into joy. A woman about to give
birth has sorrow, because her hour has come.
But when she has brought forth the child, she
no longer remembers the anguish for her joy
22 that a man is born into the world. And you
therefore have sorrow now; but I will see you
again, and your heart shall rejoice, and your
joy no one shall take from you."

"Father, the hour has come! Glorify thy Son"

ASK the FATHER in MY NAME

MAY 5 or Nov. 4

"AND IN that day you shall ask me nothing. John 16 23-33
Amen, amen, I say to you, if you ask
the Father anything in my name, he will give
it to you. Hitherto you have not asked any- 24
thing in my name. Ask, and you shall receive,
that your joy may be full.

"These things I have spoken to you in par- 25
ables. The hour is coming when I will no longer speak to you in parables, but will speak to
you plainly of the Father. In that day you shall 26

27 ask in my name; and I do not say to you that
I will ask the Father for you, for the Father
himself loves you because you have loved me,
28 and have believed that I came forth from God.
I came forth from the Father and have come
into the world. Again I leave the world and go
to the Father."

29 His disciples said to him, "Behold, now
30 thou speakest plainly, and utterest no parable.
Now we know that thou knowest all things,
and dost not need that anyone should question thee. For this reason we believe that thou
earnest forth from God."

Belief Put to the Test

31 Jesus answered them, "Do you now believe?
32 Behold, the hour is coming, and has already
come, for you to be scattered, each one to his
own house, and to leave me alone. But I am
33 not alone, because the Father is with me. These
things I have spoken to you that in me you may
have peace. In the world you will have affliction.
But take courage, I have overcome the world."

Jesus Prays for Himself

John 17 1-5 These things Jesus spoke; and raising his
eyes to heaven, he said, "Father, the hour has

come! [1]Glorify thy Son, that thy Son may glorify thee, even as thou hast given him power 2
over all flesh, in order that to all thou hast
given him he may give everlasting life. Now 3
this is everlasting life, that they may know
thee, the only true God, and him whom thou
hast sent, Jesus Christ. I have glorified thee
on earth; I have accomplished the work that 4
thou hast given me to do. And now do thou, 5
Father, glorify me with thyself, with the glory
that I had with thee before the world existed."

1. Christ glorifies the Father by faithfully accomplishing His mission. But He also glorifies Him in another way: by raising man to a state in which he also can glorify God both here and in heaven. To this end the Father has given power over all men to the Son, to open for them a way to eternal life.

PRAYS for HIS DISCIPLES

MAY 6 or Nov. 5

John 17 6-26 "I HAVE manifested thy name to the men
whom thou hast given me out of the
world. They were thine, and thou hast given
them to me, and they have kept thy word.
7 Now they have learnt that whatever thou hast
8 given me is from thee; because the words that
thou hast given me I have given to them. And
they have received them, and have known of
a truth that I came forth from thee, and they
have believed that thou didst send me.

9 "I pray for them; not for the world do I
pray, but for those whom thou hast given me,
10 because they are thine; and all things that
are mine are thine, and thine are mine; and I
11 am glorified in them. And I am no longer in
the world, but these are in the world, and I
am coming to thee. Holy Father, keep in thy
name those whom thou hast given me, that
they may be one even as we are.

12 "While I was with them, I kept them in
thy name. Those whom thou hast given me I
guarded; and not one of them perished except
the son of perdition, in order that the Scrip-
13 ture might be fulfilled. But now I am coming

to thee; and these things I speak in the world,
in order that they may have my joy made full
in themselves.
"I have given them thy word; and the world 14
has hated them, because they are not of the
world, even as I am not of the world. I do not 15
pray that thou take them out of the world, but
that thou keep them from evil. They are not of 16
the world, even as I am not of the world.
"Sanctify them in the truth. Thy word is 17
truth. Even as thou hast sent me into the 18
world, so I also have sent them into the world. 19
And for them I [1]sanctify myself, that they also
may be sanctified in truth.
"Yet not for these only do I pray, but for 20
those also who through their word are to
believe in me, that all may be one, even as 21
thou, Father, in me and I in thee; that they also
may be one in us, that the world may believe
that thou hast sent me. And the [2]glory that 22
thou hast given me, I have given to them, that

---

1. *Sanctify myself:* by offering Himself as a victim to be immolated. *That they also may be sanctified:* that they also may be set aside for God's work. *In truth:* i.e., "in contrast to all human purpose"; or for that truth which is to be the object of their mission, as it is of Christ's.

2. *Glory:* what Christ conferred upon His disciples was something of the divine nature, a further aspect of the principle of unity.

23 they may be one, even as we are one: I in them
and thou in me; that they may be perfected in
unity, and that the world may know that thou
hast sent me, and that thou hast loved them
even as thou hast loved me.

24 "Father, I will that where I am, they also
whom thou hast given me may be with me; in
order that they may behold my glory, which
thou hast given me, because thou hast loved
25 me before the creation of the world. Just
Father, the world has not known thee, but I
have known thee, and these have known that
26 thou hast sent me. And I have made known to
them thy name, and will make it known, in
order that the love with which thou hast loved
me may be in them, and I in them."

A NIGHT of AGONY

MAY 7 or Nov. 6

AFTER SAYING these things, Jesus went John 18
forth with his disciples beyond the tor- 1
rent of Cedron, †according to his custom,
to the Mount of Olives. ‡And they came to Matt. 26
a country place called Gethsemani, *where 36

† Luke 22, 39
‡ Mark 14, 32
* John 18, 1

there was a garden into which he and his disciples entered. And he said to his disciples, "Sit
down here, while I go over yonder and pray.
Luke 22 40 Pray, that you may not enter into temptation."

"Wait Here and Watch"

And he took with him Peter and James and
Mark 14 33-34 John, and he began to feel dread and to be
34 exceedingly troubled. And he said to them,
"My soul is sad, even unto death. Wait here and
Luke 22 41 watch." And he himself withdrew from them
about a stone's throw, and kneeling down, he
Mark 14 35-36 fell on the ground, and began to pray that, if it
were possible, the hour might pass from him.

Jesus Pleads with His Father

36 And he said, "Abba, Father, all things are
Luke 22 42 possible to thee. Father, if thou art willing,
Matt. 26 39 remove this cup from me. Father, if it is pos-
sible, let this cup pass away from me; yet not
Mark 14 37 as I will, but as thou willest." Then he came
and found them sleeping. And he said to Peter,
"Simon, dost thou sleep?

Spirit Willing, but Flesh Is Weak

Matt. 26 40-43 "Could you not, then, watch one hour with
41 me? Watch and pray, that you may not enter

into temptation. The spirit indeed is willing, but the flesh is weak." Again a second 42
time he went away and prayed, saying, "My
Father, if this cup cannot pass away unless I
drink it, thy will be done." And he came again 43
and found them sleeping, for their eyes were Mark 14 40
heavy. And they did not know what answer
to make to him. And leaving them he went Matt. 26 44
back again, and prayed a third time, saying
the same words over. And there appeared to Luke 22 43-44
him an angel from heaven to strengthen him.
And falling into an agony he prayed the more
earnestly.

And his sweat became as drops of blood 44
running down upon the ground.

JESUS GOES to MEET JUDAS

MAY 8 or Nov. 7

Luke 22 45-46 AND RISING from prayer he came to the
disciples, and found them sleeping for
46 sorrow. And he said to them, †"Sleep on now,
Luke 22 46 and take your rest. Why do you sleep? Rise
and pray, that you may not enter into tempta-
Mark 14 41-42 tion. It is enough; the hour has come. Behold,
the Son of Man is betrayed into the hands of
42 sinners. Rise, let us go. Behold, he who will
betray me is at hand."

† Mark 14, 41

Now Judas, who betrayed him, also knew John 18
the place, since Jesus had often met there 2-3
together with his disciples. Judas, then, tak- 3
ing the cohort, and attendants from the chief
priests and Pharisees, came there with lan-
terns, and torches, and weapons.

Betrayed by a Kiss

And while he was yet speaking, behold Judas, Matt. 26
one of the Twelve, came and with him a great 47
crowd with swords and clubs, from the chief
priests and elders of the people. ‡Judas . . .
was going before them. Now his betrayer had Mark 14
given them a sign, saying, "Whomever I kiss, 44-45
that is he; lay hold of him, and lead him safely
away." And when he came, he went straight up 45
to him, and said, "Rabbi!" and kissed him. And Matt. 26
Jesus said to him, "Friend, for what purpose 50
hast thou come? Judas, dost thou betray the Luke 22
Son of Man with a kiss?" 48

Jesus Shows His Divine Authority

Jesus therefore knowing all that was to come John 18
upon him, went forth and said to them, 4-9

‡ Luke 22, 47

5 "Whom do you seek?" They answered him,
"Jesus of Nazareth." Jesus said to them, "I am
he." Now Judas, who betrayed him, was also
6 standing with them. When, therefore, he said
to them, "I am he," they drew back and fell to
the ground.

7 So he asked them again, "Whom do you
seek?" And they said, "Jesus of Nazareth."
8 Jesus answered, "I have told you that I am he.
If, therefore, you seek me, let these go their
9 way." That the word which he said might be
fulfilled, "Of those whom thou hast given me,
Matt. 26 50 I have not lost one." Then they came forward
and set hands on Jesus and took him.

PETER CUTS OFF SERVANT'S EAR

MAY 9 or Nov. 8

BUT WHEN they who were about him saw Luke 22
what would follow, they said to him, 49
"Lord, shall we strike with the sword?" Simon John 18
Peter therefore, having a sword, drew it and 10
struck the servant of the high priest and cut

off his right ear. Now the servant's name was
Luke 22 Malchus. But Jesus answered and said, "Bear
51 with them thus far." And he touched his ear
and healed him.

John 18 Jesus therefore said to Peter, "Put up thy
11 sword into the scabbard; for all those who
Matt. 26 take the sword will perish by the sword. Or
52-53 53 dost thou suppose that I cannot entreat my
Father, and he will even now furnish me with
John 18 more than twelve legions of angels? Shall I not
11 Matt. 26 drink the cup that the Father has given me?
54-55 How then are the Scriptures to be fulfilled,
that thus it must take place?"

Jesus Rebukes His Enemies

55 In that hour Jesus said to the crowds, †to the
chief priests and captains of the temple and
elders, who had come against him, "As against
a robber have you come out, with swords and
Matt. 26 clubs. I sat daily with you in the temple teach-
55 ing, and you did not lay hands on me. ‡But
this is your hour, and the power of darkness."

† Luke 22, 52
‡ Luke 22, 53

*Now all this was done that the Scriptures of the prophets might be fulfilled.

Jesus Arrested; Disciples Flee

The cohort therefore and the tribune and John 18
the attendants of the Jews seized Jesus and 12 Mark 14
bound him. Then all his disciples left him and 50-52 51
fled. And a certain young man was following
him, having a linen cloth wrapped about his
naked body, and they seized him. But leav- 52
ing the linen cloth behind, he fled away from
them naked.

And they brought him to Annas first, for John 18
he was the father-in-law of Caiphas, who was 13-14
the high priest that year. Now it was Caiphas 14
who had given the counsel to the Jews that
it was expedient that one man should die for
the people. And Annas sent him bound to Cai- John 18
phas, the high priest. 24

* Matt. 26, 56

QUESTIONED and STRUCK
MAY 10 or Nov. 9

John 18 19-23 THE HIGH PRIEST therefore questioned Jesus
concerning his disciples, and concerning
20 his teaching. Jesus answered him, "I have spoken openly to the world; I have always taught
in the synagogue and in the temple, where
all the Jews gather, and in secret I have said
21 nothing. Why dost thou question me? Question those who have heard what I spoke to
them; behold, these know what I have said."
22 Now when he had said these things, one
of the attendants who was standing by struck
Jesus a blow, saying, "Is that the way thou dost

answer the high priest?" Jesus answered him, 23
"If I have spoken ill, bear witness to the evil;
but if well, why dost thou strike me?"

The False Witnesses

Now the chief priests and all the Sanhedrin Matt. 26
were seeking false witness against Jesus, that 59-60
they might put him to death, but they found 60
none, though many false witnesses came Mark 14
forward. For while many bore false witness 56
against him, their evidence did not agree.

But last of all two false witnesses came for- Matt. 26
ward, and said, "This man said, 'I am able to 60-61 61
destroy the temple of God, and to rebuild it
after three days.' We ourselves have heard him Mark 14
say, 'I will destroy this temple built by hands, 58-59
and after three days I will build another, not
built by hands.'" And even then their evidence 59
did not agree.

Jesus Declares Himself Son of God

Then the high priest, standing up, said to Matt. 26
him, "Dost thou make no answer to the things 62-63
that these men prefer against thee?" But Jesus 63
kept silence, and made no answer. Again the Mark 14
high priest began to ask him, and said to him, 61

"Art thou the Christ, the Son of the Blessed
Matt. 26 63-66 One? I adjure thee by the living God that thou
tell us whether thou art the Christ, the Son
64 of God." Jesus said to him, "Thou hast said it.
Nevertheless, I say to you, hereafter you shall
see the Son of Man sitting at the right hand
of the Power and coming upon the clouds of
heaven."

He Is Declared Guilty of Death

65 Then the high priest tore his garments,
saying, "He has blasphemed; what further
need have we of witnesses? Behold, now
66 you have heard the blasphemy. What do you
think?" And they answered and said, "He is
liable to death."

And when they had kindled a fire in the middle of the courtyard, and were seated together, Peter was in their midst, and warming himself.

PETER'S DENIAL

MAY 11 or Nov. 10

Matt. 26 THEN THEY spat in his face and buffeted
67 him; while others struck his face with
the palms of their hands.

Luke 22 But Peter was following *him* at a distance,
54
John 18 and so was another disciple. Now that dis-
15-17 ciple was known to the high priest, and he
entered with Jesus into the courtyard of the
high priest. But Peter was standing outside
16 at the gate. So the other disciple, who was
known to the high priest, went out and spoke
to the portress, and brought Peter in.

17 The maid, who was portress, said therefore
to Peter, "Art thou also one of this man's dis-
Matt. 26 ciples?" He said, "I am not." And he went in
58 and sat with the attendants to see the end. And
Luke 22 when they had kindled a fire in the middle of
55 the courtyard, and were seated together, Peter
was in their midst, †and warming himself.

Luke 22 But a certain maidservant saw him sitting
56
Mark 14 at the blaze, and after gazing upon him she
67 said, "Thou also wast with Jesus of Nazareth.
Matt. 26
70 ‡This man too was with him." But he denied it

† Mark 14, 54
‡ Luke 22, 56

before them all, saying, "I do not know what Luke 22
thou art saying. I do not know him. *I neither 57
know nor understand what thou art saying."
And he went outside into the vestibule; and
the cock crowed.

* Mark 14, 68

And Peter went out and wept bitterly.

PETER'S DENIAL (continued)
MAY 12 or Nov. 11

Luke 22 58 AND AFTER a little while †when he had
gone out to the gateway, another maid

† Matt. 26, 71

saw him, and said to those who were there,
"This man also was with Jesus of Nazareth."
And the maidservant, seeing him again, began Mark 14
to say to the bystanders, "This is one of them." 69-70
But again he denied it. 70

Now the servants and attendants were John 18
standing at a coal fire and warming them- 18
selves, for it was cold. And Peter also was
with them, standing and warming himself. John 18
They therefore said to him, "Art thou also one 25 Matt. 26
of his disciples?" And again he denied it with 72 Luke 22
an oath, "I do not know the man!" Someone 58-60
else saw him and said, "Thou, too, art one of
them." But Peter said, "Man, I am not."

And about an hour later another insisted, 59
saying, "Surely this man, too, was with him,
for he also is a Galilean." But Peter said, "Man, 60
I do not know what thou sayest." And after a Matt. 26 73-74
little while the bystanders came up and said
to Peter, "Surely thou also art one of them,
for even thy speech betrays thee." Then he 74
began to curse and to swear that he did not
know the man. "I do not know this man you Mark 14
are talking about." 71

One of the servants of the high priest, a John 18
relative of him whose ear Peter had cut off, 26-27

said, "Did I not see thee in the garden with
27 him?" Again, therefore, Peter denied it; and
Mark 14 72 at that moment a cock crowed a second time.
And Peter remembered the word that Jesus
had said to him, "Before a cock crows twice,
Luke 22 62-65 thou wilt deny me three times." And Peter
went out and wept bitterly.

Jesus Mocked by His Guards

63 And the men who had him in custody began
64 to mock him and beat him. And they blind-
folded him, and kept striking his face and
asking him, saying, "Prophesy, who is it that
65 struck thee?" And many other things they
kept saying against him, reviling him.

The End of Judas

JESUS before the SANHEDRIN

MAY 13 or Nov. 12

AND AS SOON as it was morning, the chief priests held a consultation with the elders, the Scribes and the whole Sanhedrin against Jesus in order to put him to death. Mark 15 1 Matt. 27 1 Luke 22 66-71

And they led him away into their Sanhedrin,
67 saying, "If thou art the Christ, tell us." And
68 he said to them, "If I tell you, you will not
believe me; and if I question you, you will
69 not answer me, or let me go. But henceforth,
the Son of Man will be seated at the right
hand of the power of God."

70 And they all said, "Art thou, then, the Son
of God?" He answered, "You yourselves say
that I am."

71 And they said, "What further need have
we of witness? For we have heard it ourselves
Luke 23 1 from his own mouth." And the whole assem-
Matt. 27 blage rose, bound him and led him away, and
2-10 delivered him to Pontius Pilate the procurator.

Remorse and Suicide of Judas

3 Then Judas, who betrayed him, when he
saw that he was condemned, repented and
brought back the thirty pieces of silver to the
4 chief priests and the elders, saying, "I have
sinned in betraying innocent blood." But they
5 said, "What is that to us? See to it thyself." And
he flung the pieces of silver into the temple,
and withdrew; and went away and hanged
himself with a halter.

The Field of Blood

And the chief priests took the pieces of silver, 6
and said, "It is not lawful to put them into the
treasury, seeing that it is the price of blood."
And after they had consulted together, 7
they bought with them the potter's field, as a
burial place for strangers. For this reason that 8
field has been called even to this day, Hacel-
dama, that is, the Field of Blood. Then what 9
was spoken through Jeremias the prophet was
fulfilled, "And they took the thirty pieces of
silver, the price of him who was priced, upon
whom the children of Israel set a price; and 10
they gave them for the potter's field, as the
Lord directed me."

JESUS before PILATE

MAY 14 or Nov. 13

John 18
28-32
THEY THEREFORE led Jesus from Caiphas to
the prætorium. Now it was early morning, and they themselves did not enter the

prætorium, that they might not be defiled,
but might eat the passover.
Pilate therefore went outside to them, and 29
said, "What accusation do you bring against
this man?" They said to him in answer, "If 30
he were not a criminal we should not have
handed him over to thee." Pilate therefore said 31
to them, "Take him yourselves, and judge him
according to your law." The Jews, then, said
to him, "It is not lawful for us to put anyone
to death." This was in fulfilment of what Jesus 32
had said, indicating the manner of his death.
And they began to accuse him, saying, "We Luke 23
have found this man perverting our nation, 2
and forbidding the payment of taxes to Cæsar,
and saying that he is Christ a king."

Jesus Questioned Secretly

Pilate therefore again entered into the præto- John 18
rium, and he summoned Jesus, and said to 33-38
him, "Art thou the king of the Jews?" Jesus 34
answered, "Dost thou say this of thyself, or
have others told thee of me?" Pilate answered, 35
"Am I a Jew? Thy own people and the chief
priests have delivered thee to me. What hast
thou done?" Jesus answered, "My kingdom is 36

not of this world. If my kingdom were of this
world, my followers would have fought that I
might not be delivered to the Jews. But, as it
is, my kingdom is not from here."

Truth Means Nothing to Pilate

37 Pilate therefore said to him, "Thou art then
a king?" Jesus answered, "Thou sayest it; I am a
king. This is why I was born, and why I have
come into the world, to bear witness to the
truth. Everyone who is of the truth hears my
38 voice." Pilate said to him, "What is truth?"

And when he had said this, he went outside
to the Jews again, and said to them, "I find no
guilt in him."

Herod Mocks Jesus

JESUS NOW SILENT

MAY 15 or Nov. 14

AND WHEN he was accused by the chief Matt. 27
priests and the elders, he made no answer. 12

Mark 15 And Pilate again asked him, saying, "Hast thou
4 no answer to make? Behold how many things
Matt. 27 they accuse thee of. Dost thou not hear how
13-14
14 many things they prefer against thee?" But he
did not answer him a single word, so that the
procurator wondered exceedingly.

Luke 23 But they persisted, saying, "He is stir-
5-16 ring up the people, teaching throughout all
Judea, and beginning from Galilee even to
6 this place." But Pilate, hearing Galilee, asked
7 whether the man was a Galilean. And learning that he belonged to Herod's jurisdiction,
he sent him back to Herod, who likewise was
in Jerusalem in those days.

Herod Mocks Jesus

8 Now when Herod saw Jesus, he was exceedingly glad; for he had been a long time desir-
ous to see him, because he had heard so much
about him, and he was hoping to see some
9 miracle done by him. Now he put many questions to him, but he made him no answer.

10 Now the chief priests and Scribes were
11 standing by, vehemently accusing him. But
Herod, with his soldiery, treated him with
contempt and mocked him, arraying him in

a bright robe, and sent him back to Pilate.
And Herod and Pilate became friends that 12
very day; whereas previously they had been
at enmity with each other.

Jesus Again before Pilate

And Pilate called together the chief priests 13
and the rulers and the people, and said to 14
them, "You have brought before me this man,
as one who perverts the people; and behold,
I upon examining him in your presence have
found no guilt in this man as touching those
things of which you accuse him. Neither 15
has Herod; for I sent you back to him, and
behold, nothing deserving of death has been
committed by him. I will therefore chastise 16
him and release him."

"BARABBAS, or JESUS?"

MAY 16 or Nov. 15

Matt. 27 15 NOW AT festival time the procurator
used to release to the crowd a prisoner, †whomever they had petitioned for.
Matt. 27 16 Now he had at that time a notorious prisoner
called Barabbas. ‡Now Barabbas was a rob-
Mark 15 ber, imprisoned with some rioters, one who
7-8 8 in the riot had committed murder. And the

† Mark 15, 6
‡ John 18, 40

crowd came up, and began to ask that he do
for them as he was wont.

Therefore, when they had gathered together, Matt. 27
Pilate said, "You have a custom that I should 17 John 18
release someone to you at the Passover. Whom 39 Matt. 27
do you wish that I release to you? Barabbas, or 17-21
Jesus who is called Christ?" For he knew that 18
they had delivered him up out of envy.

Pilate's Wife

Now, as he was sitting on the judgment-seat, 19
his wife sent to him, saying, "Have nothing
to do with that just man, for I have suffered
many things in a dream today because of him."
But the chief priests and the elders persuaded 20
the crowds to ask for Barabbas and to destroy
Jesus. But the procurator addressed them, 21
and said to them, "Which of the two do you
wish that I release to you?"

Release Barabbas!

But the whole mob cried out together, saying, Luke 23
"Away with this man, and release to us Barab- 18
bas!" But Pilate spoke to them again, wishing Luke 23
to release Jesus. "What then am I to do with 20 Matt. 27
Jesus who is called Christ?" 22

Crucify Jesus!

Luke 23 21-23 But they kept shouting, saying, "Crucify him!
22 Crucify him!" And he said to them a third
time, "Why, what evil has this man done?
I find no crime deserving of death in him. I
will therefore chastise him and release him."
23 But they persisted with loud cries, demand-
ing that he should be crucified. *They cried
out again, "Crucify him!" **and their cries
prevailed.

Mark 15 15 So Pilate, wishing to satisfy the crowd,
Luke 23 24-25 pronounced sentence that what they asked
25 for should be done. So he released to them
him who for murder and riot had been put in
prison, for whom they were asking; but Jesus
he delivered to their will.

---

* Mark 15,13
** Luke 23,23

"Behold, the Man!"

JESUS SCOURGED, CROWNED
MAY 17 or Nov. 16

PILATE, THEN, took Jesus and had him John 19 1
scourged. Now the soldiers led him away Mark 15
into the courtyard of the prætorium, and they 16
called together the whole cohort.

And they stripped him and put on him a Matt. 27 28-30
scarlet cloak; and plaiting a crown of thorns, 29
they put it upon his head, and a reed into his
right hand; and bending the knee before him
they mocked him, saying, "Hail, King of the
Jews!" And they spat on him, and took the 30
reed and kept striking him on the head.

Pilate therefore again went outside and John 19 4-15
said to them, "Behold, I bring him out to you,
that you may know that I find no guilt in him."

"Behold, the Man!"

5 Jesus therefore came forth, wearing the
crown of thorns and the purple cloak. And
6 he said to them, "Behold, the man!" When,
therefore, the chief priests and the attendants
saw him, they cried out, saying, "Crucify him!
Crucify him!" Pilate said to them, "Take him
yourselves and crucify him, for I find no guilt
7 in him." The Jews answered him, "We have a
Law, and according to that Law he must die,
because he has made himself Son of God."

Is He the Son of God?

8 Now when Pilate heard this statement, he
9 feared the more. And he again went back
into the prætorium, and said to Jesus,
"Where art thou from?" But Jesus gave him
10 no answer. Pilate therefore said to him, "Dost
thou not speak to me? Dost thou not know
that I have power to crucify thee, and that I
have power to release thee?" Jesus answered,
11 "Thou wouldst have no power at all over me
were it not given thee from above. Therefore, he who betrayed me to thee has the
greater sin."

Pilate's Last Effort

And from then on Pilate was looking for a 12
way to release him. But the Jews cried out,
saying, "If thou release this man, thou art no
friend of Cæsar; for everyone who makes
himself king sets himself against Cæsar."
Pilate therefore, when he heard these 13
words, brought Jesus outside, and sat down
on the judgment-seat, at a place called Litho-
strotos, but in Hebrew, Gabbatha. Now it was 14
the Preparation Day for the Passover, about the
sixth hour. And he said to the Jews, "Behold,
your king!" But they cried out, "Away with 15
him! Away with him! Crucify him!" Pilate said
to them, "Shall I crucify your king?" The chief
priests answered, "We have no king but Cæsar."

Via Dolorosa

SENTENCED to CRUCIFIXION
MAY 18 or Nor. 17

Matt. 27 24-25 NOW PILATE, seeing that he was doing no good, but rather that a riot was breaking

out, took water and washed his hands in sight
of the crowd, saying, "I am innocent of the
blood of this just man; see to it yourselves."
And all the people answered and said, "His 25
blood be on us and on our children." Then he John 19
handed him over to them to be crucified. And 16
so they took Jesus and led him away.

And when they had mocked him, they Matt. 27
took the cloak off him and put his own gar- 31
ments on him, and led him away to crucify
him. And bearing the cross for himself, he John 19
went forth to the place called the Skull, in 17
Hebrew, Golgotha.

Simon Helps Jesus to Carry His Cross

Now as they went out, they found a man Matt. 27
of Cyrene named Simon, coming from the 32 Mark 15
country, the father of Alexander and Rufus; 21 Luke 23
and upon him they laid the cross to bear it 26-31
after Jesus.

His Message to the Women of Jerusalem

Now there was following him a great crowd 27
of the people, and of women, who were
bewailing and lamenting him. But Jesus turn- 28
ing to them said, "Daughters of Jerusalem,

do not weep for me, but weep for yourselves
29 and for your children. For behold, days are
coming in which men will say, 'Blessed are
the barren, and the wombs that never bore,
30 and breasts that never nursed.' Then they will
begin to say to the mountains, 'Fall upon us,'
31 and to the hills, 'Cover us!' For if in the case
of green wood they do these things, what is
to happen in the case of the dry?"

JESUS CRUCIFIED

MAY 19 or Nov. 18

AND THEY brought him to the place called Mark 15 22
Golgotha. Now it was the third hour Mark 15 25
and they crucified him.

Matt. 27 34 And they gave him wine to drink mixed
with gall; but when he had tasted it, he would
not drink.

Mark 15 27 And they crucified two robbers with him,
one on his right hand and one on his left, †and
Jesus in the center. ‡And the Scripture was
fulfilled, which says, "And he was reckoned
among the wicked."

Title over the Cross

John 19 19-22 And Pilate also wrote an inscription and had
it put on the cross. And there was written,
"Jesus of Nazareth, the King of the Jews."
20 Many of the Jews therefore read this inscription, because the place where Jesus was crucified was near the city; and it was written
21 in Hebrew, in Greek and in Latin. The chief
priests of the Jews said therefore to Pilate,
"Do not write, 'The King of the Jews,' but,
22 'He said, I am the King of the Jews.'" Pilate
answered, "What I have written, I have
written."

Luke 23 34 And Jesus said, "Father, forgive them, for
they do not know what they are doing."

† John 19, 18
‡ Mark 15, 28

His Garments Divided

The soldiers therefore, when they had cru- John 19
cified him, took his garments and made of 23-24
them four parts, to each soldier a part, and
also the tunic. Now the tunic was without
seam, woven in one piece from the top. They 24
therefore said to one another, "Let us not tear
it, but let us cast lots for it, to see whose it
shall be." That the Scripture might be fulfilled which says, "They divided my garments
among them; and for my vesture they cast
lots." These things therefore the soldiers did.
And sitting down they kept watch over him. Matt. 27
36

JESUS IS BLASPHEMED

MAY 20 or Nov. 19

Luke 23 AND THE people stood looking on. Now
35 the passers-by were jeering at him,
Matt. 27 shaking their heads, and saying, "Thou who
39-42
40

destroyest the temple, and in three days
buildest it up again, save thyself! If thou art
the Son of God, come down from the cross!"
In like manner, the chief priests with the 41
Scribes and the elders, mocking, said, "He 42
saved others, himself he cannot save! If he is
the King of Israel, let him come down now
from the cross, and we will believe him. Let Luke 23
him save himself, if he is the Christ, the cho- 35
sen one of God. He trusted in God; let him Matt. 27
deliver him now, if he wants him; for he said, 43
'I am the Son of God.'"
And the soldiers also mocked him, coming Luke 23
to him and offering him common wine, and 36-37 37
saying, "If thou art the King of the Jews, save
thyself!"

The Good and the Bad Thief

And the robbers also, who were crucified Matt. 27
with him, reproached him in the same way. 44
Now one of those robbers who were hanged Luke 23
was abusing him, saying, "If thou art the 39-43
Christ, save thyself and us!" But the other in 40
answer rebuked him and said, "Dost not even
thou fear God, seeing that thou art under the
same sentence? And we indeed justly, for we 41

are receiving what our deeds deserved; but
this man has done nothing wrong."
42 And he said to Jesus, "Lord, remember me
43 when thou comest into thy kingdom." And
Jesus said to him, "Amen I say to thee, this
day thou shalt be with me in paradise."

Mother of Christ and Our Mother

John 19 25-27 Now there were standing by the cross
of Jesus his mother and his mother's
sister, Mary of Cleophas, and Mary Magda-
26 lene. When Jesus, therefore, saw his mother
and the disciple standing by, whom he loved,
he said to his mother, "Woman, behold, thy
27 son." Then he said to the disciple, "Behold, thy
mother." And from that hour the disciple took
her into his home.

"My God . . . why hast thou forsaken me?"

HIS LAST WORDS
MAY 21 or Nov. 20

IT WAS NOW about the sixth hour, and there Luke 23
was darkness over the whole land until the 44-45
ninth hour. And the sun was darkened. And at 45
the ninth hour Jesus cried out with a loud voice, Mark 15 34-35
saying, "Eloi, Eloi, lama sabacthani?" which,
translated, is, [1]"My God, my God, why hast
thou forsaken me?" And some of the bystanders 35
on hearing this said, "Behold, he is calling Elias."

"I Thirst"

After this Jesus, knowing that all things were John 19
now accomplished, that the Scripture might 28-29
be fulfilled, said, "I thirst." Now there was 29

1. The words of our Lord were a quotation of Ps. 21, 2. Taken in their context they do not express anything like despair. They do, however, express a poignant sense of dereliction.

standing there a vessel full of common wine.
Matt. 27 And immediately one of them ran and, taking
48 a sponge, soaked it in *the* wine, put it on a
Mark 15 reed and offered it to him to drink, saying,
36 "Wait, let us see whether Elias is coming to
take him down."

"It Is Consummated!"

John 19 When Jesus had taken the wine, he said, "It
30 Luke 23 is consummated!" And Jesus cried out with
46 a loud voice and said, "Father, into thy hands
I commend my spirit." And having said this,
he expired.

Nature Mourns the Divine

Matt. 27 And behold, the curtain of the temple was
51-53 torn in two from top to bottom; and the earth
52 quaked, and the rocks were rent, and the tombs
were opened, and many bodies of the saints
53 who had fallen asleep arose; and coming forth
out of the tombs after his resurrection, they
came into the holy city, and appeared to many.

The Centurion Professes His Faith

Luke 23 Now when the centurion saw what had hap-
47 pened, he glorified God, saying, "Truly this

was a just man; †truly this man was the Son of
God." ‡And those who were with him keeping
guard over Jesus, *and all the crowd that col-
lected for the sight, saw the earthquake and Matt. 27 54
the things that were happening. They were
very much afraid, and they said, "Truly he was
the Son of God," *and* began to return beating Luke 23 48-49
their breasts.

The Friends of Jesus

But all his acquaintances, and the women who 49
had followed him from Galilee, were standing
at a distance looking on. Among them were Matt. 27 56
Mary Magdalene, and Mary the mother of
James and Joseph, and the mother of the sons
of Zebedee. These used to accompany him Mark 15 41
and minister to him when he was in Galilee—
besides many other women who had come
with him to Jerusalem.

---

† Mark 15, 39
‡ Matt. 27, 54
* Luke 23,48

The BURIAL of JESUS
MAY 22 or Nov. 21

John 19 31-37 THE JEWS therefore, since it was the
Preparation Day, in order that the bodies might not remain upon the cross on the
Sabbath (for that Sabbath was a solemn day),
besought Pilate that their legs might be bro-
32 ken, and that they might be taken away. The
soldiers therefore came and broke the legs of

the first, and of the other, who had been crucified with him.
But when they came to Jesus, and saw that 33
he was already dead, they did not break his
legs; but one of the soldiers opened his side 34
with a lance, and immediately there came out
blood and water.
And he who saw it has borne witness, and 35
his witness is true; and he knows that he tells
the truth, that you also may believe. For these 36
things came to pass that the Scripture might be
fulfilled, "Not a bone of him shall you break."
And again another Scripture says, "They shall 37
look upon him whom they have pierced."

His Body Is Taken Down

Now when it was evening, there came a cer- Matt. 27 57
tain rich man of Arimathea, Joseph by name,
†a good and just man, a councillor of high Mark 15 43
rank, who was himself looking for the kingdom of God. ‡He had not been party to their
plan of action because he was a disciple of John 19 38
Jesus (although for fear of the Jews a secret

---

† Luke 23, 50
‡ Luke 23, 51

one), *and he* besought Pilate that he might
take away the body of Jesus.

Mark 15 44-45 But Pilate wondered whether he had
already died. And sending for the centurion,
he asked him whether he was already dead.
45 And when he learned from the centurion that
he was, he granted the body to Joseph.

And Wrapped in the Holy Shroud

John 19 39-40 And there also came Nicodemus (who at
first had come to Jesus by night), bringing a
mixture of myrrh and aloes, in weight about
40 a hundred pounds. They therefore took the
body of Jesus and wrapped it in linen cloths
with the spices, after the Jewish manner of
preparing for burial.

PART IV

+ The Resurrection and

Jesus has risen

Jesus appears to Magdalene

Appears to two disciples

Appears to the apostles

Jesus appears again

Ascension of Christ + +

primacy to peter

teach all nations

repent; remission of sin

the ascension of jesus

purpose of gospel

The RESURRECTION

John 19 MAY 23 or Nov. 22

41 NOW IN THE place where he was crucified
Matt. 27 there was a garden, and in the garden a
60 John 19 new tomb which *Joseph* had hewn out in the
41-42 42 rock, in which one had yet been laid. There,
accordingly, because of the Preparation Day
of the Jews, for the tomb was close at hand,
Matt. 27 they laid Jesus. Then *Joseph* rolled a large stone
60 to the entrance of the tomb, and departed.

†And the women who had come with him
Luke 23 from Galilee, ‡Mary Magdalene and Mary
55-56 56 the mother of Joseph, followed after, and

---

† Luke 23, 55
‡ Mark 15, 47

beheld the tomb, and how his body was laid. And they went back and prepared spices and ointments. And on the Sabbath they rested, in accordance with the commandment.

Sepulchre Sealed and Guarded

And the next day, which was the one after Matt. 27
the Day of Preparation, the chief priests and 62-66
the Pharisees went in a body to Pilate, saying, 63
"Sir, we have remembered how that deceiver
said, while he was yet alive, 'After three days
I will rise again.' Give orders, therefore, that 64
the sepulchre be guarded until the third day,
or else his disciples may come and steal him
away, and say to the people, 'He has risen
from the dead'; and the last imposture will
be worse than the first."
Pilate said to them, "You have a guard; go, 65
guard it as well as you know how." So they 66
went and made the sepulchre secure, sealing
the stone, and setting the guard.

The Holy Women Find It Opened

And when the Sabbath was past, Mary Mag- Mark 16
dalene, Mary the mother of James, and 1-2
Salome, bought spices, that they might go and

2 anoint him. And very early on the first day of
the week, they came to the tomb, when the
Luke 24 sun had just risen, taking the spices that they
1 Mark 16 had prepared. And they were saying to one
3 another, "Who will roll the stone back from
the entrance of the tomb for us?"

Matt. 29 And behold, there was a great earth-
2-4 quake; for an angel of the Lord came down
from heaven, and drawing near rolled back
3 the stone, and sat upon it. His countenance
was like lightning, and his raiment like snow.
4 And for fear of him the guards were terrified,
Mark 16 and became like dead men. And looking up
4 *the women* saw that the stone had been rolled
back, for it was very large.

JESUS HAS RISEN!

MAY 24 or Nov. 23

BUT ON ENTERING, *the women* did not find Luke 24 3-5
the body of the Lord Jesus. And it came 4
to pass, while they were wondering what to
make of this, that, behold, two men stood
by them in dazzling raiment. And when the 5
women were struck with rear and bowed
their faces to the ground, a young man sitting Mark 16 5-6
at the right side . . . †said to them, "Do not Matt. 28
be terrified. I know that you seek Jesus, who 5
was crucified.

† 6

Luke 24 “Why do you seek the living one among the
5-7 6 dead? He is not here, but has risen. Remember how he spoke to you while he was yet in
7 Galilee, saying that the Son of Man must be
betrayed into the hands of sinful men, and be
Matt. 28 crucified, and on the third day rise. Come,
6-7 see the place where the Lord was laid.

Going to Announce His Resurrection

7 “And go quickly, tell his disciples that he has
risen; and behold, he goes before you into
Make 16 Galilee; there you shall see him, as he told
7 Luke 24 you.” And they remembered his words. [‡]And
8 they departed and fled from the tomb, for
trembling and fear had seized them; and they
said nothing to anyone, for they were afraid.

Peter and John before Empty Tomb

John 20 *Mary Magdalene* ran therefore and came to
2-10 Simon Peter, and to the other disciple whom
Jesus loved, and said to them, “They have
taken the Lord from the tomb, and we do not
know where they have laid him.”

‡ Mark 16, 8

Peter therefore went out, and the other 3
disciple, and they went to the tomb. The two 4
were running together, and the other disciple ran on before, faster than Peter, and came
first to the tomb. And stooping down he saw 5
the linen cloths lying there, yet he did not
enter. Simon Peter therefore came following 6
him, and he went into the tomb, and saw the 7
linen cloths lying there, and the handkerchief
which had been about his head, not lying with
the linen cloths, but folded in a place by itself.

Then the other disciple also went in, who 8
had come first to the tomb. And he saw and
believed; for as yet they did not understand 9
the Scripture, that he must rise from the
dead. The disciples therefore went away again 10
to their home, wondering . . . at what had Luke 24 12
come to pass.

JESUS APPEARS to MAGDALENE

MAY 25 or Nov. 24

Mark 16 9 NOW WHEN he had risen from the dead
early on the first day of the week, he
appeared first to Mary Magdalene, out of
whom he had cast seven devils.

John 20 11-18 Mary was standing outside weeping at the
tomb. So, as she wept, she stooped down and
12 looked into the tomb, and saw two angels
in white sitting, one at the head and one at
the feet, where the body of Jesus had been
13 laid They said to her, "Woman, why art thou
weeping?" She said to them, "Because they
have taken away my Lord, and I do not know
where they have laid him."

14 When she had said this she turned round
and beheld Jesus standing there, and she did
15 is not know that it was Jesus. Jesus said to her,
"Woman, why art thou weeping? Whom dost
thou seek?" She, thinking that he was the gar-
dener, said to him, "Sir, if thou hast removed
him, tell me where thou hast laid him and I
16 will take him away." Jesus said to her, "Mary!"

Turning, she said to him, "Rabboni!" (that
is to say, Master). Jesus said to her, "Do not 17
touch me, for I have not yet ascended to
my Father, but go to my brethren and say to
them, 'I ascend to my Father and your Father,
to my God and your God.'"

Mary Magdalene came, and announced 18
to the disciples, †as they were mourning and
weeping, ‡"I have seen the Lord, and these
things he said to me."* And they, hearing that
he was alive and had been seen by her, did not
believe it.

He Appears to Other Holy Women

Mary Magdalene and Joanna and Mary, the Luke 24 10
mother of James, and the other women who
were with them, departed quickly from the Matt. 28 8-10
tomb in fear and great joy, and ran to tell his
disciples. And behold, Jesus met them, say- 9
ing, "Hail!" And they came up and embraced
his feet and worshipped him. Then Jesus said 10
to them, "Do not be afraid; go, take word
to my brethren that they are to set out for

---

† Mark 16, 10
‡ John 20, 18
* Mark 16, 11

Luke 24 10-11 Galilee; there they shall see me." *They* were
11 telling these things to the apostles. But this
tale seemed to them to be nonsense, and they
did not believe the women.

Guards Are Bribed to Lie

Matt. 28 11-15 Now while they were going, behold, some of
the guard came into the city and reported to
12 the chief priests all that had happened. And
when they had assembled with the elders
and had consulted together, they gave much
13 money to the soldiers, telling them, "Say, 'His
disciples came by night and stole him while
14 we were sleeping.' And if the procurator hears
of this, we will persuade him and keep you
15 out of trouble." And they took the money, and
did as they were instructed; and this story has
been spread abroad among the Jews even to
the present day.

He took the bread and blessed and broke and began handing it to them. And their eyes were opened, and they recognized him.

APPEARS to TWO DISCIPLES

MAY 26 or Nov. 25

Luke 24 AND BEHOLD, two of them were going that
13-35 very day to a village named Emmaus,
14 which is sixty stadia from Jerusalem. And
they were talking to each other about all
15 these things that had happened. And it came
to pass, while they were conversing and
arguing together, that Jesus himself also drew
16 near and went along with them; but their
eyes were held, that they should not recog-
17 nize him. And he said to them, "What words
are these that you are exchanging as you walk
and are sad?"

18 But one of them, named Cleophas,
answered and said to him, "Art thou the only
stranger in Jerusalem who does not know
the things that have happened there in these
19 days?" And he said to them, "What things?"

And they said to him, "Concerning Jesus of
Nazareth, who was a prophet, mighty in work
20 and word before God and all the people; and
how our chief priests and rulers delivered
him up to be sentenced to death, and crucified him.

Their Lack of Faith and Hope

"But we were hoping that it was he who 21
should redeem Israel. Yes, and besides all this,
today is the third day since these things came
to pass. And moreover, certain women of our 22
company, who were at the tomb before it was
light, astounded us, and not finding his body, 23
they came, saying that they had also seen a
vision of angels, who said that he is alive. So 24
some of our company went to the tomb, and
found it even as the women had said, but him
they did not see."

But he said to them, "O foolish ones and 25
slow of heart to believe in all that the prophets
have spoken! Did not the Christ have to suffer 26
these things before entering into his glory?"

Jesus Confirms Their Faith

And beginning then with Moses and with all 27
the Prophets, he interpreted to them in all the
Scriptures the things referring to himself. And 28
they drew near to the village to which they
were going, and he acted as though he were
going on. And they urged him, saying, "Stay 29
with us, for it is getting towards evening, and
the day is now far spent." And he went in with

30 them. And it came to pass when he reclined
at table with them, that he took the bread
and blessed and broke and began handing it
31 to them. And their eyes were opened, and
they recognized him; and he vanished from
32 their sight. And they said to each other, "Was
not our heart burning within us while he was
speaking on the road and explaining to us the
Scriptures?"

They Become Active Witnesses

33 And rising up that very hour, they returned
to Jerusalem, where they found the Eleven
gathered together and those who were with
34 them, saying, "The Lord has risen indeed, and
35 has appeared to Simon." And they themselves
began to relate what had happened on the journey, and how they recognized him in the break-
Mark 16 13 ing of the bread. And even then they (*the other
disciples*) did not believe.

APPEARS to the APOSTLES

MAY 27 or Nov. 26

WHEN IT WAS late that same day, the first John 20
of the week, though the doors where 19
the disciples gathered had been closed for fear Luke 24
of the Jews, Jesus stood in their midst, and 36
said to them, "Peace to you! It is I, do not be
afraid." And when he had said this, he showed John 20
them his hands and his side. 20

He Rebukes Their Unbelief

And he upbraided them for their lack of faith Mark 16
and hardness of heart, in that they had not 14
believed those who had seen him after he
had risen. But they were startled and panic- Luke 24
stricken, and thought that they saw a spirit. 37-39
And he said to them, "Why are you dis- 38
turbed, and why do doubts arise in your hearts? 39
See my hands and feet, that it is I myself. Feel
me and see; for a spirit does not have flesh and
bones, as you see I have." But as they still disbe- Luke 24
lieved and marvelled for joy, he said, "Have you 41-43
anything here to eat?" And they offered him a 42
piece of broiled fish and a honeycomb. And 43
when he had eaten in their presence, he took
what remained and gave it to them.

Gladly Do They Now Believe

John 20 20 The disciples therefore rejoiced at the sight
Luke 24 of the Lord. And he said to them, "These are
44-45 the words which I spoke to you while I was
yet with you, that all things must be fulfilled
that are written in the Law of Moses and the
Prophets and the Psalms concerning me."
45 Then he opened their minds, that they might
understand the Scriptures.

"As the Father Has Sent Me, I Send You"

John 20 He therefore said to them again, "Peace be
21-29 to you! As the Father has sent me, I also send
22 you." When he had said this, he breathed
upon them, and said to them, "Receive the
23 Holy Spirit; whose sins you shall forgive, they
are forgiven them; and whose sins you shall
retain, they are retained."

Thomas Doubts

24 Now Thomas, one of the Twelve, called the
Twin, was not with them when Jesus came.
25 The other disciples therefore said to him,
"We have seen the Lord." But he said to
them, "Unless I see in his hands the print of
the nails, and put my finger into the place

"My Lord and my God!"
"Blessed are they who have not seen, and yet have believed."

of the nails, and put my hand into his side, I
will not believe."

26 And after eight days, his disciples were
again inside, and Thomas with them. Jesus
came, the doors being closed, and stood in
their midst, and said, "Peace be to you!"

Believing without Seeing

27 Then he said to Thomas, "Bring here thy finger, and see my hands; and bring here thy
hand, and put it into my side; and be not
28 unbelieving, but believing." Thomas answered
29 and said to him, "My Lord and my God!" Jesus
said to him, "Because thou hast seen me, thou
hast believed. Blessed are they who have not
seen, and yet have believed."

JESUS APPEARS AGAIN

MAY 28 or Nov. 27

AFTER THESE THINGS, Jesus manifested him- John 21
self again at the sea of Tiberias. Now he 1-14
manifested himself in this way. There were 2
together Simon Peter and Thomas, called the
Twin, and Nathanael, from Cana in Galilee,

and the sons of Zebedee, and two others of
his disciples.

While They Are Fishing

3 Simon Peter said to them, "I am going fish-
ing." They said to him, "We also are going with
thee." And they went out and got into the boat.
4 And that night they caught nothing. But when
day was breaking, Jesus stood on the beach;
yet the disciples did not know that it was
5 Jesus. Then Jesus said to them, "Young men,
have you any fish?" They answered him, "No."

How Their Net Is Filled

6 He said to them, "Cast the net to the right of
the boat and you will find them." They cast
therefore, and now they were unable to draw
7 it up for the great number of fishes. The disciple whom Jesus loved said therefore to Peter,
"It is the Lord." Simon Peter therefore, hearing that it was the Lord, girt his tunic about
him, for he was stripped, and threw himself
8 into the sea. But the other disciples came with
the boat (for they were not far from land,
only about two hundred cubits off), dragging
the net full of fishes.

When, therefore, they had landed, they 9
saw a fire ready, and a fish laid upon it, and
bread. Jesus said to them, "Bring here some 10
of the fishes that you caught just now." Simon 11
Peter went aboard and hauled the net onto
the land full of large fishes, one hundred and
fifty-three in number. And though there were
so many, the net was not torn.

He Invites Them to Eat

Jesus said to them, "Come and breakfast." And 12
none of those reclining dared ask him, "Who
art thou?" knowing that it was the Lord. And 13
Jesus came and took the bread, and gave it to 14
them, and likewise the fish. This is now the
third time that Jesus appeared to the disciples
after he had risen from the dead.

PRIMACY to PETER

MAY 29 or Nov. 28

John 21 15-23 WHEN, THEREFORE, they had breakfasted, Jesus said to Simon Peter, "Simon, son

of John, dost thou love me more than these
do?" He said to him, "Yes, Lord, thou know- 16
est that I love thee." He said to him, "Feed
my lambs." He said to him a second time,
"Simon, son of John, dost thou love me?" He
said to him, "Yes, Lord, thou knowest that I
love thee." He said to him, "Feed my lambs."
A third time he said to him, "Simon, son of 17
John, dost thou love me?" Peter was grieved
because he said to him for the third time, "Dost
thou love me?" And he said to him, "Lord, thou
knowest all things, thou knowest that I love
thee." He said to him, "Feed my sheep.

Jesus Predicts Peter's Martyrdom

"Amen, amen, I say to thee, when thou wast is 18
young thou didst gird thyself and walk where
thou wouldst. But when thou art old thou
wilt stretch forth thy hands, and another will
gird thee, and lead thee where thou wouldst
not." Now this he said to signify by what man- 19
ner of death he should glorify God. And having spoken thus, he said to him, "Follow me."
Turning round, Peter saw following them 20
the disciple whom Jesus loved, the one who,
at the supper, had leaned back upon his breast

and said, "Lord, who is it that will betray
21 thee?" Peter therefore, seeing him, said to
22 Jesus, "Lord, and what of this man?" Jesus said
to him, "If I wish him to remain until I come,
what is it to thee? Do thou follow me."
23 This saying therefore went abroad among
the brethren, that that disciple was not to die.
But Jesus had not said to him, "He is not to
die"; but rather, "If I wish him to remain until
I come, what is it to thee?"

"Make disciples of all nations, baptizing them in the name of the Father, and of the Son, and of the Holy Spirit, teaching them to observe all that I have commanded you."

TEACH ALL NATIONS

MAY 30 or Nov. 29

Matt. 28 16-18 BUT THE eleven disciples went into Galilee, to the mountain where Jesus had
17 directed them to go. And when they saw him
18 they worshipped him; but some doubted. And
Jesus drew near and spoke to them saying,
"All power in heaven and on earth has been
Mark 16 15 given to me." And he said to them, "Go into
the whole world and preach the gospel to
every creature.

Believe and Observe

Matt. 28 18-20 "Make disciples of all nations, baptizing them
in the name of the Father, and of the Son, and
20 of the Holy Spirit, teaching them to observe
all that I have commanded you.

Mark 16 16-18 "He who believes and is baptized shall
be saved, but he who does not believe shall
17 be condemned. And these signs shall attend
those who believe: in my name they shall cast
18 out devils; they shall speak in new tongues;
they shall take up serpents; and if they drink
any deadly thing, it shall not hurt them; they
shall lay hands upon the sick and they shall
get well.

"And behold, I am with you all days, even unto the consummation of the world." Matt. 28 20

ASCENSION of JESUS

MAY 31 or Nov. 30

Luke 24 46-51 AND HE SAID to them, "Thus it is written; and thus the Christ should suffer,

and should rise again from the dead on the
third day; and that repentance and remission 47
of sins should be preached in his name to all
the nations, beginning from Jerusalem. And 48
you yourselves are witnesses of these things.
And I send forth upon you the promise of my 49
Father. But wait here in the city, until you are
clothed with power from on high."

Ascension of Jesus

Now he led them out towards Bethany, and 50
he lifted up his hands and blessed them. And 51
it came to pass as he blessed them, that he
parted from them and was carried up into Mark 16
heaven, and sits at the right hand of God. 19

Apostles in Prayer and Action

And they worshipped him, and returned Luke 24
to Jerusalem with great joy. And they were 52-53 53
continually in the temple, praising and blessing God. But they went forth and preached Mark 16
everywhere, while the Lord worked with 20
them and confirmed the preaching by the
signs that followed.

Purpose of Gospel

John 20 30-31 Many other signs also Jesus worked in the
sight of his disciples, which are not written
31 in this book. But these are written that you
may believe that Jesus is the Christ, the Son
of God, and that believing you may have life
in his name.

John 21 24-25 This is the disciple who bears witness concerning these things, and who has written
these things, and we know that his witness is
25 true. There are, however, many other things
that Jesus did; but if every one of these should
be written, not even the world itself, I think,
could hold the books that would have to be
written.

Study Guide and Daily Practice

BY THE

REV. JOHN A. O'BRIEN, PH. D.

Notre Dame University

This Appendix to Christ in the Gospel assists your efforts in two ways. It forms your scheme of Scripture study, and it outlines your method of meditation thereon. Time spent in prayerful recollection of the inspired texts will be blessed and rewarded by God with such an insight into the mysteries of salvation as you have never before enjoyed.

HOW TO USE

AFTER a careful reading of the Gospel selection appointed for the day, turn to the corresponding date in the Appendix. Review your lesson by asking yourself the questions listed. If you can supply the correct answers, you will have absorbed the Gospel message. Then note the recommendations for "Religious Practices" and determine that, with God's help, you will observe them to the best of your ability. Finally, select one of these recommendations as a point for your meditation. Give as much time as you can to quiet consideration of this point, asking God to show you its application to the needs of your life. Make a firm resolve to follow the way of life which God will show you.

DEC. 1—What is meant by the "Word"? Was He uncreated and eternal? What was in Him? What is meant by the "light"? By the "darkness"? Who was sent by God? What was John's mission? What enlightens every man? Who did not know Jesus? Who did not receive Him? What did He give to those who received Him? How did Jesus become our Brother? What did John testify concerning Jesus? What came through Moses? Through Jesus? Whom did Jesus reveal?

RELIGIOUS PRACTICES

1. Use *Christ in the Gospel* every day. Read the selection, answer each question, and perform the religious practices suggested, without fail. Never allow an exception to this daily procedure.
2. If you are using this book by yourself, and not as a member of a discussion group, set aside each day a ten minute period for this purpose and adhere faithfully to your schedule.
3. Secure a copy of *A Commentary on the New Testament,* prepared by the biblical scholars who brought out the revised edition of The New Testament, by sending to the publisher, Sadlier, 11 Park Place, New York, N.Y. Use that Commentary when reading the daily selection from the Gospel.

DEC. 2—To whom does St. Luke address his account? For what purpose? What does he propose to set forth? Who was Zachary? Who was his wife? Had they any prospect of a son? Why? Zachary was chosen to do what? Who appeared to him? Whose birth did the angel foretell?

RELIGIOUS PRACTICES

1. Cultivate a devotion to St. John the Baptist.
2. Examine your conscience each night to keep yourself blameless like Zachary and Elizabeth.

DEC. 3—What did the angel announce concerning the character of John? Whom would he bring back to God? In the spirit and power of whom would he walk? What would he prepare for the Lord? What did Zachary say to the angel? The angel's reply? How was Zachary punished for doubting? Why did the people wonder? What did Elizabeth say?

RELIGIOUS PRACTICES

1. Recite daily the Act of Faith with ever increasing fervor.
2. Drive away any doubts which ever arise to assail your faith.

DEC. 4—To whom was the angel Gabriel sent? To whom was Mary betrothed? How did the angel greet Mary? How did the angel reassure Mary? Whose birth did the angel foretell? What throne will be given to Jesus? What wonderment did Mary express? What did the angel reply? How did Mary express her consent? Some of the words of what two well known prayers occur in this selection?

RELIGIOUS PRACTICES

1. Say the *Hail Mary* with a richer understanding of its origin and of its beauty.
2. Imitate our Blessed Mother in her willingness to do God's will at all times.
3. Recite the Rosary daily in her honor.

DEC. 5—Whom did Mary visit? What happened within Elizabeth when she heard Mary's greeting? How did Elizabeth reply? Why did she say that Mary was blessed? Why did Mary magnify her Lord? What does she say God has done to the mighty? The lowly? The hungry? The rich? To Israel?

RELIGIOUS PRACTICES

1. Memorize the *Magnificat* and recite it daily with great devotion.
2. Meditate often upon the great honor bestowed upon Mary in choosing her to be the Mother of God.
3. Imitate her purity and pray to her each day for this great virtue.

DEC. 6—Mary remained with Elizabeth how long? What name had the people chosen for Elizabeth's son? What name did his mother choose? What did Zachary write? When was speech restored to him? What wonderment did these events arouse in the people? What is the burden of Zachary's hymn? How should the people serve the Lord? What was the mission he prophesied for John?

RELIGIOUS PRACTICES

1. Learn by heart a hymn of praise to God and recite it daily.
2. Try to win at least two converts for Christ each year.

DEC. 7—By whose power was Christ conceived? What was Joseph minded to do? What reassurance did the angel give him? What was the child's name to be? What does that name mean? What prophecy was thus fulfilled? Explain what is meant by "she brought forth her firstborn son"? Who decreed the census? Whither did Joseph and Mary go? Where was Jesus born? Why?

RELIGIOUS PRACTICES

1. Meditate each day upon the great mystery of the Incarnation.
2. Say daily, and especially in time of temptation, the prayer: "Jesus, Mary, and Joseph, help me!"

DEC. 8—To whom did the angel appear? What was his message? What was the saying of the angelic host? What did the shepherds say to one another? Whom did they find? How did this help them to understand what had been told to them? Where did Mary keep these things? Why did the shepherds praise and glorify God?

RELIGIOUS PRACTICES

1. Memorize the message of the angel and the words of praise uttered by the angelic host.
2. Reflect often upon the humility of a divine Being who deigned to be born in a manger.
3. Recite the *Gloria* in the Mass with increased understanding and devotion.

DEC. 9—The name, Jesus, was given by whom? When was Jesus taken to Jerusalem? Why? What holy man was awaiting the coming of our Lord? What revelation had been granted to Simeon? What is meant by the custom of the Law? What did Simeon exclaim? What did he predict? What prophetess was there? What did she do day and night?

RELIGIOUS PRACTICES

1. Cultivate a special reverence for the Holy Name of Jesus. Recite it devoutly during the day.

2. Join the Holy Name Society and promote reverence for the Holy Name among others, especially by your example.

DEC. 10—What distinguished visitors came to Jerusalem when Jesus was born? Whom were they seeking? Why was King Herod troubled? Where did prophecy indicate the Savior would be born? What did Herod say to the Magi? What led them to the manger at Bethlehem? What gifts did they bring? Did they return to Herod? Why? What did the angel say to Joseph? How long did he remain there? Whom did Herod slaughter? Why? What prophecy was thus fulfilled?

RELIGIOUS PRACTICES

1. Receive Holy Communion every Sunday, and daily, if possible.
2. Give a generous offering for the support of the Church at Sunday Mass.

DEC. 11—What was the angel's message to Joseph? What did Joseph do? Why did he settle in Nazareth? How did the child Jesus grow? Why did His parents go to Jerusalem? How did Jesus become lost? Where did they find Him? What was He doing? What did His mother say to Him? His reply? Jesus came with Mary and Joseph to what city? In what did He advance?

RELIGIOUS PRACTICES

1. Show your parents every mark of respect and obey them promptly.
2. Imitate the humility and obedience of Jesus.
3. Say a *Hail Mary* each day for your parents.

DEC. 12—What did John preach in the region about the Jordan? What was the prophecy of Isaias? Who went out to John? What did John do to them? How was John clothed? What did John say to the Pharisees and Sadducees? What did the crowds ask John? His answer? What did the publicans say to John? His answer? What did the soldiers ask John? His response?

RELIGIOUS PRACTICES

1. Practice charity by giving something each month to the poor and needy.

2. Make a generous offering to the collection taken up for the home and foreign missions.

DEC. 13—What were the people wondering about John? What did the priests and Levites ask him? His reply? What did they continue to ask him? His answers? Whom did John finally say he was? What did the Pharisees then ask him? With what did John baptize? Whom did John say was mightier than he? With what did the Messias baptize? Why did Jesus come to John? What did John say to Him? Jesus' reply? What did the voice from heaven testify?

RELIGIOUS PRACTICES

1. Perform some act of penance and self-denial each day.
2. Meditate upon the message of repentance brought by John the Baptist.

DEC. 14—How long did Jesus fast? Who came to Him? How did he tempt Jesus? What did Christ reply? Where did the devil then lead Jesus? How did he tempt the Savior? What did Jesus reply? Where did the devil then take Jesus? How did he tempt Him? What did Jesus reply? Who ministered then to Jesus?

RELIGIOUS PRACTICES

1. Guard against temptation by shepherding your thoughts and guarding your senses.
2. In time of temptation say immediately, "Jesus, Mary, and Joseph, come to my help!" Then flee from the danger.
3. Cultivate a special devotion to your guardian angel, saying a prayer to him each day.

DEC. 15—When John saw Jesus the next day, what did he exclaim? What further witness did he bear? Memorize John's testimony to Christ's divinity. Who followed Jesus? What invitation did Christ extend to them? Name one of the two who followed Jesus.

RELIGIOUS PRACTICES

1. Meditate often upon the divinity of Jesus Christ.
2. Spread the knowledge of that truth among men.
3. Make often during the day the devout ejaculation, "My Jesus, my God, and my All!"

DEC. 16—What did Andrew say to his brother Simon? What did Jesus say to Simon? Whom else did Jesus call to be an apostle? What did Philip tell Nathanael? Nathanael's reply? What tribute did Jesus pay Nathanael? Nathanael acknowledged Jesus to be whom? What was the first promise Jesus made to Nathanael? The second promise?

RELIGIOUS PRACTICES

1. Meditate often upon the promptness with which the apostles left all things and followed Christ.
2. Emulate their zeal by striving to win each year at least two converts for Christ.

DEC. 17—Where did the wedding take place? Who were there? What embarrassing happening occurred? What did Jesus say to Mary? What did Mary tell the attendants to do? What orders did Jesus give? What miracle did Christ perform? What did the chief steward remark? Who believed in Christ? Whither did Christ then proceed?

RELIGIOUS PRACTICES

1. Meditate often upon the kind and sympathetic intercession of the Blessed Virgin.
2. Imitate the example of Christ by helping your neighbor in need.

DEC. 18—What feast was at hand? What did Jesus find in the temple? What did He do to them? What did He say to them? What did the disciples then recall? What did the Jews demand? What sign of authority did Jesus give them? To what was Jesus referring? When did the disciples recall those words of Christ? Why did many believe in Jesus? Did Jesus trust Himself to them? Why?

RELIGIOUS PRACTICES

1. Have a great respect for the house of God, and act always with great reverence while in it.
2. Send flowers for the decoration of the altars for the great feasts of the Church.

DEC. 19—Who came at night to see Jesus? What did he say to Jesus? How did Jesus answer him? How can a man be born again? What further question did Nicodemus ask? What line of reasoning did Jesus then present to him? What comparison is drawn between the act of Moses in the desert and the sacrifice of Christ on the cross? To what extent did God manifest his love for the world? Why did God send His Son into the world? Why is faith so important? What is the judgment? What does everyone who does evil hate?

RELIGIOUS PRACTICES

1. Pray each day for a deeper and stronger faith.
2. Read books of religious instruction which will enlighten and deepen your faith.
3. Secure a copy of *The Faith of Millions,* from Our Sunday Visitor Press, Huntington, Ind., read it, and loan it each month to a non-Catholic friend.

DEC. 20—Jesus and His disciples went where? What did they do? Who also was baptizing? What discussion arose? What did John's disciples say? What was John's reply? Why must Christ increase but John decrease? What was the testimony of Jesus? What is the reward for faith in Jesus? The punishment for lack of such faith? When did Jesus leave Judea?

RELIGIOUS PRACTICES

1. Strive daily to imitate the humility of John the Baptist.
2. Seek not your own glory but the glory of Christ Jesus, our Lord.

DEC. 21—Describe the location of Jacob's well. What did Jesus say to the Samaritan woman? Her reply? Jesus promises what kind of water? What astonishment does the Samaritan woman show? What is the difference between natural water and the water which Jesus promises? What does the Samaritan woman ask? How does Jesus show that He is a searcher of the hearts and minds of people?

RELIGIOUS PRACTICES

1. Prefer always spiritual values to merely material ones.
2. Stir up in you a thirst for souls, striving to bring them closer to Christ.
3. Secure a copy of *Winning Converts,* a Symposium on Methods of Convert Making, P. J. Kenedy & Sons, N.Y. and follow its suggestions for winning converts.

DEC. 22—What did the woman say to Jesus? His reply? Salvation is from whom? How will true worshippers worship the Father? Whom did Jesus reveal Himself to be? At what did the disciples wonder? Why? What did the woman say to the people? What did Jesus reveal His food to be? What pressing invitation did Jesus extend to His disciples? Why did many of the Samaritans at first believe in Christ? Why later on?

RELIGIOUS PRACTICES

1. Say a daily prayer for the missioners at home and abroad.
2. Aid them with your funds and with your zeal.
3. Subscribe to The *Extension Magazine,* Chicago, Ill. and follow its suggestions for helping our home missionaries.

DEC. 23—To what did Jesus bear witness? Who received Him? Why? What did the official implore? What did Jesus reply? How did Jesus heal the son? How did the official know that the cure was wrought by Jesus? What was the prophecy of Isaias? What was the burden of Jesus' teaching?

RELIGIOUS PRACTICES

1. Do each day something that is hard for you to do, in order to strengthen your will.
2. Make the Stations of the Cross each week.
3. Subscribe to *The Field Afar,* Maryknoll, N. Y., and follow its suggestions for helping our missionaries in foreign lands.

DEC. 24—Whom did Jesus see casting a net? What did Jesus do in the boat? What request did Jesus make of Simon? Simon's reply? What did they catch? What did Simon Peter say? What henceforth was Simon to catch?

RELIGIOUS PRACTICES

1. Meditate daily upon the wonderful power of God.
2. Emulate the faith of Peter kneeling at the feet of Christ.
3. Secure a copy of Father Stedman's *My Sunday Missal* from the Confraternity of the Precious Blood, 5300 Ft. Hamilton Parkway, Brooklyn, H.Y., and use it at Mass.

DEC. 25—Why were the people in the synagogue astonished

at the teaching of Jesus? What did the unclean spirit cry out? How did Christ rebuke him? The effect? What did the people then say? Whom did Jesus then cure? Who were then brought to Jesus? How did He cure them? What was the prophecy of Isaias? What testimony did the unclean spirit bear?

RELIGIOUS PRACTICES

1. Remember the sick with a visit, flowers, and prayer.
2. Bear your own sickness with patience and resignation, thus converting it into spiritual merit.

DEC. 26—Where did Jesus go before daybreak? Why? Relate the conversation between Simon and Jesus. Describe the manifold ministry of Jesus in Galilee. What did the leper say to Jesus? What did Jesus do? What did He say? What charge did Jesus give to the cleansed leper? What did the leper do? Why did great crowds gather? Where was Jesus?

RELIGIOUS PRACTICES

1. Retire into your own mind each day for an examination of conscience.
2. Write out your resolution of improvement, and put it into practice immediately.
3. Secure a copy of *Pathways to Happiness,* from Our Sunday Visitor Press, Huntington, Ind., and follow out its suggestions.

DEC. 27—Who gathered together at Capharnaum to hear Jesus? Who was brought to Jesus? What did Jesus say to him? How did the Scribes and Pharisees argue? How did Jesus meet their arguments? What did He say to the paralytic? What did Jesus prove by this miracle? What did the astonished crowd exclaim?

RELIGIOUS PRACTICES

1. Acknowledge the divinity of Christ by saying at the Elevation in the Mass the words of St. Thomas, "My Lord and my God!"
2. Reflect often upon the wonderful power of pardoning which Christ conferred upon His priests.

DEC. 28—Who was Matthew? What did Jesus say to him? How did Matthew respond? Who were at table with Jesus and His disciples? How did the Pharisees and the Scribes react to their presence? How did Jesus answer their complaint? What question was raised in regard to fasting? How did Jesus answer it? What parable did Jesus relate unto them? What is the meaning of the parable?

RELIGIOUS PRACTICES

1. Deny yourself occasionally candy or some other delicacy which you like.
2. Donate the money thus saved for the work of the missions.
3. Subscribe to *The Catholic Digest,* Catholic Digest Bldg., St. Paul, Minn. Read it carefully each month, and then pass it on.

DEC. 29—What pool is at Jerusalem? Who were waiting there? Why? Who was cured? Whom did Jesus encounter at the pool? Narrate the conversation which ensued. Of what did the Jews accuse Jesus? Why? What did the Jews say to the man who had been healed? Whither did Jesus go? What did Jesus say to the cured man?

RELIGIOUS PRACTICES

1. Render any assistance possible to a crippled person.
2. Say a daily prayer for all who are in sickness and pain.

DEC. 30—Why were the Jews persecuting Jesus? How did Jesus answer them? What is the second reason why the Jews were seeking to put him to death? Discuss the relationship of Jesus to His Heavenly Father. He who does not honor the Son does not honor whom? Who has everlasting life? Who shall hear the voice of the Son of God? Who shall come forth unto the resurrection of life? Jesus seeks the will of whom?

RELIGIOUS PRACTICES

1. Observe Sunday by reading some good spiritual book.
2. Make Sunday a day of spiritual growth, visiting our Lord in the Blessed Sacrament in the afternoon or evening.

DEC. 31—What does Jesus say of the witness concerning Him? What does Jesus say of John? Why does He call him a lamp? What witness is greater than John? How do the works of Jesus bear witness concerning Him? How do the Scriptures bear witness concerning

Jesus? How does Jesus rebuke them for their unbelief? What does Jesus say of Moses?

RELIGIOUS PRACTICES

1. Emulate the example of John the Baptist by being a lamp for Jesus.
2. Bear witness to your faith in Him by your reverence in the use of His Holy Name.
3. Secure a copy of the pamphlet, *The Holy Name,* Our Sunday Visitor Press, Huntington, Ind., and follow its suggestions.

JAN. 1—What charge did the Pharisees bring against the disciples of Jesus? How did Jesus defend the action of His disciples? Who break the Sabbath and are guiltless? Why? Memorize Christ's saying, "The Sabbath was made for man, and not man for the Sabbath." Whom did Jesus encounter in the synagogue? What did the Jews ask Jesus? What did Jesus say to the man with the withered hand? What did Jesus then remark to the Jews? Give the reasoning preceding the conclusion of Jesus that it is lawful to do good on the Sabbath. What did Jesus do for the man with the withered hand?

RELIGIOUS PRACTICES

1. Abstain from unnecessary servile work on Sunday.
2. Visit the sick on that day.

JAN. 2—What were the Pharisees planning to do? Whither did Jesus go? What did He tell His disciples? Why? What did the unclean spirits cry out? What prophecy of Isaias was fulfilled? How long did Jesus pray? Whom did Jesus choose? What are the names of the twelve apostles?

RELIGIOUS PRACTICES

1. Familiarize yourself with the prophecies concerning Jesus.
2. Meditate often upon the striking manner in which these prophecies were fulfilled and thus demonstrated the divinity of Christ.

JAN. 3—From what places did people come to hear Jesus? Whom did he heal? What is the reward promised for the poor in spirit? For the meek? For them who mourn? For them who hunger? For the merciful? For the pure of heart? For the peacemakers? For those who suffer persecution for justice' sake?

For the reproached, the persecuted, and the slandered? Punishment is threatened whom?

RELIGIOUS PRACTICES

1. Memorize the eight beatitudes and often meditate upon them.
2. Pray for peace among men, and among nations, and work for the same.
3. Secure a copy of *The Way to Peace,* Catholic Information Society, 214 W. 31st St., N. Y. 1, N. Y. and study it carefully.

JAN. 4—Who are called the salt of the earth? Why? Who are called the light of the world? Why? Why should one let his light shine before men? Did Christ come to destroy the Law? Who shall be called the least in the Kingdom of Heaven? The great in the Kingdom of Heaven? How does Christ condemn hatred and anger? How does Christ emphasize the supremacy of charity?

RELIGIOUS PRACTICES

1. Make it a point never to speak ill of your neighbor, or call him bad names.
2. Cultivate a constant spirit of friendliness and good will towards your neighbors.
3. Secure a copy of *Why Not Be a Scholar?* Queen's Work Press, 3115 So. Grand Blvd., St. Louis 18, Mo., and follow its suggestion.

JAN. 5—What was said to the ancients? What does Christ say on this subject? What does Christ say about the occasions of sin? What does Christ teach concerning divorce? What is the difference between separation and divorce? What does Christ say about perjury and swearing? What does Christ say about pardoning? About avoiding revenge? About traveling the second mile?

RELIGIOUS PRACTICES

1. Shepherd your thoughts carefully to avoid all temptation.
2. Strive to return good for evil, love for hatred.

JAN. 6—Contrast Christ's law of love with conceptions which prevailed among the ancients. What is the Golden Rule? Memorize it. How are we to surpass the publicans? Whom are we to love? We are to be merciful like Whom? What is the proper motive for our charity? Why are we to give alms in secret?

RELIGIOUS PRACTICES

1. Strive daily to put into practice the Golden Rule.

2. Examine your conscience on this point every evening before retiring.

JAN. 7—How do the hypocrites love to pray? How should we pray? Why? What prayer did Christ formulate for us? Why is it a model prayer? If we forgive men their offenses, Who will forgive us? How are we to fast? Contrast the method recommended to us with that employed by the hypocrites. What kind of treasure should we lay up for ourselves? Why?

RELIGIOUS PRACTICES

1. Recite each morning and evening the *Lord's Prayer.*

2. Meditate upon the rich significance of each part of it, and try to put its full meaning into practice.

JAN. 8—What is the lamp of the body? Why? Why cannot one serve God and mammon? For what should we not show too great anxiety? Why? What lesson may we learn from the birds of the air? From the lilies of the field? For what should we seek first of all? Why? Why should we refrain from judging others? Why should we forgive our neighbor?

RELIGIOUS PRACTICES

1. Learn to work with all your might and at the same time trust in the Divine Providence with all your strength.

2. Cultivate a spirit of peace, tranquillity, and freedom from anxiety about worldly affairs.

JAN. 9—Can a blind man guide a blind man? Why? Why should we first cast out the beam from our own eye? What does Christ say about not profaning holy things? Why should we have confidence in prayer? What line of reasoning does Jesus develop on this point? What is the twofold gate? The twofold way?

RELIGIOUS PRACTICES

1. Pray with great confidence in the efficacy of your coming

to God in supplication and in petition.

2. Show the greatest respect for sacred things and holy places.

3. Secure a copy of *Character Formation,* Paulist Press, 401 W. 59 St., N.Y., and follow its suggestions.

JAN. 10—Of whom are we to beware? Jesus cites what standard by which we may judge? Of what does the mouth speak? What contrast does Jesus draw between work and word? Who is likened to the wise man who built his house upon a rock? Who is likened to a foolish man who built his house on sand? What happens to that house? How did the teaching of Jesus differ from that of the Scribes and Pharisees?

RELIGIOUS PRACTICES

1. Meditate often upon the necessity of *doing* the will of God instead of rendering merely lip service.

2. Examine your conscience to see if the fruits of your conduct are good or evil.

JAN. 11—Who was at the point of death? What entreaty did the centurion send to Jesus? How did they recommend the centurion to Jesus? What promise did Jesus give them? What was the second message which the centurion sent to Jesus? How did Jesus comment on it? How did Jesus rebuke the chosen people? What did Jesus say to the centurion?

RELIGIOUS PRACTICES

1. Pray devoutly each day the prayer recited just before Holy Communion, "Oh Lord, I am not worthy . . ."

2. Emulate the humility and faith of the centurion in your own life.

3. Secure a copy of *Why Not Be a Saint?* The Queen's Work Press, 3115 So. Grand Blvd., St. Louis 18, Mo., and follow its suggestions.

JAN. 12—Who was being borne in funeral procession? What did Jesus say to the widowed mother? What did He do? How did the people begin to glorify God? What did John's disciples say to Christ? What miracles did the disciples of John the Baptist witness? How did Jesus answer them? The miracles of Christ proved what?

RELIGIOUS PRACTICES

1. Extend sympathy, consolation and the assurance of prayers to those who have suffered the loss of a relative or close friend.
2. Have a Requiem Mass offered up *each* month for the repose of your parents, relatives, and friends.

JAN. 13—What did Jesus ask the crowds concerning John? What high tribute did Jesus pay to John? Contrast the action of the people and the publicans with that of the Pharisees and the lawyers. How has the Kingdom of Heaven been seized? The men of this generation are likened to what? Of what was John the Baptist accused? Of what was Jesus accused?

RELIGIOUS PRACTICES

1. Say often the prayer, "I do believe, Lord: help my unbelief."
2. Meditate often on the life of John the Baptist, and imitate his deeds of penance and self-denial.

JAN. 14—What did the penitent woman do to the feet of Jesus? What did the Pharisee say? What consideration did Jesus propose to Simon, the Pharisee? What contrast did Jesus draw between the treatment He received from Simon and that received from the penitent woman? How did Jesus reward the penitent woman? What did He say to her? What comment did those who were at the table make? What final word did Jesus address to Mary Magdalene?

RELIGIOUS PRACTICES

1. Meditate often upon the profound contrition of the penitent woman.
2. Recall when going to confession the mercy and the forgiveness which Christ lavished upon the penitent woman.
3. Arouse deep sorrow, perfect contrition for your sins before going to confession.

JAN. 15—Who were with Jesus? How did Christ's friends try to restrain Him? What cure did Jesus effect? What comments did it provoke? How did Jesus refute the calumnies of the Pharisees? Those who are not with Jesus are in what relation to Him? Those who do not gather with Jesus are doing what?

RELIGIOUS PRACTICES

1. Have an undivided loyalty to Jesus and to His divine commands.
2. Choose to suffer any pain or shame rather than offend Jesus in any way whatsoever.

JAN. 16—What is meant by blasphemy against the Spirit? Why will not such a sin be forgiven? By what is a tree judged? How does Christ condemn hypocrisy? What does Christ say about idle speech? Who were seeking Jesus? Who are the true brethren of Jesus?

RELIGIOUS PRACTICES

1. Learn to weigh your words carefully in order to avoid all evil speech.
2. If you cannot say something good about a person, keep silent.
3. Secure a copy of *What's the Truth About Catholics?* from Our Sunday Visitor Press, Huntington, Ind., read and loan it to others.

JAN. 17—What did Jesus do in the boat? What parable did He unfold to them? Explain and apply the parable. Why did Jesus speak in parables? What prophecy of Isaias was thus fulfilled? What privilege did Jesus extend to His disciples?

RELIGIOUS PRACTICES

1. Meditate upon the importance of sowing early in life the seeds of virtue.
2. Often reflect upon the truth that as one sows so also shall one reap.

JAN. 18—What parable did Jesus unfold to them? Who quickly falls away? Why? The one sown among thorns is likened to whom? Who is the one sown upon good ground? Where should a lamp be placed? Why? Why should we heed what we hear?

RELIGIOUS PRACTICES

1. Meditate often upon the reward which the just and righteous shall receive.
2. Reflect often upon the punishment which will be meted out to the wicked.
3. Secure a copy of *Happiness! But Where?* from St. Anthony's Guild Press, Paterson, N. J., and follow its suggestions.

JAN. 19—The Kingdom of God is as what? Who gives fertility to the earth? The Kingdom of Heaven is like what? Explain and apply this parable. Narrate the conversation between the servants and the householder. What do the weeds symbolize? The wheat?

RELIGIOUS PRACTICES

1. Reflect often upon the truth that the mills of God grind slowly; that they grind exceedingly fine.
2. See in everything that grows a symbol of the creative and directive power of God.

JAN. 20—Who is the sower of the good seed? Of the bad seed? Who are the reapers? How close did your explanation of the parable come to that given by Jesus? How is the Kingdom of Heaven like unto a treasure? How is it like a merchant in search of fine pearls? Jesus teaches by what means? What prophecy was thus fulfilled?

RELIGIOUS PRACTICES

1. Reflect often that your holy Catholic faith is a treasure beyond all price.
2. Guard that faith with the same zeal with which you would guard your most precious possessions.
3. Avoid all companionship and reading material which would endanger or weaken that faith.

JAN. 21—The Kingdom of Heaven is like what? Why? What is done finally with the good? With the bad? What does Jesus say about the wise Scribe? How did Jesus test the faith of His disciples? What did Jesus say to them? What did Jesus say to the sea? What was the comment of the disciples?

RELIGIOUS PRACTICES

1. Strengthen and deepen your faith in God so that you will never doubt or fear.
2. Remember that God and one constitute a majority.
3. In time of anxiety, recall the words of Christ, "Why are you fearful, O you of little faith?"

JAN. 22—Whom did Jesus encounter? Describe the behavior of the man with the evil spirit. What did Jesus say to the unclean spirit? What plea did the evil spirit make? The evil spirits were cast where? What happened then? What was the effect upon the people? What did Jesus say to the man freed from the unclean spirit? Did he obey the command of Jesus?

RELIGIOUS PRACTICES

1. Strive to remain always in the love and the friendship of Almighty God.
2. Regard sin as the greatest evil that can befall you.
3. Secure a copy of *God: Can We Find Him?* from The Paulist Press, 401 W. 59th St., N. Y., and read it carefully.

JAN. 23—Who came to Jesus? What entreaty did he make? Who touched the cloak of Jesus? What did she say? What happened? What did Jesus ask? What reply did Peter and the disciples make? Who confessed the truth? What did Jesus say to her?

RELIGIOUS PRACTICES

1. Remember that Jesus can hear us today as easily as he heard those who walked by His side.
2. Meditate often upon the truth that all things are possible to those who have faith.

JAN. 24—What word was brought to the ruler of the synagogue? What did Jesus say? What did Jesus do? What did He say? What was the reaction of the crowd? What did Jesus say to the girl? What happened immediately? What request did Jesus make? What plea did the two blind men make? Relate the conversation between them and Jesus. Whom did Jesus next cure? What was said by the crowds? By the Pharisees?

RELIGIOUS PRACTICES

1. Remember that spiritual blindness is worse than physical blindness.
2. Keep your spiritual clear-sightedness by doing deeds of love, kindliness, and piety each day.
3. Secure a copy of *My Daily Psalm Book*, 5300 Ft. Hamilton Parkway, Brooklyn 19, N. Y., and read it daily.

JAN. 25—To what town did Jesus come? What did he read from the volume of Isaias? What did Jesus say to the people in the synagogue? How did his own townsmen scoff at Jesus? What did Jesus say to them? Where is a prophet without honor? To whom was Elias sent? What leper was cleansed? What did the people do with Jesus? At what did Jesus marvel? Why?

RELIGIOUS PRACTICES

1. Read each day a chapter from *The Imitation of Christ*, by Thomas a Kempis.
2. Have a five minute period at noon and at night for the examination of conscience.

JAN. 26—Why was Jesus moved with compassion? What did Jesus say to His disciples? Memorize that utterance of the divine Master. What power did He confer upon His twelve disciples? Whither did Jesus send them? What instructions did He give them? Where did He tell them to stay? What were they to do if shown hospitality? If not shown hospitality?

RELIGIOUS PRACTICES

1. Meditate often upon the saying of Jesus, "The harvest indeed is great, but the laborers are few."
2. Consult with your spiritual director in regard to your vocation and follow his guidance.
3. Help the laborers for Christ by your prayers, alms and good works.

JAN. 27—Jesus warned His disciples that they must expect what? Who will inspire their message? Why will they be hated? What reward is promised to him who has persevered? How are they to keep in step with Christ? How are they to preach? Where?

RELIGIOUS PRACTICES

1. Meditate often upon the blow given you during Confirmation, reminding you to be ready to suffer persecution for the sake of Christ.
2. Preach by your conduct in your daily life, as well as by words, the truth of Christ.
3. Secure a copy of the revised edition of *The New Testament*, Confraternity of the Precious Blood, Brooklyn, N. Y., and use it.

JAN. 28—Whom should you not fear? Whom should you fear? Why? What will Jesus do for those who acknowledge Him before men? For those who disown Him? What did

Jesus come to bring? How does he show that by a sword He means division within a family? What kind of love does Jesus demand? What will happen to the man who loses his life for Christ's sake? The man who receives Christ's messengers, receives whom? Who shall not lose his reward?

RELIGIOUS PRACTICES

1. Reflect often upon the all-embracing Providence of God that has numbered the hairs of our head.

2. Memorize and meditate upon the saying of Jesus, "He who finds his life will lose it, and he who loses his life for my sake, will find it."

3. Honor and aid those who are consecrated to the service of God, remembering the reward which Christ has promised for so doing.

JAN. 29—What had John said to Herod? Who laid snares for John? Why did Herod fear John? What did Herod promise to the daughter of Herodias? How did he confirm that promise? What did her mother tell her to ask for? Why was Herod unwilling to displease her? What did he do?

RELIGIOUS PRACTICES

1. Avoid evil companions as they are always a danger to your virtue.

2. Cultivate the friendship and companionship of those who aid and inspire you to a life of virtue.

JAN. 30—Jesus and His disciples preached what? Did what? Who heard of the deeds of Jesus? What did Herod say? Why was he perplexed? What did he say? What invitation did Jesus extend to His apostles? Why? Why did great crowds follow Jesus? Whither did He go?

RELIGIOUS PRACTICES

1. Avoid all rash oaths and promises.

2. Make an annual retreat, so that you can thus secure a careful inventory of the condition of your soul.

3. Secure a copy of *The Reformation* from The Paulist Press, 401 W. 59th St., N. Y., study it carefully, and then loan it to others.

JAN. 31—Why did Jesus have compassion on the crowd? What did Jesus say to His disciples? Their reply? What did Jesus ask Philip? Philip's reply? How much food did they find there? What miracle did Jesus work? What did Jesus order His disciples to do? Why? What was the number of people who had eaten? What did the people say? Whither did Jesus send His disciples? Whither did He go?

RELIGIOUS PRACTICES

1. Reflect often upon the mighty power of God that is able to work such miracles as the multiplication of the loaves.
2. Regard food as something that is precious, and never to be wasted.

FEB. 1—Where were the apostles? Who came walking towards them? What did the apostles exclaim? How did Jesus calm them? Relate the conversation between Peter and Jesus. What happened? What did Peter cry out? What did Jesus do and say? What did those in the boat say? Why had they not understood about the loaves?

RELIGIOUS PRACTICES

1. Draw comfort and strength from the knowledge that God is always present with us.
2. Reflect often on the saying of Jesus, "Take courage; it is I, do not be afraid."

FEB. 2—When the people recognized Jesus, what did they do? Where did they lay the sick? Why? How did the crowd discover that Jesus had walked across the sea? What did they then do? What did they say to Jesus? How did Jesus answer them? What does Jesus tell them is the work of God? What did they then ask for? How did Jesus answer them?

RELIGIOUS PRACTICES

1. Meditate often upon the manner in which Jesus prepared the minds of the people for the great truth concerning the Holy Eucharist.
2. Prepare your mind and heart with equal care and diligence to receive Holy Communion with the deepest devotion.
3. Secure a copy of *Our Daily Bread*, Our Sunday Visitor Press, Huntington, Ind., and follow its suggestions.

FEB. 3—What did the Jews then ask for? What did Jesus tell them was the bread of life? Why had Jesus come down from Heaven? What is the will of His Father? How did the Jews murmur about the claims of Jesus? How did Jesus answer them? Whom does Jesus say has life everlasting?

RELIGIOUS PRACTICES

1. Reflect often upon the words of Jesus, "I am the bread of life."
2. So live that you may be worthy to receive that heavenly bread often as nourishment for your soul.

FEB. 4—How does the manna in the desert differ from the bread of life? The bread that Jesus promises to give is what? How did the Jews argue among themselves? What did Jesus reply? What pledge of our resurrection did Jesus give? What will happen to him who eats worthily the bread of life?

RELIGIOUS PRACTICES

1 Meditate often upon the wonderful gift which Jesus gives us in the Holy Eucharist.
2. Ask yourself frequently if you are making generous use of that wonderful gift.
3. Read daily a chapter in *The Imitation of Christ* by Thomas a Kempis.

FEB. 5—How did some of the disciples of Jesus murmur? What response did Christ make to them? Whose words are spirit and life? Jesus knew what from the beginning? What does Jesus say to them? Who went away? What did Jesus then say to the apostles? How did Peter answer? Memorize that answer of Peter. Jesus said that one of the twelve was what? Why? What were the Jews seeking to do to Jesus?

RELIGIOUS PRACTICES

1. Meditate often upon the memorable reply of Peter and make that reply your own.
2. Remember that one proves himself a traitor to Jesus by committing mortal sin.
3. Secure a copy of *What Think You of Christ?*, Our Sunday Visitor Press, Huntington, Ind., read it carefully, and loan it to others.

FEB. 6—What complaint did the Pharisees and the Scribes make? Why? What did the Pharisees and the Scribes say to Jesus? What response did Jesus make? What did they let go of? What did they hold fast to? What did they nullify? What did they keep? What had Moses said? How did the Pharisees frustrate the Law of Moses? What did they thus make void?

RELIGIOUS PRACTICES

1. Distinguish carefully between the law of God and the law of man.
2. Remember always that the law of God has the highest claim upon our loyalty.

FEB. 7—What defiles a man? Why? What did the disciples say to Jesus? How did He reply? What did Peter ask? What explanation did Jesus give? What comes out of the heart of man? What does not defile a man?

RELIGIOUS PRACTICES

1. Watch your speech carefully, remembering that it can be a source of untold mischief.
2. Keep your mind and your heart clean, for they are the source of your thoughts and actions.
3. Secure a copy of *Choosing a Partner for Marriage*, Ave Maria Press, Notre Dame, Ind., and read it carefully.

FEB. 8—What did the mother cry out to Jesus? What did His disciples ask Him to do? What did Jesus reply? Explain the meaning of that reply. What did the mother again beseech Jesus to do? How did He answer her? Her rejoinder? How did Jesus reward her faith? How did Jesus heal the deaf-mute? What did Jesus charge them to do? The result? What did the people say in wonderment?

RELIGIOUS PRACTICES

1. Imitate the example of the Canaanite mother by Daily Practice persisting in your prayer.
2. Pray always with the condition that what you ask is really for your benefit.

FEB. 9—Whom did the crowd bring to Jesus? What did He do for them? Why did Jesus have compassion for the multitude? How much food did the disciples bring to Jesus? What did

Jesus do to it? The fragments filled how many baskets? How many had eaten?

RELIGIOUS PRACTICES

1. Cultivate a hunger for the truth of Jesus Christ.
2. Strive to satisfy that hunger by studying the teachings of Christ and by receiving Him frequently in Holy Communion.

FEB. 10—What did the Pharisees and the Sadducees ask of Jesus? How did He answer them? What kind of a generation demands a sign? Explain the reference to Jonas the prophet. Who will condemn this generation of men? Why? What caution did Jesus give the disciples? How did they construe that warning? What did Jesus then say to them? What did Jesus mean by the leaven of the Pharisees and Sadducees?

RELIGIOUS PRACTICES

1. Beware of books which would injure or destroy your faith in Jesus and in His teachings.
2. Encourage Catholic authors by purchasing a good book on religion every few months.

FEB. 11—Whom did they bring to Jesus? What did Jesus ask him? The man's response? What did Jesus then do? What did He tell him to do? What did Jesus ask His disciples? Their response? What did Jesus then ask? How did Peter answer? How did Christ confirm the correctness of that answer? What signal honor did He then bestow by way of reward upon Peter? What do the keys symbolize?

RELIGIOUS PRACTICES

1. Reflect often upon the memorable saying of Peter, "Thou art the Christ, the Son of the living God."
2. Make that profession of faith your own, and live up to it.
3. Secure a copy of *The Spirit of Catholicism*, Macmillan Co., N. Y., study it carefully, and loan it to others.

FEB. 12—What did Jesus reveal to His disciples? How did Peter chide Jesus? How did Christ rebuke Peter? What great truth did Christ then preach to the disciples and to the crowd? What can a man give in exchange for his soul?

Of whom will the Son of Man be ashamed? He will render to everyone according to what? Some will not taste death until when?

RELIGIOUS PRACTICES

1. Meditate often upon the supreme importance of saving your immortal soul.
2. Be willing to take up your cross each day and follow Jesus.
3. Secure a copy of *The Ladder of Handicaps*, Paulist Press, 401 W. 59th St., N.Y. 19, N.Y. and read it often.

FEB. 13—Whom did Jesus take with Him to the mountain? Who appeared at His side? What did Peter say to Jesus? What did a voice out of the cloud say? How did Jesus reassure them? How did Jesus caution them? What did they discuss among themselves? What did the disciples ask Jesus? How did He answer them? They understood then that Jesus had spoken of whom?

RELIGIOUS PRACTICES

1. When kneeling before Christ in the Blessed Sacrament, say the words of Peter to Jesus, "Master, it is good for us to be here."
2. Reflect often upon the words uttered by God in Heaven concerning the divinity of Jesus, "This is my beloved Son, in Whom I am well pleased; hear Him."

FEB. 14—What question did Jesus ask the crowd? What did a man in the crowd reply? How did the father plead for his child? What did Jesus say about that generation? What did He ask of the boy's father? The answer? What did Jesus say about the efficacy of faith? What did the father cry out? How did Jesus free the boy from the evil spirit? What did the disciples ask Jesus privately? What did Jesus reply? A certain kind of demon can be cast out only by what?

RELIGIOUS PRACTICES

1. Meditate often upon the words of Jesus, "If thou canst believe, all things are possible to him who believes."
2. Make your frequent prayer the words of the father of the boy, "I do believe; help my unbelief."

FEB. 15—What did the brethren of Jesus say to Him? Why did the world hate Jesus? Where did Jesus go privately? Where were the Jews looking for Jesus? What was the whispered comment about Jesus? When did Jesus go into the temple?

RELIGIOUS PRACTICES

1. Do your deeds chiefly for the sake of God and only secondly to have them come to the attention of men.
2. Be prepared to suffer, like Jesus, contradiction and contempt.

FEB. 16—What response did Jesus make? Why do men seek to put Jesus to death? What did Jesus say to the crowd? What did the people of Jerusalem say about Jesus? What did Jesus cry out in the temple? Did many of the people believe in Jesus? What did they say? What did Jesus say to the crowd? What did the Jews say among themselves?

RELIGIOUS PRACTICES

1. Often reflect upon the many false charges brought against Jesus.
2. Imitate His patience and resignation in bearing with false and malicious gossip.

FEB. 17—What invitation did Jesus extend to men? To what did He refer? How did the people disagree concerning Christ? What did the chief priests and Pharisees say to the attendants? Their response? How did the Pharisees chide them? How did Nicodemus defend Christ? How did they answer Nicodemus?

RELIGIOUS PRACTICES

1. Reflect often on the invitation of Jesus, "If anyone thirst, let him come to me and drink."
2. Satisfy your thirst by receiving Jesus often in Holy Communion.
3. Secure a copy of *Religion: Does It Matter?* The Paulist Press, 401 W. 59th St., N. Y., read it carefully, and loan it to others.

FEB. 18—Whom did the Scribes and Pharisees bring to Jesus? How did they seek to entrap Jesus? What did Jesus do? What did He say to them? What did the crowd do? Why? Relate the conversation of

Jesus with the sinful woman. Whom did Jesus say that He was? What objection did the Pharisees utter? How did Jesus answer it? What two bear witness to Jesus? What did they ask Jesus? How did He reply? Why did no one seize Jesus?

RELIGIOUS PRACTICES

1. Meditate often on the saying of Jesus, "Let him who is without sin among you be the first to cast a stone at her."

2. Memorize and say each day the words of Jesus, "I am the light of the world. He who follows me does not walk in the darkness, but will have the light of life."

FEB. 19—What did Jesus say to the Jews? What did the Jews say among themselves? How did Jesus emphasize the importance of believing in Him? What did Jesus then say to the Jews? Did they understand that He was speaking about the Father? When will the Jews know that Jesus is the Son of Man? Who is with Jesus? What shall make men free? What difficulty did the Jews propose to Jesus? How did Jesus answer them?

RELIGIOUS PRACTICES

1. Meditate often upon the saying of Jesus, "If you abide in my word, you shall be my disciples indeed."

2. Reflect upon the second part of that saying of Jesus, "You shall know the truth, and the truth shall make you free."

3. Strive to learn the truth about Jesus and to proclaim it to the world.

FEB. 20—Why do the Jews seek to kill Jesus? Whom do the Jews say is their father? What does Jesus say in reply? From whom does Jesus say He has come? The Jews have made whom their father? Who is it that hears the word of God?

RELIGIOUS PRACTICES

1. Love your earthly father, and love God as your Heavenly Father.

2. Endeavor always to carry out the will of your Father as faithfully as Jesus carried out the will of His Father.

3. Secure a copy of *God in the Home*, The Paulist Press, 401 W. 59th St., N.Y., read it carefully, and loan it to others.

FEB. 21—What accusation did the Jews bring against Jesus? How does Jesus answer the charge? What reward does He promise to anyone who keeps His word? What further objection did the Jews bring? How did Jesus meet it? How can Abraham be said to have seen Christ's day? What third difficulty did the Jews raise? How did Jesus meet it? What did the Jews then attempt to do?

RELIGIOUS PRACTICES

1. Reflect often upon the saying of Jesus, "If anyone keep my word, he will never see death."
2. Meditate upon God's eternity as mirrored in the words of Jesus, "Before Abraham came to be, I am."

FEB. 22—What question did the disciples ask Jesus? What answer did He give them? How did Jesus heal the man born blind? What did the neighbors then say? What response did the man make? On what day did Jesus cure the man of his blindness? What did the Pharisees ask that man? What charge did they bring against Jesus? What did the man who was cured of his blindness say about Christ?

RELIGIOUS PRACTICES

1. Reflect often on the saying of Jesus, "Night is coming, when no one can work."
2. Bestir yourself to work diligently for God and the salvation of souls while you have health and strength.
3. Secure a copy of *Falling in Love*, Ave Maria Press, Notre Dame, Ind., and read it carefully and loan it to others.

FEB. 23—Whom did the Jews now question? What answer did the parents give? Why did the parents urge the Jews to question their son? What did the Jews say to the man the second time? What was his reply? Were the Jews now satisfied? What did the man now ask them? Sneering at him, the Jews said what? How does the man cured of his blindness reason with the Jews? How did he clinch his argument? What did the Jews then say and do to him? Relate the conversation of Jesus with the man cured of blindness. Why did Jesus say He had come into this world?

RELIGIOUS PRACTICES

1. Meditate upon the saying of the man cured of blindness, "If this man were not from God, He could do nothing."

2. Make your own the words of the man born blind but cured by Christ, "I believe, Lord."

3. Like the man thus cured, fall down on your knees and worship God.

FEB. 24—Whom did Jesus say is a thief and a robber? Whom does Jesus say is a shepherd? Why do the sheep follow their shepherd? Why will they not follow a stranger? For what purpose did Jesus come? Sketch the difference between the good shepherd and the hireling. Who is the good shepherd? Whom must Jesus also bring? What division arose among the Jews?

RELIGIOUS PRACTICES

1. Reflect often upon the saying of Jesus, "I came that they may have life, and have it more abundantly."

2. Help Jesus fulfill His mission mirrored in the words, "Them also I must bring, and they shall hear my voice, and there shall be one fold and one shepherd."

3. Secure a copy of *Converts: How to Win Them*, Our Sunday Visitor Press, Huntington, Ind., and follow its suggestions.

FEB. 25—How does Jesus foretell His death? His resurrection? What question did they ask Peter? What comment did Jesus make? What did He direct Peter to do? Why did Jesus pay the temple tax? How did Jesus correct the secret ambition of the apostles? Jesus urges them to become as humble as who? Who is the greatest in the Kingdom of Heaven? Whoever receives a little child for Jesus' sake, receives whom?

RELIGIOUS PRACTICES

1. Pay all your just debts to the state and to your fellow men.

2. Seek to become as humble and meek as a little child that you may find favor with God.

FEB. 26—What did John tell Jesus? What did Jesus reply? What warning does Jesus utter against scandal? Whom did the Son of Man come to save?

Relate the parable of the lost sheep. How does Jesus urge His followers to cast off all sinful influence? What members of the body is it better to lose than to lose the salvation of one's soul? Tell the parable of the salt.

RELIGIOUS PRACTICES

1. Exercise the greatest vigilance in order to avoid giving scandal to anyone.
2. Sacrifice any object or possession which offers an occasion of sin to you.
3. Secure a copy of *Mirror of Christ: St. Francis of Assisi*, from St. Anthony's Guild Press, Paterson, N. J., and read it carefully.

FEB. 27—In what manner are we to correct an erring brother? If he refuses to hear the Church, how is he to be regarded? What power of forgiveness did Christ confer upon His apostles? How did Christ emphasize the power of united prayer? How often are we to forgive our brother? Relate the parable of the unmerciful servant. How did the master rebuke the unmerciful servant? What will our Heavenly Father do to us if we do not forgive our brothers from our hearts?

RELIGIOUS PRACTICES

1. Say the Rosary together each evening as a family prayer.
2. Harbor no grudges, but forgive your enemies from your heart.

FEB. 28—What did James and John ask Jesus? How did He rebuke them? What did the Scribe say to Jesus? How did Jesus answer him? What invitation did Jesus extend to him? What excuse did the man offer? What did Jesus say to him in reply? What excuse did another offer Jesus? How did Jesus answer him?

RELIGIOUS PRACTICES

1. Reflect often upon the invitation of Jesus, "Follow me."
2. Memorize and meditate upon the words of Jesus, "No one, having put his hand to the plow and looking back, is fit for the kingdom of God."
3. Consult your confessor concerning the possibility of your having a vocation to the religious life.

FEB. 29—How did our Lord send forth His laborers? What

did He tell them about the harvest? What are His disciples to carry with them? How are they to enter a house? Is the laborer worthy of wages? What are the disciples to say to the people? How are the disciples to act in regard to the towns which do not receive them?

RELIGIOUS PRACTICES

1. Esteem it an honor to offer hospitality to every missionary and laborer for Christ.

2. Reflect often about the abundant harvest and the scarcity of laborers, and try to help meet the situation.

3. Send every Christmas an offering to The Fathers of the Foreign Missions, Maryknoll, N. Y., to help in the work of the missions.

MAR. 1—What did Jesus reproach? Why? What did He say to those towns? What warning did Jesus address to Capharnaum? The person who hears the disciples of Jesus hears whom? What report do the disciples carry back to Jesus? What did He say to them in reply? Why should one rejoice? Why does Jesus praise the Father? What invitation does Jesus extend to all who labor? What does He promise them?

RELIGIOUS PRACTICES

1. Reflect often upon the fact that priests are the ambassadors of Jesus Christ, as mirrored in His words, "He who hears you, hears me."

2. In moments of weariness recall the invitation of Jesus, "Come to me, all you who labor and are burdened, and I will give you rest."

3. Secure a copy of *Fools for God*, Our Sunday Visitor Press, Huntington, Ind., read it carefully, and loan it to others.

MAR. 2—What did Jesus say to His disciples? How did a certain lawyer seek to test Jesus? What did Jesus ask him? How did the lawyer reply? Did Jesus approve the answer? Who is your neighbor? Tell the story of the good Samaritan. What is its lesson? What did Jesus finally say to the lawyer?

RELIGIOUS PRACTICES

1. Reflect often upon the great commandment, "Thou shalt

love the Lord thy God with thy whole heart."

2. Meditate likewise upon the second commandment, "Thou shalt love thy neighbor as thyself."

3. Strive to make your whole life the fulfillment of these two commandments.

MAR. 3—Jesus visited at the home of whom? What did Mary do? What did Martha do? What was Martha's complaint? How did Jesus answer her? What did one of the disciples ask Jesus? What prayer did Jesus teach the disciples to say? Is it wise to persevere in prayer? How did Jesus show that it is well to persevere in prayer? How does Jesus show the disciples that their Heavenly Father knows how to shower good gifts upon them?

RELIGIOUS PRACTICES

1. Reflect often upon the words of Jesus, "Ask, and it shall be given to you."

2. Persevere in your prayers but always with the implied condition that what you are asking for is really for your good.

MAR. 4—What did the Jews ask Jesus? How did He answer them? What things did Jesus say bore witness concerning Him? Who are one? What did the Jews attempt to do? What did Jesus ask them? How did the Jews reply? Explain the line of reasoning which Jesus then developed for them. To what proof of His divinity did Jesus appeal? What did many say concerning John? Concerning Jesus?

RELIGIOUS PRACTICES

1. Reflect often upon the saying of Jesus, "My sheep hear my voice, and I know them and they follow me. And I give them everlasting life."

2. Show your loyalty and your love of Jesus not merely by your words, but by your deeds.

MAR. 5—By what power did the Jews say that Jesus was casting out devils? How did Jesus answer them? How does Jesus show that one must follow Him wholeheartedly? How did Jesus say that it shall be with that evil generation? What did a certain woman say to Jesus? How did He answer her? Where does one put a lamp? Why? What is the lamp of the body? Of what should we take care?

RELIGIOUS PRACTICES

1. Meditate often upon the saying of Jesus, "He who is not with me is against me; and he who does not gather with me scatters."
2. Memorize the words of Jesus, "Blessed are they who hear the word of God and keep it."

MAR. 6—What was the question in the mind of the Pharisee? Why? What did Jesus say to him? What was the hypocrisy of the Pharisees? How did Jesus denounce it? What did one of the lawyers say to Jesus? How did Jesus rebuke those who burden mankind? What did the wisdom of God declare? What key did the lawyers take away? Of what double crime were the lawyers guilty? What was the reaction of the Pharisees and the lawyers?

RELIGIOUS PRACTICES

1. Remember that Jesus looks beyond the exterior into the heart and soul of man.
2. Strive always to keep your heart pure and to do all that you do for the love and honor of God. Let that be the intention behind all your thoughts, words and deeds.
3. Secure a copy of *Why Not Investigate the Catholic Religion?* Our Sunday Visitor, Huntington, Ind., read it and loan it to others.

MAR. 7—Of what did Jesus warn the disciples to beware? Why? Whom should they not fear? Of whom should they be afraid? Why? How does Jesus illustrate the knowledge and the love of God? Whom will the Son of Man acknowledge? Whom will He disown? Who will not be forgiven? Who will teach the disciples what they are to say?

RELIGIOUS PRACTICES

1. Meditate often upon the love, providence and solicitude of God, as mirrored in the words of Jesus, "The very hairs of your head are all numbered."
2. Profess your faith in God courageously, remembering the promise of Jesus, "Everyone who acknowledges me

before men, him will the Son of Man also acknowledge before the angels of God."

MAR. 8—What does one of the crowd say to Jesus? How did He answer him? Of what are we to beware? Why? Relate the parable of the rich fool. What lesson does it teach? Why should we not be over-solicitous for temporal things? What lesson should we learn from the lilies of the field? What are we to seek first? Why?

RELIGIOUS PRACTICES

1. Guard against too great solicitude for material possessions.
2. Meditate often upon the saying of Jesus, "Take heed and guard yourselves from all covetousness, for a man's life does not consist in the abundance of his possessions."

MAR. 9—Jesus teaches us to work for what kind of treasure? Where is one's heart to be found? How does Jesus stress the need for preparation and vigilance? One should be ready for what? What did Peter ask Jesus? How did Jesus reply? What servant will the master reward? Why? What kind of servant will the master punish? Why? From whom will much be required? Why?

RELIGIOUS PRACTICES

1. Live in such a state of virtue and holiness that you will be ready at any moment at which the Master might call you.
2. Remember that the best preparation for death is a virtuous life, sanctified by the frequent reception of Jesus in Holy Communion.
3. Secure a copy of *Why Attend Sunday Mass?* Our Sunday Visitor, Huntington, Ind., read it, and loan it to others.

MAR. 10—Jesus came to cast what upon the earth? What kind of division did Jesus come to bring? Why? What signs do the people know how to read? What do they not judge rightly? They should take pains to do what? In this discourse Jesus teaches the people that they should reconcile themselves to whom?

RELIGIOUS PRACTICES

1. Learn to suffer contradiction and vexation for the sake of Jesus.

2. Kindle your zeal for the salvation of souls with a spark of the fire which Jesus cast upon the earth—the faith of Christ.

MAR. 11—What word was brought to Jesus? Jesus urged the people to do what? Under what penalty? Relate the parable of the fruitless fig tree. What lesson does it teach? Whom did Jesus heal? With what words? What did the ruler of the synagogue say? How did Jesus answer him? Who were put to shame? Who rejoiced?

RELIGIOUS PRACTICES

1. Remember that by our fruit we shall be judged and that there can be no substitutes for good works.
2. Do penance for your sins, recalling the saying of Jesus, "Unless you repent, you will all perish."
3. Secure a copy of *Preparing for Marriage*, Ave Maria Press, Notre Dame, Ind., and read it and loan it to others.

MAR. 12—To what did Jesus liken the kingdom of God? How is the kingdom of God like unto leaven? What question was asked Jesus? How did He answer it? What sentence will be passed upon the workers of iniquity? Who will be the first? Who the last?

RELIGIOUS PRACTICES

1. Make yourself a leaven, purifying and sweetening the stream of community life by your civic virtue and your good example.
2. Strive to pay at least a brief visit to Jesus in the Blessed Sacrament each day.
3. Say *The Grace Before Meals* and the *Thanksgiving After Meals* with unfailing regularity.

MAR. 13—What warning did the Pharisees bring to Jesus? What answer did He give to them? What does Jesus say about Jerusalem? For what purpose were they watching Jesus? What question did Jesus ask the lawyers and the Pharisees? What did Jesus do? How did Jesus justify His action?

RELIGIOUS PRACTICES

1. Meditate upon the blessings of Jesus by making the Stations

of the Cross at least once a week.

2. Remember that man was not made for the Sabbath, but that the Sabbath was made for man.

MAR. 14—Jesus observed that the Jews were seeking what places at the table? What did He advise them to do? Why? Who shall be humbled? Who shall be exalted? Whom did Jesus recommend as persons to be invited to a dinner? Why? What did one of those at the table say to Jesus? What excuses were offered for not accepting the invitation? What did the master of the house then say to his servant? What report did the servant make? What further command did the master of the house give? Who were not to taste of his supper?

RELIGIOUS PRACTICES

1. Purify your motives in all works of charity, so that you shall receive your reward from God alone.

2. Do not spurn with false excuses the invitation of Jesus to come to Him frequently in Holy Communion.

MAR. 15—The followers of Christ must be ready to make what sacrifice? Who cannot be His disciple? Before beginning to erect a building, we should do what? What does the prudent king, in setting out to battle, do? What are the disciples of Jesus asked to renounce? If salt loses its strength, what is it fit for? What lesson does Jesus teach by means of this illustration?

RELIGIOUS PRACTICES

1. We must give our supreme love and loyalty to Jesus, giving Him the first place in our hearts.

2. Reflect often upon the saying of Jesus, "And he who does not carry his cross and follow me, cannot be my disciple."

MAR. 16—What did the Pharisees and the Scribes murmur about? Jesus answered them by relating what parable? What great truth does the parable bring out? A woman who loses a drachma does what? What does she say upon finding it? Who rejoices when one sinner repents?

RELIGIOUS PRACTICES

1. Reflect often upon the mercy and the love of Jesus for a sinner, as mirrored in the words of Jesus, "There will be joy in heaven over one sinner who repents, more than over ninety-nine just who have no need of repentance."

2. Strive each month to bring back to the practice of religion a person who has strayed away.

3. If you know of any person who is not attending Mass because of an irregular marriage, bring him to a priest to have the marriage rectified, if possible.

MAR. 17—What did the younger son say to his father? What did the father do? Where did the younger son go? What happened to him? When the son came to himself, what did he say? What did he do? How did the father receive him? What complaint did the elder brother make? What did the father say in reply?

RELIGIOUS PRACTICES

1. In your sorrow for your past sins, make your own the words of the prodigal son, "Father, I have sinned against heaven and before thee. I am no longer worthy to be called thy son; make me as one of thy hired men."

2. Meditate likewise upon the mercy and love of Jesus, as mirrored in the words of the forgiving father, "Rejoice, for this thy brother was dead, and has come to life; he was lost, and is found."

3. Secure a copy of *St. Augustine*, The Paulist Press, 401 W. 59th St., N.Y., read it carefully, and loan it to others.

MAR. 18—What did the rich man say to his steward? Why? What did the steward say within himself? What did he do? How did the master commend the worldly wisdom of his steward? What lesson does it teach us? One who is faithful in a little thing is faithful also in what? Can a servant serve two masters? Why?

RELIGIOUS PRACTICES

1. In our striving for spiritual riches, let us imitate the shrewdness displayed by worldlings in their business affairs.

2. Give generously of your means to God, remembering

that we hold our material possessions only as stewards.

MAR. 19—What did Jesus say to the Pharisees? Who knows the heart of man? How does Jesus condemn divorce? What did Jesus say of the unmerciful rich man? Of the deserving poor man? What was the position of both of these in the next life? What did the rich man cry out? What did Abraham say in reply? What further request did the rich man make? What did Abraham tell him in reply? Was the rich man satisfied? How does Abraham end the discussion?

RELIGIOUS PRACTICES

1. Reflect often that upon the use you make of the present time will depend your eternity.
2. Endeavor to store up for yourself riches in heaven by doing good each day upon earth.

MAR. 20—Who was sick in Bethany? What message did Mary and Martha send to Jesus? What did Jesus say in reply? Whom did Jesus love? What did the disciples ask Jesus? How did He answer them? How does Jesus reveal to the disciples that Lazarus is dead? What did Thomas say?

RELIGIOUS PRACTICES

1. Remember in your prayers, morning and night, the sick and the dying.
2. Face always toward the light and the shadows will flee behind you, remembering the saying of Jesus, "If a man walks in the day, he does not stumble."

MAR. 21—Who went out to meet Jesus? What did she say to Him? What did Jesus reply? Who is the resurrection and the life? What profession of faith did Martha make? What message did Martha bring to Mary? What did the Jews say when Mary went to meet Jesus?

RELIGIOUS PRACTICES

1. Reflect often on the saying of Jesus, "I am the resurrection and the life."
2. Cultivate a love for Jesus in this life, that you may reign with Him forever in eternity.

MAR. 22—What did Mary say to Jesus? How did the Jews know that Jesus loved Lazarus?

What did Jesus ask to be done at the cave? What objection did Martha raise? How did Jesus answer her? What did Jesus say in prayer to His Heavenly Father? What did He say to Lazarus? What was the result? What was the effect of this miracle upon the Jews?

RELIGIOUS PRACTICES

1. Reflect often upon your own resurrection from the grave.
2. Remember that it is well to think more of your soul than of your body, because the former will live forever.

MAR. 23—What did the chief priests and the Pharisees say? What did Caiphas say to the council? Whom did Caiphas prophesy was to die for the nation? To what place did Jesus withdraw for safety? Whom were the Jews at Jerusalem looking for? What did they say to one another? What did Jesus say to His disciples about scandal? How often are we to forgive our brother?

RELIGIOUS PRACTICES

1. Before acting, think of the effect that your action may have on others. Will it edify or scandalize them?
2. Do not harbor resentment against one who has offended you, but show your willingness to forgive him, as you yourself wish to be forgiven by those whom you have offended.
3. Secure a copy of *Cardinal Newman*, The Paulist Press, 401 W. 59th St., N.Y., read it, and loan it to others.

MAR. 24—What did the apostles ask of our Lord? How did Jesus answer them? Present the line of reasoning which Jesus used to show His disciples that they should consider themselves unprofitable servants. Whom did Jesus encounter? What favor did they ask of Him? What did Jesus say to them? How many returned to express gratitude to Jesus? What did Jesus say to him? How did He commend the leper's faith?

RELIGIOUS PRACTICES

1. Utter frequently the petition of the apostles to our Lord, "Increase our faith."
2. Often reflect upon how much Jesus wishes the expression of

our gratitude, as mirrored in His words, "Were not the ten made clean? But where are; he nine?"

MAR. 25—What did the Pharisees ask our Lord? Jesus told them that the kingdom of God is where? How does Jesus warn His disciples to beware of false christs? What must the Son of Man first do? How will unbelievers be punished? How will God's judgment come? What will happen to him who tries to save his life? What will happen to him who loses his life for Christ's sake?

RELIGIOUS PRACTICES

1. Reflect often upon the saying of Jesus, "For behold, the kingdom of God is within you."
2. Have a good conscience and you will always have joy and peace.
3. Secure a copy of *Jesus, King of Love*, The National Center of the Enthronement, Sacred Hearts Academy, Fairhaven, Mass., read it carefully, and loan it to others.

MAR. 26—Jesus tells the people that they must do what? What story does He relate to them? What lesson does it teach? What two men went up to the temple to pray? What was the prayer of the Pharisee? Of the publican? Which one did Jesus commend? Why?

RELIGIOUS PRACTICES

1. Make your own the prayer of the publican, "O God, be merciful to me the sinner!"
2. Practice humility and seek always the lowest place.

MAR. 27—What did the Pharisees ask Jesus? What did He answer them? What did they say that Moses permitted them? What did Almighty God say to our first parents? What did Jesus say that no man was to put asunder? What objection did the Pharisees offer? How did Jesus answer it? What did Jesus again emphasize to His disciples? What comment did His disciples make? How did Jesus praise the excellence of virginity?

RELIGIOUS PRACTICES

1. Reflect upon the divine origin of matrimony, as mirrored in the words of Almighty God, "For this cause a man shall leave his father and mother,

and cleave to his wife, and the two shall become one flesh."

2. Champion the law of Christ concerning the indissolubility of the marriage bond, as mirrored in His words, "What therefore God has joined together, let no man put asunder."

MAR. 28—What did they bring to Jesus? Why? What did the disciples do? What did Jesus say to them? What did Jesus do to the little children? What question did a young man put to Jesus? What answer did Jesus give? What did Jesus say is necessary in order to enter into life? State the commandments mentioned by Jesus. What one thing was lacking in the young man? What invitation did Jesus extend to him? Did he accept? Why?

RELIGIOUS PRACTICES

1. Treat little children with the kindliness and love with which Christ treated them, as mirrored in His memorable words, "Let the little children come to me, and do not hinder them, for of such is the kingdom of God."

2. Be willing to make any sacrifice to follow Jesus.

MAR. 29—Who will find it difficult to enter the kingdom of God? Why? What did the disciples say to Jesus? How did He answer them? What question did Peter put to Jesus? What reward does Jesus promise those who have left all things to follow Him?

RELIGIOUS PRACTICES

1. Do not allow your mind and heart to be wrapped up in material possessions.

2. Meditate often on the hundredfold reward which Jesus promises to those who have left all things to follow Him.

3. Secure a copy of *Which Is Christ's True Church?* Our Sunday Visitor Press, Huntington, Ind., read it, and loan it to others.

MAR. 30—The kingdom of heaven is like unto what? What did the householder say to the man whom he found standing idle at the eleventh hour? What wages did all the workers receive? Why did they murmur? What was the reply of the employer? What lesson does the parable teach?

RELIGIOUS PRACTICES

1. Do not attempt to judge the reward due your fellow men.

Leave that to God Who alone is able to judge the true merits of every man's work.

2. Seek not yourself, but seek Jesus in all that you do and strive for.

MAR. 31—Whither were Jesus and His disciples going? What did Jesus tell His disciples was going to happen? What did James and John ask of Jesus? What did their mother ask for them? What did Jesus tell James and John and their mother? How did Jesus teach them a lesson in humility and in service? Whoever wishes to become great shall be what? Whoever wishes to be first shall be what? Why did the Son of Man come?

RELIGIOUS PRACTICES

1. Seek always the lowest place, mindful of the words of Jesus, "Whoever wishes to become great shall be your servant."

2. Seek to give rather than to receive, to serve rather than to be served, mindful of the saying of Jesus, "For the Son of Man also has not come to be served but to serve, and to give His life as a ransom for many."

APR. 1—Who was trying to see Jesus? Describe Zacchæus. What did he do in order to see Jesus? What did Jesus say to him? How did the people murmur? What did Zacchæus say to Jesus? What reply did Jesus make? What did the Son of Man come to seek? What did the blind man cry to Jesus? What did the disciples say to the blind man? What favor did the blind man ask of Jesus? What did Jesus say and do?

RELIGIOUS PRACTICES

1. Imitate the energy and resourcefulness shown by Zacchæus to see Jesus, and try to keep Him always in your heart.

2. Let your frequent prayer be that of the blind man, "Rabboni, that I may see."

3. Say the above prayer particularly when your cross is heavy and the way is dark.

APR. 2—A nobleman went to seek what? What instructions did he give to his servants? What did the citizens say of the nobleman? How did he reward the industrious servants? How did he punish his slothful servant? How did he punish his enemies?

RELIGIOUS PRACTICES

1. Make the most of your talents, be they few or many, in order to bring honor, praise, and glory to God.

2. Remember that God will demand a strict accounting for the use of your time and your talents.

APR. 3—Where and with whom was Jesus taking supper? Who anointed the feet of Jesus? What objection did Judas make? How did Jesus justify the action of Mary? What shall be told in memory of Mary? Why did many people come to see Jesus? Why also did many believe in Him?

RELIGIOUS PRACTICES

1. Try always to make single the eye of your intention, so that whatever you do, you do for the sake of Jesus and not on account of Lazarus.

2. Show a reverence for Jesus similar to that shown by Mary, by receiving Jesus in frequent Holy Communion.

3. Secure a copy of *The Real Presence: Fact or Fiction?* Our Sunday Visitor Press, Huntington, Ind., read it, and loan it to others.

APR. 4—What instructions did Jesus give to two of His disciples? What did the owners of the colt say to the disciples? How did they reply? What happened then? What prophecy was thus fulfilled? Did the disciples at first understand? Did they understand later on?

RELIGIOUS PRACTICES

1. Imitate the humility and meekness of Jesus, who said, "Learn of me, for I am meek and humble of heart."

2. Show your meekness and humility not only to superiors but to your subordinates as well.

APR. 5—How did the crowd acclaim Jesus? What did they cry out? Who bore witness to Jesus? What did the Pharisees say among themselves? What did the Pharisees ask Jesus to do? How did Jesus reply? Why did Jesus weep over Jerusalem? What did He say of Jerusalem?

RELIGIOUS PRACTICES

1. Emulate the enthusiasm of the crowd in welcoming Jesus, saying with them, "Blessed is he who comes in the name of the Lord!"

2. Emulate likewise the zeal of the disciples in proclaiming Jesus to the world, mindful of the saying of Jesus, "I tell you that if these keep silence, the stones will cry out."

APR. 6—When Jesus entered Jerusalem, what did the crowds cry out? What did the chief priests and the Scribes say to Jesus? How did He answer them? What did Jesus place a curse upon? Why? What did the fig tree symbolize? What did Jesus do to the money-changers in the temple? What did Jesus say His house shall be called? What had the money-changers made of it? The chief priests and the Scribes sought to do what? Why?

RELIGIOUS PRACTICES

1. Show the greatest respect for the house of God, refraining from any conversation or levity while in it.

2. Help our missionaries at home and abroad, that increasingly fufilled may be the words of Jesus, "My house shall be called a house of prayer for *all* the nations."

3. Secure a copy of *The Holy Eucharist and Reason*, Our Sunday Visitor Press, Huntington, Ind., read it carefully, and loan it to others.

APR. 7—What did the Gentiles ask of Philip? What did Jesus say? What happens to him who loves his life? What happens to him who hates his life in this world? What reward is promised to anyone who serves Jesus? How did the eternal Father testify to His Son? If Jesus be lifted up from the earth, what will He draw to Him? Narrate the conversation of Jesus with the crowd.

RELIGIOUS PRACTICES

1. Meditate often upon the saying of Jesus, "He who loves his life, loses it; and he who hates his life in this world, keeps it unto life everlasting."

2. Strive while you are young to form habits of virtue and holiness of life, mindful of the saying of Jesus, "Walk while you have the light, that darkness may not overtake you."

APR. 8—How did Jesus teach His disciples the power

of faith? What did Jesus teach concerning the power of prayer? In what spirit should you pray? What question did the chief priests and elders of the people ask Jesus? How did Jesus answer them? Relate the parable of the two sons. To whom did Jesus apply the truth contained in this parable? Why?

RELIGIOUS PRACTICES

1. In times of doubt and difficulty recall the words of Jesus, "Have faith in God."

2. Have unbounded faith and confidence when you pray, mindful of the words of Jesus, "All things whatever you ask for in prayer, believe that you shall receive, and they shall come to you."

3. Secure a copy of *Why Pray for the Dead?* Our Sunday Visitor Press, Huntington, Ind., and follow out its suggestions.

APR. 9—What did the vineyard workers do to the first servant who came to them? To the second? To the third? What did the vineyard workers say when the owner's son came to them? What did they do? How did Jesus apply this parable to the Jews? The stone which the builders rejected has become what? The kingdom of God will be given to whom? What was the reaction of the chief priests and the Pharisees to the parable of Jesus?

RELIGIOUS PRACTICES

1. Memorize the sentence which you think contains the most important truth presented in your daily reading of the Gospel.

2. Write that sentence in a notebook, and review those selected truths each week, thus keeping them fresh in your mind.

APR. 10—The kingdom of heaven is like unto what? What invitation did the king extend? What excuses did the people offer for not accepting? What did the people do to the king's servants who invited them? How did the king punish the people? Who finally came to the wedding feast? What did the king say to the man who had not worn a wedding garment? What did he do to him?

RELIGIOUS PRACTICES

1. Always come on time to Mass, planning to arrive ten

minutes or so ahead of time, to avoid the danger of being late.
2. Assist at Mass with great devotion, using a missal or prayer book.

APR. 11—The Pharisees took counsel together for what purpose? What did they say to Jesus? How did Jesus handle their tricky question? What are we to render to Cæsar? To God? What was the reaction of the people?

RELIGIOUS PRACTICES

1. Love your country and seek always to promote its true welfare and happiness.
2. Become an active member of one of the societies in your parish church.
3. Secure a copy of *How to Get Married,* Our Sunday Visitor Press, Huntington, Ind., read it carefully, and loan it to others.

APR. 12—What truth did the Sadducees deny? What difficulty did they urge against the resurrection? How did Jesus answer their difficulty? Does marriage take place after the resurrection? Who are equal to the angels? What did Moses teach concerning the resurrection of the dead? What did certain of the Scribes say when the Master had finished?

RELIGIOUS PRACTICES

1. Make the Sign of the Cross carefully, without haste, and with reflection concerning its meaning.
2. Make a Morning Offering of all your thoughts, words, and deeds in union with Christ for the salvation of the world.

APR. 13—What did the Scribe ask Jesus? What is the greatest and the first commandment? What is the second commandment? What comment did the Scribe make? How did Jesus commend him? How did Jesus teach that He was both human and divine?

RELIGIOUS PRACTICES

1. Meditate on the mighty truth that Jesus is both God and Man, and that He founded the Catholic Church, of which you are privileged to be a member.
2. Take your membership in a study club seriously, and learn the doctrines of the church so well that you can explain them to others.

3. Secure a copy of *Does It Matter Much What Man Believes?* Our Sunday Visitor Press, Huntington, Ind., read it carefully and loan it to others.

APR. 14—What did Jesus say to the crowds and to His disciples concerning the Scribes and the Pharisees? What is the difference between their words and their deeds? What is the motive behind their works? How did the Scribes and Pharisees constitute stumbling-blocks for others? For what shall they receive the greater judgment? The Scribes and Pharisees turn a convert into what? How do they trifle with sacred oaths?

RELIGIOUS PRACTICES

1. Be careful to do all your work not out of the motive of human vanity, but for love of God.
2. Avoid hypocrisy in every form, being sincere and frank in all your deeds.

APR. 15—What trifles do the Scribes and the Pharisees perform? What important duties do they leave undone? What kind of piety do they neglect? Upon what do they place too much emphasis? How do they appear outwardly? What are they really like within? How does Jesus condemn their arrogance and presumption? How did they treat the prophets sent to them? What is their final lot?

RELIGIOUS PRACTICES

1. Make it a point to attend Benediction of the most Blessed Sacrament whenever possible, thus cultivating a special devotion to Jesus in the Holy Eucharist.

APR. 16—Whose offering did Jesus especially commend? Why? What two prophecies of Isaias were fulfilled? Why did not the rulers profess their belief in Jesus publicly? Jesus has come into the world to be what? Jesus has come into the world to do what? What word will condemn the unbeliever on the last day?

RELIGIOUS PRACTICES

1. If you have only a little, imitate the example of the poor widow, and thus be assured of Christ's great reward.

2. Do not be afraid to profess openly your belief in Christ, preferring the glory of God to the esteem of man.

3. Doff your hat when passing a Catholic Church to show your reverence for Jesus in the Blessed Sacrament.

APR. 17—What did one of the disciples say to Jesus? How did He answer the disciple? What did some of the apostles ask Jesus privately? Jesus warned the apostles against whom? Why should they not fear wars? What kind of a fate is in store for the apostles, according to the warning of Jesus? Who will teach them what to say in the critical hour?

RELIGIOUS PRACTICES

1. Renew your faith in the final victory of Christ and of His kingdom.

2. Renew your baptismal vows from time to time, thus keeping them fresh in your mind and prompting you to fulfill them.

3. Subscribe to *The Ave Maria*, Notre Dame, Ind., and after reading, pass it on to others.

APR. 18—Who will be hated by all? Why? Who will betray one another? Who will lead many astray? How are the followers of Christ to act during persecution? What kind of tribulation and distress shall overwhelm the world? What city will be trodden down by the Gentiles?

RELIGIOUS PRACTICES

1. Learn how to baptize and be ready to assume the responsibility in case of necessity.

2. When you are sponsor for a child in baptism, know your obligations and live up to them.

3. Secure a copy of *The Life of Christ*, St. Anthony's Guild Press, Paterson, N. J., read it carefully, and loan it to others.

APR. 19—Who will arise and try to deceive the people? How will the Son of Man come? How will the heaven and the earth be affected? Who will come with great power and majesty? Whom will He send forth? To do what?

RELIGIOUS PRACTICES

1. So live in virtue and holiness of life that you would be ready to meet your God at any time.

2. Think often of eternity and ask yourself upon arising each morning, "Where shall I spend eternity?"

APR. 20—What parable is to be learned from the fig tree? Whose words will not pass away? Does anyone know the time of the end of the world? Who? Why should the people take heed to themselves? Why should the people watch and pray? At what hour will the Son of Man come?

RELIGIOUS PRACTICES

1. Exercise restraint and temperance in all things, mindful of the words of Jesus, "But take heed to yourselves, lest your hearts be overburdened with self-indulgence and drunkenness and the cares of this life."
2. Abstain from intoxicating liquor until you are at least twenty-one.
3. Secure a copy of *Drinking Is Dangerous*, Our Sunday Visitor Press, Huntington, Ind., and follow its suggestions.

APR. 21—What message does Jesus bring to all? What does He say about the man preparing for a long journey abroad? What kind of a servant will the master set over all his goods? What will the master do to the wicked servant? Narrate the story of the wise and the foolish virgins. What important truth does it bring out?

RELIGIOUS PRACTICES

1. Remember that in the spiritual life, as in our earthly life, eternal vigilance is the price of liberty and of victory.
2. Be sure to make an annual retreat to check up on the condition of your soul.

APR. 22—Contrast the conduct of the man with the five talents and the one with the one talent. What did the master say to the man with the five talents? With the two talents? How did the master punish the lazy servant? What lesson does the parable of the talents teach us?

RELIGIOUS PRACTICES

1. Often ask yourself, "What use am I making of the talents which God has given to me?"
2. Remember that God will expect more from those to whom He has given more talents.

APR. 23—Who will be gathered before the Son of Man? What will He do to them? What will Jesus say to those on His right hand? What will the just ask Jesus? What answer will be given to them? What will the Son of Man say to those on His left hand? Their questions? How will the Son of Man answer them?

RELIGIOUS PRACTICES

1. See in the faces of the poor and lowly the countenance of Jesus, and treat them accordingly.
2. Meditate often upon the saying of Jesus, "As long as you did it for one of these, the least of my brethren, you did it for me."
3. Secure a copy of *Now I See*, Sheed and Ward, N.Y., read it carefully, and loan it to others.

APR. 24—Where did Jesus pass the night? What prediction did Jesus make to His disciples? What did the rulers plot to do to Jesus? What did the chief priests give to Judas to have him betray Jesus? On what day was it customary to sacrifice the Passover? What instruction did Jesus give to Peter and John? How did the disciples prepare for the Last Supper?

RELIGIOUS PRACTICES

1. Reflect often that the person who commits a mortal sin is playing again the role of Judas.
2. Prepare your mind and heart carefully before receiving Jesus in Holy Communion.

APR. 25—Who were with Jesus at the Last Supper? What did Jesus say to His apostles? What dispute arose among them? How did Jesus settle the dispute? Jesus declares He is in their midst as one who does what? Jesus appoints His disciples to what?

RELIGIOUS PRACTICES

1. Remember that humility is the foundation of all the virtues and strive to practice humility every day.
2. Prefer always to serve rather than to be served, mindful of the saying of Jesus, "I am in your midst as He who serves."

APR. 26—Whose hour had come? Jesus washed the feet of whom? What protest did

Peter make? How did Jesus answer him? Was Peter satisfied? What did Jesus then say to Peter? Peter's response? Why did Jesus say, "You are not all clean"? What did Jesus invite the apostles to do?

RELIGIOUS PRACTICES

1. Visit the poor and the needy in their homes, thus familiarizing yourself with their wants, so that you may be able to help them the more effectively.
2. Reflect often upon the humility of Jesus, recalling how He insisted upon washing the feet of His apostles.

APR. 27—One who eats bread with Jesus has done what? Jesus foretells that one of the apostles is about to do what? What did the apostles ask Jesus? How did He answer them? What did Peter ask John? How did Jesus reveal the identity of the traitor? What did Jesus tell Judas to do? Which apostle had charge of the purse?

RELIGIOUS PRACTICES

1. Do not allow any worldly fame or possession to cause you to falter in your loyalty to Jesus.
2. Bring a friend, unaffiliated in an active manner with any church, to Mass with you on Sunday and invite him to learn more about the Catholic religion.
3. Secure a copy of *Making Marriage Stick,* Ave Maria Press, Notre Dame, Ind. and after reading, loan it to others.

APR. 28—With what words did Jesus institute the Holy Eucharist? Jesus declares that he will not drink henceforth of this fruit of the vine until when? When Judas had gone out, Jesus said what? What new commandment did Jesus give to His disciples? How would men know that they were the disciples of Jesus?

RELIGIOUS PRACTICES

1. Reflect often upon the supreme gift which Jesus instituted for mankind, namely, the Holy Eucharist.
2. Heed the invitation of Jesus to receive Him often in Holy Communion.

APR. 29—What did Jesus say to Simon Peter? What did Simon Peter say in reply? How did Jesus answer him? In what words did Jesus predict Peter's denial? Why did Jesus pray for Peter? What did Jesus command Peter to do? Peter protested that he would not do what? Relate the conversation which then took place between Jesus and the apostles.

RELIGIOUS PRACTICES

1. Reflect often that the great commandment which Jesus gave to His followers is the commandment to love one another.
2. Try every day to grow in love of your neighbor and to manifest that love in a helpful manner.

APR. 30—How did Jesus console His disciples? Jesus is going to prepare what for His disciples? What did Thomas say to Jesus? How did Jesus answer him? What did Philip say to Jesus? In what striking manner did Jesus affirm His divinity? Jesus promises that the disciples who believe in Him will be able to do what? In whose name are we to ask for anything?

RELIGIOUS PRACTICES

1. Reflect often upon the saying of Jesus, "I am the way, and the truth, and the life."
2. Endeavor always to walk in that way.
3. When you ask anything, ask for it always in the name of Jesus.

MAY 1—How do we best show our love for Jesus? Whom will the Father send to them? For what purpose? Jesus promises that He will not leave them as what? Why? He who loves Jesus will be loved by whom? What did Judas ask Jesus? How did Jesus answer him? Who will teach the disciples all things? How did Jesus bestow His peace upon them? What did Jesus tell the disciples before it came to pass?

RELIGIOUS PRACTICES

1. Seek always to show your love for Jesus by obeying His commandments, mindful of His words, "If you love me, keep my commandments."
2. Strive always to be worthy of that peace which Jesus promised to give His followers when He said, "Peace I leave with you, my peace I give to you."
3. Secure a copy of *The Conquest of Fear,* The Paulist Press, 401 W. 59th St., N.Y., and follow its suggestions.

MAY 2—Who is the true vine? The vine-dresser? Why is union with Jesus so necessary for fruitfulness? What will be done with anyone who does not abide in Jesus? Under what conditions will one's petition be granted? What commandment does Jesus give to them? What is the supreme expression of love? Why does Jesus call them friends? Jesus has appointed them that they should do what?

RELIGIOUS PRACTICES

1. Reflect often upon the truth that Jesus is the vine and that we are the branches, and that we can bear fruit only as long as we remain united with Jesus.

2. Honor and revere the man who lays down his life for his country, being mindful of the words of Jesus, "Greater love than this no one has, that one lay down his life for his friends."

MAY 3—Why does the world hate the followers of Jesus? What does Jesus ask His disciples to remember? What word in the Law was fulfilled? The Advocate will bear witness concerning whom? Why I did Jesus speak these things to His disciples? Why will persecution and death be meted out to the disciples of Jesus?

RELIGIOUS PRACTICES

1. Recall often the meaning of the blow upon your cheek given to you at Confirmation, reminding you to be ready and willing to suffer persecution and death for the sake of Jesus Christ.

2. Bear witness before all the world to your faith in Jesus and try always to win souls for Christ.

3. Read a chapter of *Winning Converts* each month and endeavor to carry out its suggestions as to how you can win a convert for Christ.

MAY 4—Why is it expedient for Jesus to depart? What will the Advocate do? When the Advocate comes, what will he teach? What did the disciples say to one another? How did Jesus counsel them against discouragement?

RELIGIOUS PRACTICES

1. Cultivate a special devotion to the Holy Ghost and pray

that. He may come into your heart and strengthen you.

2. Do not allow yourself to be discouraged or grow weary of well-doing, but keep in mind always the saying of Jesus, "I will see you again, and your heart shall rejoice, and your joy no one shall take from you."

3. Memorize the above saying of Jesus, and repeat it often to yourself.

MAY 5—Jesus instructs the disciples to petition the Father in the name of whom? What hour is coming? Why does the Father love the disciples? What did the disciples say to Jesus? How is the belief of the disciples soon to be put to test? Why did Jesus speak these things to them? Why should they take courage? What prayer does Jesus address to the Father? Everlasting life consists in what?

RELIGIOUS PRACTICES

1. Reflect often upon the saying of Jesus, "But take courage, I have overcome the world."

2. When you make the Sign of the Cross, do so carefully and reverently, meditating upon the great mystery of the Blessed Trinity made known to us by Jesus.

MAY 6—How does Jesus pray for His disciples? They have known what? Why did Jesus pray for His disciples? Whom did Jesus guard? Who perished? Why did the world hate the disciples of Jesus? Jesus prays that the disciples may be sanctified in what? How does Jesus pray for His church? For what does Jesus especially ask? How will the world know that Jesus was sent by the Father? Jesus asks that the disciples may be with whom? Why? Jesus has made known whose name? Why?

RELIGIOUS PRACTICES

1. Remember that the chief mark of Christ's church is that of unity—unity of belief and unity of practice.

2. Strive earnestly to win souls for Jesus, mindful of His prayer, "That all may be one, even as thou, Father, in me and I in thee."

MAY 7—Whither did Jesus and His disciples go? What did

Jesus say to them? What apostles did Jesus take with Him? What did He say to them? What did He do? What plea did He make to His Father? What did Jesus say to Peter? Why did Jesus urge Peter to watch and pray? Jesus went and prayed how many times? Who appeared to Jesus? The sweat of Jesus became as what?

RELIGIOUS PRACTICES

1. Reflect often upon the saying of Jesus, "Watch and pray, that you may not enter into temptation."

2. Strengthen your will by doing each day something that is hard and difficult, and that you are not strictly obliged to do.

MAY 8—Jesus found His disciples doing what? What did He say to them? Who is at hand? Who came with Judas? How did Judas betray Jesus? What response did Jesus make? What did Jesus say to the crowd? Their response? What did Jesus repeat to the crowd? What word was fulfilled? What did the crowd finally do to Jesus?

RELIGIOUS PRACTICES

1. Consider how Judas faced the sacred sign of affection by using it to betray Jesus.

2. Be careful during courtship to avoid danger to yourself and to your friend by following the wise and prudent "hands off" policy.

3. Secure a copy of *A White Courtship,* Our Sunday Visitor Press, Huntington, Ind., read it, and loan it to others.

MAY 9—What did the disciples ask Jesus? What did Simon Peter do? What did Jesus say to His disciples? What did He do? What did Jesus say to Peter? How did Jesus rebuke His enemies? What did the crowd do to Jesus? Who deserted Jesus? To whom did they bring Jesus? What counsel had Caiphas given to the Jews?

RELIGIOUS PRACTICES

1. Reflect often upon the words of Jesus condemning those who resort to unjust warfare, "All those who take the sword will perish by the sword."

2. Study the teachings of the Pope on peace, as embodied in the booklet, *The Way to Peace.*

3. Work earnestly for the establishment of the international institutions, such as a world court and a world sheriff, necessary for the abolition of war as an instrument of national policy.

MAY 10—The high priest questioned Jesus concerning what? How did Jesus answer him? Whom did He advise the high priest to question? What did one of the attendants do and say to Jesus? How did Jesus answer him? The chief priests were seeking whom? Why? What did the two false witnesses testify against Jesus? What did the high priest ask Jesus? Did Jesus reply? What did the high priest say a second time to Jesus? What finally did Jesus say in reply? What did the high priest do? What did the high priest say? What sentence is passed upon Jesus?

RELIGIOUS PRACTICES

1. Recall often to mind the question of the high priest, Caiphas, "I adjure thee by the living God that thou tell us whether thou art the Christ, the Son of God."
2. Remember the simple and direct answer of Jesus, "Thou hast said it."
3. Remember always that the Catholic Church teaches with divine authority because her Founder Jesus Christ is divine.
4. Use every opportunity to proclaim the divinity of Christ and of His Church to the world.

MAY 11—How did they treat Jesus? Who were following Jesus at a distance? What did the maid say to Peter? What answer did Peter make? What did he do? What did a certain maidservant say to Peter? What reply did Peter make? Whither did he go? What happens then?

RELIGIOUS PRACTICES

1. Reflect often upon the indignities and insults heaped upon Jesus.
2. Be willing to bear persecution and insults for the sake of Jesus, remembering that the disciple is not above the Master.

MAY 12—What did the maid say of Peter? What did Peter say? What did the servants and the attendants say to Peter? Did Peter admit the charge? An hour later another insisted what? What did Peter reply? What did the bystanders say about Peter's speech? What did Peter do? What did the servant of the high priest say to Peter? Peter's reply? Peter recalls what words of Jesus? Did Peter repent? How did the guards mock Jesus?

RELIGIOUS PRACTICES

1. Be willing to withstand the social pressure of a hostile crowd by conforming your actions to the commandments of God.

2. Reflect often upon the insults which Jesus willingly endured for love of us.

3. Secure a copy of *Youth's Struggle for Decency*, Our Sunday Visitor Press, Huntington, Ind., read it, and loan it to others.

MAY 13—What question did they put to Jesus before the Sanhedrin? What reply did Jesus make? How did Jesus proclaim His divinity? Upon what charge did the Sanhedrin condemn Jesus? What did Judas say to the chief priests? Their reply? What did Judas do with the thirty pieces of silver? How did Judas die? What was done with the thirty pieces of silver? What prophecy was thus fulfilled?

RELIGIOUS PRACTICES

1. Meditate often upon the divinity of Jesus and pledge to Him your supreme and abiding loyalty.

2. Reflect upon the tragic fate of Judas and promise that you will never betray your Lord by committing mortal sin.

MAY 14—They led Jesus from Caiphas where? What did Pilate ask the Jews? Their answer? What did Pilate then suggest? What did the Jews reply? What charges did the Jews then bring against Jesus? What question did Pilate put to Jesus secretly? How did Jesus answer him? Why did Jesus say that He came into the world? What report did Pilate make to the Jews concerning his investigation of Jesus?

RELIGIOUS PRACTICES

1. Meditate often upon the patience with which Jesus bore

the false charges made against Him.

2. Deem it an honor to suffer persecution and calumny for the sake of Jesus.

MAY 15—What did Pilate ask Jesus? Did Jesus make any reply? What further charge did the Jews bring against Jesus? Why did Pilate send Jesus to Herod? Why was Herod glad to see Jesus? How did Herod mock Jesus? What happened when Herod sent Jesus back to Pilate? What report did Pilate make to the Jews? What did he decide to do with Jesus?

RELIGIOUS PRACTICES

1. Do some daily act of penance and self-denial in atonement for your sins.

2. Abstain from smoking until you are twenty-one as an act of penance as well as for the health of your body and mind.

3. Secure a copy of *Sharing the Faith,* Our Sunday Visitor Press, and read it carefully.

MAY 16—What was the custom at the festival time? Who was Barabbas? What did Pilate say to the Jews? What message did Pilate's wife send? Whom did the crowd ask Pilate to release? Why? What did the crowd demand be done with Jesus? What did Pilate first do with Jesus? Did Pilate finally yield to the cries of the crowd?

RELIGIOUS PRACTICES

1. Make it a rule never to speak a harsh or angry word to any member of your family or to your neighbor.

2. Never strike a person. Avoid the harsh and angry words which often lead to a quarrel.

3. Secure a copy of *Marriage: Catholic or Mixed?* Our Sunday Visitor Press, Huntington, Ind., read it, and loan it to others.

MAY 17—Tell what the soldiers did to Jesus. How did they mock him? What did Pilate say to the Jews concerning Jesus? How was Jesus attired? What did the Jews cry out upon seeing Jesus? What did Pilate suggest? What did the Jews demand? Relate the conversation between Pilate and Jesus. What was Pilate looking for? What did the Jews say to Pilate? What did Pilate say to the

Jews concerning Jesus? What did the Jews cry out?

RELIGIOUS PRACTICES

1. Treat your parents always with the greatest respect and love.
2. Surprise them from time to time with a little gift as token of your love and gratitude.
3. Secure a copy of *The Christian Mother,* Our Sunday Visitor Press, Huntington, Ind., autograph it, and on Mother's Day present it to your mother as a token of your love.

MAY 18—Why did Pilate wash his hands in the presence of the crowd? What did he say to the crowd? What reply did the Jews make? Whither did the Jews lead Jesus? Who helped Jesus carry His cross? Who were following Jesus? What did Jesus say to the women of Jerusalem?

RELIGIOUS PRACTICES

1. Read a good book on the Catholic religion every few months, and pass it on to others to read.
2. Read the Catholic paper of your diocese each week.
3. Subscribe to *Our Sunday Visitor,* and read it all, particularly the Youth Section.

MAY 19—Whither did the Jews take Jesus? What did they do with Him? Who were crucified beside Him? What word of Scripture was thus fulfilled? What inscription did Pilate put on the cross? In what languages was it written? What did the chief priests say to Pilate? Pilate's reply? What did Jesus say? How did the soldiers divide the garments of Jesus? What saying of Scripture was thus fulfilled?

RELIGIOUS PRACTICES

1. Meditate often upon the sufferings, and death of Jesus, thus vividly recalling His love for you.
2. Have a crucifix in your room and gaze upon it occasionally during the day making ejaculations of love for Jesus crucified.

MAY 20—What did the Jews say to Jesus hanging upon the cross? How did the chief priests and the elders mock Jesus? What did the soldiers say to Jesus? What did the bad thief say to Jesus? How did the good thief rebuke him? What did the good thief say to Jesus? What promise did Jesus make to him? Who was standing by the cross of Jesus? What did Jesus say to His mother? To the disciple?

RELIGIOUS PRACTICES

1. Meditate often upon the repentance of the good thief, and the readiness with which Jesus pardoned him.

2. Reflect often upon the love which Jesus manifested for His mother, placing her under the care of His beloved disciple. Try each day to increase your love, devotion and kindliness toward your father and your mother.

MAY 21—What did Jesus cry out at the ninth hour? What did the bystanders say? What did Jesus say? What did they offer Jesus? After taking the wine, Jesus said what? Then what did Jesus cry out with a loud voice? How did nature mourn the death of Jesus? How did the centurion profess his faith in Jesus? What did those who were keeping guard over Jesus say? What friends of Jesus were standing at a distance, looking on?

RELIGIOUS PRACTICES

1. Carry your rosary beads on your person and recite the Rosary each day.

2. Kiss devoutly the crucifix on your Rosary as a token of your love for Jesus crucified, every time you begin and end the Rosary.

MAY 22—What request did the Jews make of Pilate? What did they do to the bodies of the two thieves? To the body of Jesus? What sayings of Scripture were thus fulfilled? Who was Joseph of Arimathea? What request did he make of Pilate? Did Pilate grant it? Who also came? What did they do with the body of Jesus?

RELIGIOUS PRACTICES

1. Reflect often how sin, like the lance of the soldier, pierces the side of Jesus.

2. When you make your purpose of amendment in connection with confession, see that it is made earnestly and prove your sincerity by keeping

that purpose of amendment. Remember that the sincerity of one who makes a promise and then repeatedly breaks it, may well be questioned.

MAY 23—Where did they bury the body of Jesus? What did they place over the entrance to the tomb? What women came to the tomb? What did they do? What request did the chief priests and the Pharisees make of Pilate? What reply did Pilate make? What holy women came to the tomb early on Sunday morning? What did they say to one another? What did the women find at the tomb?

RELIGIOUS PRACTICES

1. Read a short sketch of the life of a saint each day, particularly of the saint whose feast is celebrated that day.
2. Meditate upon the virtues of that saint and endeavor to imitate them.
3. Secure a copy of *Can Priests Forgive Sins?* Our Sunday Visitor Press, Huntington, Ind., read it carefully, and loan it to others.

MAY 24—Whom did the holy women find at the entrance to the tomb? What did the young man say to them? He instructed the women to carry the news to whom? What did Mary Magdalene say to Peter and John? Describe the speed with which they went to the tomb. Who reached there first? Who entered first? Why? What did Peter and John see? What effect did this have upon them?

RELIGIOUS PRACTICES

1. Meditate often upon the resurrection of Jesus from the dead, and see in it a promise of your own resurrection.
2. Reflect often upon the saying of Jesus, "I am the resurrection and the life, he who believes in Me shall never die."
3. Think often upon the shortness of your earthly life and the length of eternity. Resolve to use your time here so that you may spend your eternity with God in Heaven.

MAY 25—Jesus appeared first to whom? Whom did Mary see at the tomb? What did they say to her? Her reply? What did Jesus say to Mary? What reply did Mary make? How did Mary recognize Jesus? What did Jesus tell Mary to do? Did the disciples believe Mary? What did Jesus say to the holy women? Did the apostles believe the story which the women brought to them? What report did the guards bring to the chief priests? What did the chief priests and the elders instruct the soldiers to say? What did they give the soldiers?

RELIGIOUS PRACTICES

1. Meditate often upon the mercy, forgiveness and love which Jesus manifested toward the penitent woman, Mary Magdalene.
2. Never remain in a state of sin, but fly with all possible speed to confession.
3. Strive always to keep yourself in the state of grace, and to grow daily in holiness of life.

MAY 26—Jesus walked with two of His disciples to what village? Did the disciples recognize Jesus? Why? How did the disciples describe Jesus of Nazareth? The disciples were hoping that Jesus would have done what? What did Jesus say to them? How did Jesus confirm their faith? What did the two disciples say to each other? What did they tell the other disciples?

RELIGIOUS PRACTICES

1. Pray each day that God may so deepen and strengthen your faith as to make you acutely sensitive to spiritual values.
2. Say an Our Father and a Hail Mary for the success of the missionaries bringing the faith of Jesus to other lands and peoples.
3. Secure a copy of *The Priesthood: A Divine Institution,* Our Sunday Visitor Press, Huntington, Ind., read it carefully, and loan it to others.

MAY 27—Where did Jesus appear to the apostles? What did He say to them? What did He show them? How did he rebuke their unbelief? How did Jesus prove to them that He was flesh and blood? What did Jesus then say to the apostles? What did He do to their mind? What tremendous power did He then confer upon the apostles? Which one of the apostles was absent when Jesus came? What did Thomas say? What happened eight days later?